Introduction to Game Physics with Box2D

Introduction to
Game Physics
with Box2D

Ian Parberry

CRC Press
Taylor & Francis Group
Boca Raton London New York

CRC Press is an imprint of the
Taylor & Francis Group, an **informa** business

AN A K PETERS BOOK

CRC Press
Taylor & Francis Group
6000 Broken Sound Parkway NW, Suite 300
Boca Raton, FL 33487-2742

Version Date: 20121128

International Standard Book Number: 978-1-4665-6576-0 (Paperback)

Library of Congress Cataloging-in-Publication Data

Parberry, Ian.
    Introduction to game physics with Box2D / Ian Parberry.
        p. cm.
    "An A K Peters book."
    Includes bibliographical references and index.
    ISBN 978-1-4665-6576-0 (pbk.)
        1. Computer games--Programming. 2. Computer animation--Mathematics. 3.
Physics--Data processing. I. Title.

    QA76.76.C672P36 2013
    794.8'1526--dc23   2012036762

Visit the Taylor & Francis Web site at
http://www.taylorandfrancis.com

and the CRC Press Web site at
http://www.crcpress.com

For my daughters Lizzie, Kate, and Maggie.

Study hard what interests you the most
in the most undisciplined, irreverent
and original manner possible.
— Richard Feynman

Contents

Preface

This is a book that is very much in the spirit of the Feynman quote on the dedication page, an undisciplined, irreverent, and original book on how to program the physics used in 2D video games. If you are looking at it for the first time, then your mind is probably abuzz with questions.[1] Here are brief answers to some of the more obvious ones.

Why 2D Game Physics?

2D game physics is a practical and useful thing to know. It is practical because it has been used in successful commercial 2D video games.[2] It is useful because even if you are not interested in 2D game physics in its own right, you'll find that moving from 2D to 3D game physics is relatively easy.[3]

Why Box2D?

Box2D is a popular Open Source 2D game physics package that has been used in successful commercial 2D video games.[4]

Why is This Book in Two Parts?

I imagine you, the reader, to be the novice standing at the left of this picture who wants to be the trained and capable 2D game physics programmer on

....

[1] If not, then it should be. Question everything. (Your response to that statement should of course be *Why?*)

[2] At least one of them involving cranky birds.

[3] Compared to, say, the difficulty of moving from 2D to 3D graphics.

[4] Including the one with the cranky birds.

the right. Between these two there is a morass of things to know about,
like vectors and positions, bodies, angles, and floating-point numbers.

Box2D is a bridge to help you get to the other side.

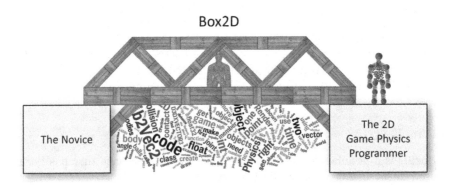

I could write a book that tells you how this bridge is constructed, but how
many people want to be a bridge builder? All you want to do is use and
maybe modify the bridge, not build a new one. You need to know a little
about how it's built, but you don't need to understand it at the same level
that a bridge builder would. Instead, I'm going to show you how the two
ends of the bridge are constructed, and I'm going to let you swing across
the middle because rope swings are a lot more fun than building bridges.

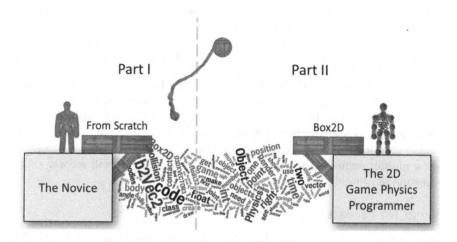

Is There Code Online?

Yes. You can download the source code used in this book and also see short video clips and get supplementary material from [Parberry 12].

What Platform is the Code Written For?[5]

The code is written in C++ for Microsoft Visual Studio 10, and comes with a full set of Visual Studio Solutions and Projects. It uses DirectX 9 for graphics.

Why Does This Book Have So Much Code in It?

This book is aimed at mid-level programmers. The best way for a mid-level programmer to improve is to read somebody else's code. Read my code, adopt the things that resonate with you, and invent your own style that overcomes what you see as the drawbacks in mine.[6]

Why Does This Book Have So Much Math in It?

I'm afraid you can't get away from it, game physics needs a lot of math. I'm going to try to connect up all the pieces of math that you need and take a few stabs at explaining *why* they are true so that you can hopefully

....

[5]Yes, I know that this should read, "For What Platform is the Code Written?" Winston Churchill was once criticized by a subordinate for ending a sentence with a preposition like this. He is reputed to have replied, "That is the kind of insubordination up with which I will not put." So bite me.

[6]I will admit that my style is a bit cramped by the limitations of the printed page. My code usually has longer lines, about double the width of what you see here.

visualize them all, see the connections, and understand how they work rather than memorize them or look them up in a table.

● What Does This Book Give Me That I Can't Find Online?

It's true that you'll find lots of manuals, tutorials, and code demos on 2D game physics and Box2D online. They're free, and some of them are excellent. What this book does is address many of the same subjects but as a unified, cohesive whole. It also addresses some of the gaps in the online knowledge base, for example, that of actually building a game based on a physics engine once you understand it. Section 1.1 will answer this question in more detail.

● What Do I Need to Know Before I Start?

You need to know some math and some programming. This is not a book for the faint of heart. Section 1.2 will answer this question in more detail.

● What Will I Know When I'm Finished?

If you've paid attention, read carefully, and experimented with the code samples, then you will know the basics of 2D game physics and how to go about using Box2D to make a 2D physics-based game. Section 1.3 will answer this question in more detail.

● Why Are Some Exercises Starred?

They are the tricky ones.

● Who is Ian Parberry?

I'm a full professor in the Department of Computer Science and Engineering at the University of North Texas. I got my PhD in 1984. Since then, I've published 65 refereed research papers in academic journals and conferences, 23 of them on game development. This is my seventh book, my fourth about game development. Google me.

● What Does He Know about Teaching Game Programming?

I've been teaching game programming classes since 1993. Alumni from these classes can be found in game development positions in the Console, PC, Online, Casual, Serious, and Casino game markets. They have 245 credits on 143 games that have sold over 180 million copies, grossing over $9 billion in revenue. My most distinguished alumnus is Jason West, co-founder of the Call of Duty franchise.

 1

Read Me First

Before we get started, let's take a look at why this book exists, what I expect you to know before you can start reading it, what the stuff inside will be like stylistically, and what you can expect to get out of it if you put a reasonable amount of effort into it.

1.1 Why Does This Book Exist?

One thing that has changed in academia over the last 30 years is that we professors are no longer the Source of All Knowledge. In 1984 when I started out as a young assistant professor, the books and papers that we taught from were sparse and often difficult to obtain. Happily, the Internet has changed all that. Knowledge is everywhere. What we need to teach students now is *understanding*,[1] not *knowledge*, which is something that we would have liked to have done all along, but we were stunned into complacency by the burden of memorization, repetition, and standardized tests.

Students thrive when they have an easy on-ramp to understanding difficult material. Let's use a visual metaphor to explain what I mean. When students are faced with a large block of new and difficult material (below, left) that they want to get on top of, they turn to manuals, tutorials, newsgroups, books, papers, whatever information they can gather together on the subject both online and in what we old-timers laughingly call the Real World. What they usually end up with is a jumble of mismatched

....

[1]How would I define *understanding*? See my 1997 paper [Parberry 97].

and odd-shaped pieces of knowledge that are frustrating to put together
(right):

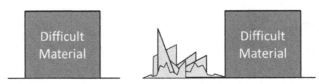

Some of the documents that they find get too hard too fast, which means
a steep on-ramp (below left). That could be because the author is very
smart and has forgotten what it's like to be a beginner, or because he
or she is writing for a very smart audience. On the other hand, some of
the documents stay at a very shallow level, which can be slow and boring
and not of much help in getting on top of the difficult material (right).
These are often written by authors who think it is useful to teach very
young children how to do trivial things with a computer, while ignoring
the really difficult question of how to get them from there to the top of
the block. (I suppose it's another example of Douglas Adams' "Somebody
Else's Problem" field in action.)

Sometimes the author just isn't very good at presenting the material,
switching from very easy stuff to very hard stuff without warning (left)
or leaving gaps that the average reader finds insurmountable (right):

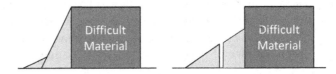

Even worse, the material could be so badly organized that it's hardly an
on-ramp at all. This often happens with new authors when their level of
excitement is high and their organizational and pedagogical skills are low:

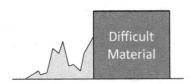

In my experience, students want an on-ramp that is neither too steep nor too flat, leading them almost to the top of the difficult material on a path that is as smooth and continuous as possible:

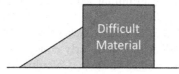

An on-ramp for game physics should probably be in 2D because it has almost all of the richness and complexity of 3D game physics, but it is, in a sense, only two-thirds as difficult since it is only missing a dimension. This is not so with game math (geometry and linear algebra). You could say that 2D game math is only one-third as hard as 3D game math because the former has only one axis of rotation while the latter has three. The Irish mathematician Sir William Rowan Hamilton (1805–1865) discovered this to his dismay when he tried to generalize the concept of 2D rotations as complex numbers into three dimensions.[2]

You can imagine how happy I was when I found Box2D, Erin Catto's excellent Open Source 2D physics engine [Catto 12]. It is, in my opinion, the ideal code base for teaching game physics. It is much less complex than a 3D physics engine, which means that students have a chance of mastering it during part of a 15-week semester. It requires only the addition of a 2D rendering engine to make a game, which is ideal for classroom use because, in my experience, a 2D minigame can be constructed in a few thousand lines of C++ code, whereas even a very simple 3D game starts at tens of thousands of lines of C++ code (for example, SAGE [Parberry et al. 07]).

Box2D is a *real* game physics engine in the sense that it has been used in some successful commercial games. Students like getting experience with a real piece of software instead of classroom code wherever they can. Best of all, Box2D is Open Source (which means it is free), it has a large and active online community behind it (which means it is relatively stable and bug-free), and it has been ported to multiple platforms (which means you can use it in your classes no matter what platform your students are proficient in).

So why this book? Box2D comes with an excellent online manual, but it's more useful for people who know what they're doing than it is to newbies. There are lots of tutorials and code examples online, but they are fragmentary and of variable quality, running the gamut from incoherent to excellent. My intention is to put all of this material together and craft it into a relatively smooth on-ramp for beginners.

....

[2]He thought that he would need two imaginary parts, but he was blocked until he realized in 1843 that three imaginary parts are necessary and sufficient. The resulting objects were called *quaternions*. See [Dunn and Parberry 11] for more information.

• 1.2 Preconditions

Let's talk about what you need to know before you can start reading this book. These are what a programmer would call *preconditions* and an educator would call *prerequisites*.

I hope you're not afraid of mathematics. You should be familiar with a certain amount of high-school and early college mathematics, most importantly, linear algebra and geometry. Calculus up to the Fundamental Theorem of Calculus would be helpful too, but all I really expect from you in this area is a vague feeling of déjà vu. I'll also be using a certain amount of what used to be called *mechanics*, a subject usually taught in applied mathematics or physics classes. If you can remember being taught $s = ut + at^2/2$, then you are probably good to go.

Since this is a book about programming, I expect you to be able to write and debug code. Speaking of debugging, I am often struck by the fact that while we spend hours teaching students how to program, we spend very little time teaching them how to debug, yet even professional programmers seem to find themselves spending half[3] their time debugging. Some instructors never mention it, some give it passing mention, some even make it seem that having bugs is a shameful thing that should never be mentioned in polite society.[4] See Appendix B for some of my debugging tips.

To get the most out of this book you must be familiar with the C++ programming language and the object-oriented philosophy upon which it is based. The supplementary code that goes with this book will be written using Microsoft Visual Studio 10 and DirectX 9.0. If you are unfamiliar with these, I suggest that you get familiar with them fast. To get a job in the game industry, you need to be flexible and omnivorous about programming. You should be able to program for the major programming environments[5] and, more importantly, be able to learn new ones fast. Your mantra should be "If it takes code, then I can program it."

• IMPORTANT POINT •

You need to have Visual Studio 10 and the DirectX 9.0 SDK installed on your computer before you can begin working with the source code. Obviously you need a PC running Windows. Visual Studio 10 is commercial software, but if you are a student, your school may very well have an MSDNAA subscription, in which case you can get it for free. The DirectX 9.0 SDK is a free download.

Sometimes it makes more sense pedagogically to look at more abstract algorithms and data structures rather than code. It might help to familiar-

. . . .

[3] "Half" here is a technical term meaning "lots of," or "beaucoup de" in French.
[4] Like having bedbugs.
[5] By "programming environment," I mean target hardware, target operating system, programming language, and development tools.

ize yourself with balanced trees by consulting a standard Algorithms text such as [Cormen et al. 01] before you read Section 8.4.

1.3 Postconditions

You're probably interested in what you'll gain from mastering this book. These are what a programmer would call *postconditions* and an educator would call *outcomes*. Let me list the expected outcomes chapter by chapter.

Part I: Introduction to Game Physics

Part I is designed to help you come to grips with the trials and tribulations of programming game physics from scratch, by hand, with no libraries or outside help. It consists of three chapters.

Chapter 2: Mathematics for Game Physics

We start off pedal to the metal by examining the mathematical foundation of game physics and how it can be applied in practice. We'll be doing some geometry, linear algebra, and calculus. Thanks to René Descartes, we learn that geometry and linear algebra are really the same thing, which is really great news. The expected outcomes for Chapter 2 are

1. understanding of vectors, angles, and reflection;
2. recollection of the suppressed memories of how much we hated the linear algebra and geometry classes we took in school;
3. realization that we didn't need to pay for two classes when they're really the same thing;
4. understanding of exactly why `atan2(a,b)` is better than `atan(a/b)`;
5. a vague recollection that sines and cosines have something to do with horses and hippies;
6. understanding the concepts of Euler integration and Verlet integration and their roles in game physics;
7. knowledge of the mathematical technique of relaxation;
8. realization that despite the hairy math and the scary names, Verlet integration and Gauss-Seidel relaxation are just a couple of lines of code.

Chapter 3: A Rigid Body Physics Game

Now we put the concepts learned in Chapter 2 to the test by coding the end game in eight-ball pool. The expected outcomes for Chapter 3 are

1. knowledge of simple methods for the computation of motion and impulse,
2. ability to recognize where code for 2D physics fits into a game,
3. familiarity with the supporting game code used throughout this book,
4. sudden desire to play eight-ball in real life.

Chapter 4: A Soft Body Physics Toy

Having been introduced to the theory of Verlet integration and Gauss-Seidel relaxation in Chapter 2, we now examine code for a Ball and Spring Toy, which allows you to play with various springy things and a ragdoll robot named Woodie. The expected outcomes for Chapter 4 are

1. familiarity with the use of Verlet integration for programming game physics,
2. experience with applying Gauss-Seidel relaxation to implement springs and sticks,
3. familiarity with using Verlet integration and Gauss-Seidel relaxation to implement ragdoll physics.

Part II: Game Physics with Box2D

Now that you've mastered the basics in Part I, you are ready for Part II, which shows you how to use Box2D to go beyond the baby steps in Part I. It consists of four chapters.

Chapter 5: Getting Started

Chapter 5 gets you started with Box2D by showing you how to download it and integrate it with your game code. After running you quickly through the basic concepts, this chapter demonstrates the process with a quick toy that lets you drop balls and books out of the sky. The expected outcomes for Chapter 5 are

1. Box2D correctly downloaded and integrated with Visual Studio,
2. knowledge of the basic concepts used in Box2D,
3. understanding that physics units should not be pixels,
4. experience with using Box2D in a simple application.

Chapter 6: A Tale of Three Modules

Chapter 6 goes into some details of the three modules that make up Box2D, the *Common Module*, the *Collision Module*, and the *Dynamics Module*. The expected outcomes for Chapter 6 are

1. knowledge of the what basic functions are included in the math library in the Common Module;
2. understanding of the role of the Collision Module, what contact manifolds are, and how broad-phase collision detection works;
3. knowledge of the shapes that Box2D provides;
4. understanding of the role of the Dynamics Module, what the Physics World is, and what fixtures and bodies are;
5. understanding of what the Integrator and the Constraint Solver do, and what parts of the Ball and Spring Toy in Chapter 4 they correspond to;
6. knowledge of the joints that Box2D provides.

Chapter 7: The Cannon Game

The Cannon Game gives the player control of a cannon in a world with a tempting tower of books. The player's job is to knock down the tower in 60 seconds or less by firing cannonballs at it. The expected outcomes for Chapter 7 are

1. knowledge of how to use Box2D to create a simple game;
2. familiarity with Box2D bodies, fixtures, and joints;
3. ability to knock down a tower of books with a cannon.

Chapter 8: The Collision Module

Chapter 8 drills down a little into the Collision Module. It starts by looking more closely at contacts and contact manifolds before introducing the *contact listener*, which is an efficient way of having Box2D notify your program about collisions. It finishes with some heavy geek stuff about AABBs and dynamic trees. The expected outcomes for Chapter 8 are

1. deeper understanding of how a contact manifold works,
2. understanding of why the `userData` field in `b2BodyDef` is so useful,
3. understanding of what a contact listener is and of what events are likely to cause its `PreSolve` function to be called,
4. knowledge of how to get information from a contact manifold in the contact listener's `PreSolve` function,
5. experience with using a contact listener to monitor collisions,
6. knowledge of what AABBs are and how dynamic trees work.

Part III: Appendices

Part III consists of four appendices containing things that are useful but tangential to the major theme of this book. This is like the bonus scene at the end of a movie except that you don't have to sit through the credits to see it.

Appendix A: For Math Geeks Only

Appendix A contains a neat proof of identities for $\sin(\alpha+\beta)$ and $\cos(\alpha+\beta)$. The expected outcomes for Appendix A are

1. recollection of the suppressed memories of how much we *really* hated the linear algebra and geometry classes we took in school.

Appendix B: The Blacke Arte of Program Debugging

Appendix B has some observations about debugging, a Blacke Arte if ever there was one. The expected outcomes for Appendix B are

1. appreciation for the debug `printf`,
2. less stress when bugs appear,
3. inexplicable fondness for pipes and deerstalker hats.

Appendix C: There Are, in Fact, Dumb Questions

Appendix C introduces an important concept, the idea of actually sitting down and *experimenting with code* until you understand it. That way you don't have to ask so many dumb questions. The expected outcomes for Appendix C are

1. reduction in the need to ask dumb questions,
2. increased confidence in your own abilities,
3. increased appearance of competence.

Appendix D: Bullet Physics

Appendix D is a brief primer on using Bullet physics, just to pique your interest. The expected outcomes for Appendix D are

1. understanding that Bullet physics and Box2D are quite similar,
2. increased desire to go out and learn 3D game physics,
3. realization that having learned 2D game physics and Box2D from this book, you now know enough go out and learn 3D game physics and Bullet physics by yourself.

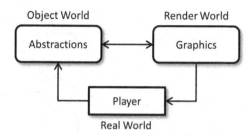

Figure 1.1 • The two principal Game Engine Worlds and how they relate to each other and to the Real World.

• 1.4 Programming Style

Stylistically, I'm going to be taking what Buddhists calls the middle road between academic ivory-towerism and wishful thinking about programming on one side and the harsh realities of professional coding on a budget and a deadline on the other side.

• 1.4.1 Object-Oriented Programming

I intend to use object-oriented programming (OOP) as a method of *data-hiding*. The ideal is that each C++ class knows only what it needs to know and gives out that information only in certain prescribed ways. Other classes that need to operate on that information must either ask the class that owns it to give it out or ask it to perform that operation for it. This has two advantages. The first is that it provides a measure of bug deterrence by limiting the unexpected consequences of a new class meddling with information that is needed elsewhere in the program. Secondly, it helps limit the amount of spaghetti code in which it is not clear what segment of code has responsibility for which abstract operation.

However, I'm not going to be rigid about data hiding. There are some things that are going to be right out there in a global variable—pointers to things deep in the mesh of objects and inheritance that can cause endless disruption if they are accidentally or intentionally abused. However, hiding them would involve convoluted code that is hard to understand and in the Real World, there would be enough of them to cause a significant performance hit.

I'll be using OOP to encapsulate my game code into two separate Game Engine Worlds: Object World, which is a world of abstractions about the objects in the game; and Render World, which is a world of sprites, pixels, and display devices. Render World is tied to the Real World through devices; the player gets information from the Render World via the video screen. The two worlds and their relationships are shown in Figure 1.1.

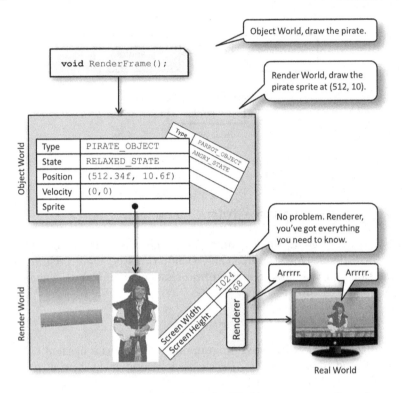

Figure 1.2 • How Object World and Render World cooperate to draw the screen in the Real World.

Since the Object World contains only abstractions that are completely device-independent, moving from one graphics platform to another (say, from DirectX to OpenGL) should involve changing only the Render World.

Let's look at a quick run-through of how Object World and Render World interact in Figure 1.2. It begins with the game loop somewhere in a file that we'll call `MyGame.cpp`. Within that loop, your code will call a function `RenderFrame` to render a frame of animation to the video screen. `RenderFrame` at some point will ask Object World to draw the objects in the game, including a pirate. `RenderFrame` can't ask Render World to draw the pirate yet, because while Render World contains the pirate's sprite read in from a file, it doesn't know the pirate's location. Object World knows that, so it tells it to Render World, which now has all of the information that it needs to know. It has a renderer, which it uses to draw the pirate to the screen.

It is worth noting that the two Game Engine Worlds measure things in their own units, using their own rulers. The Render World is tied to the graphics hardware, which may use integers for pixel coordinates and RGB color quads, and floating point numbers for pixel and vertex shader calculations. Since Object World is a world of abstractions, the programmer is almost completely free to use whatever unit of measurement that he or she finds convenient. It is tempting to use screen coordinates even for a 3D world that is many thousands of screen-widths wide. While this is relatively harmless for single-screen games such as the ones you will see in this book, it can ultimately be very harmful, as we will see later.

1.4.2 Variable Naming Convention

You were probably taught in programming class that "variable names should reflect their function." I'm guessing that you mostly ignored that advice while making a half-hearted attempt to use sensible-ish names often enough to make the instructor happy, or at least not so unhappy that he or she deducts the 10 points allocated for the somewhat nebulous concept of "program style." Here are the naming conventions that I will try to abide by in this book.[6]

My global variable names will start with "g_" and my member variable names will start with "m_". These will be followed by a few lowercase letters that indicate the variable's type (for example, n for an integer, f for a floating point number, b for a Boolean, and p for a pointer), followed by a descriptive name in lowercase and uppercase letters, used judiciously to separate out words, starting with an uppercase letter. When you are reading my code, you will be able to tell instantly that, for example, m_bIsFinished must be a Boolean member variable that records whether or not something is finished, g_pObjectList is a global pointer variable that points to a list of objects, and count is just a local variable or function parameter that is in use only temporarily.

You will see me making occasional use of global variables, a practice that is frowned upon by many academics. My approach to global variables is this: if, like the Highlander, "there can be only one," then you may as well make it global, particularly if you would otherwise end up passing it as a parameter to scads of functions.

1.5 Supplementary Material

You will find supplementary material including source code online at [Parberry 12].

....

[6]You may be tempted to call me obsessive, at least until you're awake at 4am on a deadline trying to read code that you wrote three months ago.

Part I

Introduction to Game Physics

2

Mathematics for Game Physics

Game physics uses mathematics as a tool. I'm afraid you can't get away from it, so take a deep breath and let's go. I'll try to start this off as simply as possible, but things are going to get complicated fast. Section 2.1 shows you some of the most important things from geometry and linear algebra that you are going to need in game physics: vectors, trigonometry, the Pythagorean Theorem and Identity, the Law of Cosines, and orientation. Section 2.2 is about reflection, meaning that we're going to be bouncing balls off things to see how they behave. The proper name for this is *collision response*. Section 2.3 is about digital calculus, mainly integration, which is the part of calculus that people often find the scariest. Starting with Euler integration, we thankfully find that we don't need to integrate at all, we just need to sum. That's good because computers are excellent at adding things up fast. Verlet integration is another useful way to not do integration. Game physics is sometimes about satisfying constraints using a technique called *relaxation* covered in Section 2.4. It turns out that we can take a pretty relaxed approach to that.

● 2.1 Geometry and Linear Algebra

The French philosopher and mathematician René Descartes (1596–1650) is noted for, amongst other things,[1] noticing that linear algebra and geometry are in fact one and the same thing. Anything you can do with linear algebra you can also do with geometry, and vice versa. This is not immediately obvious because Linear Algebra World is a world of symbolic mathematics

....

[1] For example, he's the "I think, therefore I am" guy.

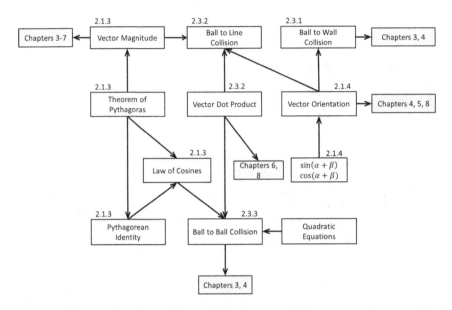

Figure 2.1 • Summary of the main results in this section, with their dependencies and places in which we will apply them.

that has things like vectors and matrices in it, whereas Geometry World is a world of pictures that has things like lines and angles in it.

It's handy for us that they are the same thing because linear algebra is what goes on inside your computer, and geometry is what you see on the screen. The video card is the piece of hardware that translates from one to the other, and it is thanks to Descartes' observation that it can do it at all. The CPU talks to the video card using linear algebra, and the video card responds by painting geometry on the screen.

There's so much to learn here that it's hard to keep it all in your head. You're probably also wondering why these two branches of mathematics are useful in a 2D physics game. Figure 2.1 gives a high-level block diagram of the main results in this section, how they rely on each other, and where we will use them later.

2.1.1   What's Our Vector, Victor?

A *vector* is a list of scalars,[2] typically written with square brackets around them like this $[0, 1]$. The *dimension* of a vector is the number of numbers in the list. For example, $[0, 1]$ has two dimensions, and $[0, 3, 42]$ has three dimensions. We're mostly interested in two-dimensional vectors in this

....

[2]Which for us means a floating-point number.

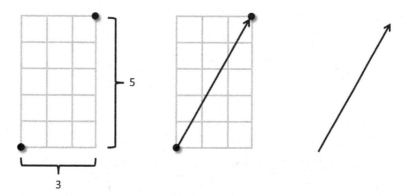

Figure 2.2 • The Linear Algebra World vector [3, 5] is drawn in Geometry World by measuring 3 units across and 5 units up from an initial point (left) and drawing an arrow from the initial point to the other one (center). The vector is the arrow (right), not the other stuff.

book because that's enough to describe 2D space. Remember how I said that linear algebra is what goes on inside a computer? That's reflected in the fact that a vector corresponds very naturally to an array in most programming languages. D3DX has a structure **D3DXVECTOR2** that we will use to implement 2D vectors in code. A **D3DXVECTOR2** v has two floating-point fields v.x and v.y.

That's the Linear Algebra World version of a vector. The Geometry World version of a vector is a picture of an arrow. To draw the vector [a, b], you start at some arbitrary point on a flat plane; pick some arbitrary unit such as nanometers, inches, furlongs, or parsecs; go a units to the right of your point and b units up and make a second point; then draw an arrow from your first point to your second one. For example, Figure 2.2 shows how the Linear Algebra World vector [3, 5] is drawn in Geometry World. We'll adopt the habit of naming vectors with letters of the alphabet, putting an arrow over them so that we remember they are vectors, for example, the vector named $\vec{v}$.

Multiplication of a vector $\vec{v} = [v_x, v_y]$ by a scalar s gives you a vector. Simply multiply the components of the vector by the scalar:

$$s.\vec{v} = s.[v_x, v_y] = [s.v_x, s.v_y].$$

Scalar division is defined as scalar multiplication by the reciprocal of the scalar.

$$\vec{v}/s = [v_x, v_y]/s = [v_x/s, v_y/s].$$

The addition or subtraction of two vectors gives you a vector. The Linear Algebra World definition of vector addition says that you just add them

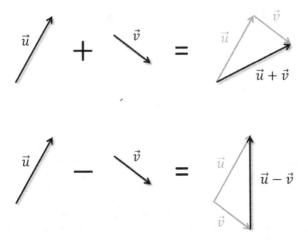

Figure 2.3 • The Geometry World definition of vector addition and subtraction.

component by component. That is, if $\vec{u} = [u_x, u_y]$ and $\vec{v} = [v_x, v_y]$, then

$$\vec{u} + \vec{v} = [u_x + v_x, u_y + v_y].$$

Vector subtraction is similar. Another way of looking at it is that you add $\vec{u}$ and $-1.\vec{v}$.

$$\vec{u} - \vec{v} = [u_x - v_x, u_y - v_y].$$

The Geometry World definition of vector addition is shown in Figure 2.3 (top). Place the tail of $\vec{v}$ on the head of $\vec{u}$. Then, $\vec{u} + \vec{v}$ is the vector that goes from the tail of $\vec{u}$ to the head of $\vec{v}$. The Geometry World definition of vector subtraction is shown in Figure 2.3 (bottom). Place the tail of $\vec{v}$ on the tail of $\vec{u}$. Then, $\vec{u} - \vec{v}$ is the vector that goes from the head of $\vec{v}$ to the head of $\vec{u}$.

D3DXVECTOR2s can be added using the overloaded addition operator + and multiplied by a scalar using the overloaded multiplication operator *. Here are some examples:

```
D3DXVECTOR2 u, v, w;
v = D3DXVECTOR2(3.1415f, 7.0f);
u = 42.0f * v;
w = u + D3DXVECTOR2(v.x, 99.0f);
u += w;
```

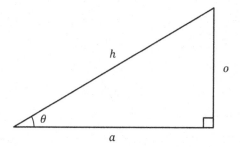

Figure 2.4 • A right triangle with sides of length a, o, and h, with θ the angle opposite the side of length o.

2.1.2 Oh, Trig

Trigonometry is the mathematics that relates the sizes of the sides of a triangle to the angles between them. For example, consider the right-angled triangle in Figure 2.4, with sides of length o, a, and h as labeled, and one of the (non-right) angles called θ. The side of length o is called the *opposite side*, the one of length a is called the *adjacent side* relative to θ, and the one labeled h is called the *hypotenuse*. Then, we define the trigonometric functions *sine, cosine,* and *tangent* as follows:

$$\sin \theta = o/h,$$
$$\cos \theta = a/h,$$
$$\tan \theta = o/a.$$

The best way to remember this is to look at the letters underlined below. They form the word "sohcahtoa":

$$\underline{s}in\ \theta = \underline{o}/\underline{h},$$
$$\underline{c}os\ \theta = \underline{a}/\underline{h},$$
$$\underline{t}an\ \theta = \underline{o}/\underline{a}.$$

Sohcahtoa is such a weird word that you might be able to remember it automatically. But if not, there are two handy mnemonics:

> Some Old Horse Caught Another Horse Taking Oats Away.
> Some Old Hippy Caught Another Hippy Toking On Acid.

The inverses of the trigonometric functions are called *arcsine, arccosine,* and *arctangent*:

$$\theta = \arcsin \frac{o}{h} = \arccos \frac{a}{h} = \arctan \frac{o}{a}.$$

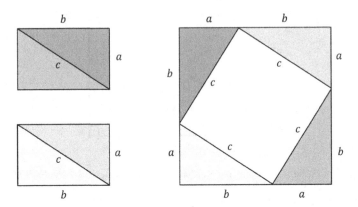

Figure 2.5 • A geometric proof of the Theorem of Pythagoras.

The C++ programming language handily provides us with useful functions `sin`, `cos`, `tan`, `asin`, `acos`, and `atan`. Of particular interest is the `atan2` function that takes two parameters `x` and `y` and computes the arctangent of `y/x`. We'll find that one very useful in due course.

2.1.3 Theorem of Pythagoras

The Theorem of Pythagoras says that if you have a right-angled triangle with sides of length a, b, and c, where c is the length of the hypotenuse, then

$$a^2 + b^2 = c^2.$$

Figure 2.5 contains a geometric proof of the Theorem of Pythagoras. The two rectangles on the left have total area $2ab$. The big square on the right has area $(a + b)^2$ since its sides have length $a + b$. But looking inside you will see that the white internal square has area c^2 and the gray triangles are the same as the gray triangles on the left and therefore have area $2ab$. Both of these methods of measuring the area of the square on the right must give the same answer; therefore,

$$(a + b)^2 = c^2 + 2ab$$
$$a^2 + 2ab + b^2 = c^2 + 2ab$$
$$a^2 + b^2 = c^2.$$

Looking at it another way,

$$c = \sqrt{a^2 + b^2}.$$

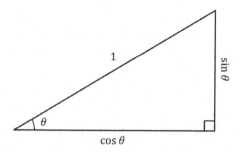

Figure 2.6 • A geometric proof of the Pythagorean Identity.

This gives us a way to compute the length, often called the *magnitude* or *norm* of a vector $\vec{v}$, written $\|\vec{v}\|$. If $\vec{v} = [v_x, v_y]$,

$$\|\vec{v}\| = \sqrt{v_x^2 + v_y^2}.$$

A vector is described as being *normalized* if it has length 1. A normalized vector is usually written with a circumflex[3] over it, like this: $\hat{v}$. To normalize a vector $\vec{v} = [v_x, v_y]$, simply do a scalar division by its magnitude.

$$\hat{v} = \frac{\vec{v}}{\|\vec{v}\|} = \frac{\vec{v}}{\sqrt{v_x^2 + v_y^2}}.$$

We can see now that multiplying a vector $\vec{v}$ times a scalar s increases the length of $\vec{v}$ by a factor of s, that is, $\|s\vec{v}\| = s\|\vec{v}\|$, since

$$\|s\vec{v}\| = \|[sv_x, sv_y]\| = \sqrt{s^2(v_x^2 + v_y^2)} = s\sqrt{v_x^2 + v_y^2} = s\|\vec{v}\|.$$

Function **D3DXVec2Length** computes the length of a **D3DXVECTOR2**. The square-root operation is sufficiently expensive that we should avoid it when we can easily do so. Often, it is just as easy to work with the squares of vector lengths as it is to work with lengths themselves.[4] If so, then we can use the faster **D3DXVec2LengthSq** function instead. **D3DXVec2Normalize** normalizes a **D3DXVECTOR2**, that is, makes its length equal to 1.

Another thing we can derive from the Theorem of Pythagoras is the so-called *Pythagorean Identity:*

$$\sin^2\theta + \cos^2\theta = 1,$$

which can be proved by applying the Theorem of Pythagoras to a right-angled triangle with hypotenuse of length 1 (see Figure 2.6).

....

[3]A hat. ,
[4]We'll see some examples later.

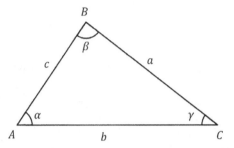

Figure 2.7 • Triangle on which to illustrate the Law of Cosines.

The Theorem of Pythagoras only works for right-angled triangles, but there is a useful generalization that works for any triangle, called the *Law of Cosines*. I'm going to use the following notation in the rest of this section. I'll label points with letters of the alphabet, A, B, C, etc. The triangle constructed by drawing line segments between points A, B, and C will be called $\triangle ABC$. The angle in $\triangle ABC$ at point B will be called $\angle ABC$, with the B in the middle. The distance between points A and B will be called $\|AB\|$. Now that we've gotten that out of the way, we can continue.

Suppose we have a triangle $\triangle ABC$ in which $\|AB\| = c$, $\|AC\| = b$, $\|BC\| = a$, $\angle CAB = \alpha$, $\angle ABC = \beta$, $\angle BCA = \gamma$, as shown in Figure 2.7. The Law of Cosines says that

$$a^2 = b^2 + c^2 - 2bc\cos\alpha,$$
$$b^2 = a^2 + c^2 - 2ac\cos\beta,$$
$$c^2 = a^2 + b^2 - 2ab\cos\gamma.$$

Let's see if we can prove the first of the three parts of the Law of Cosines, $a^2 = b^2 + c^2 - 2bc\cos\alpha$. Let's face it, the other two parts are exactly the same if you just rename the points, sides, and angles. The whole problem is that $\triangle ABC$ is not a right-angled triangle, but we can divide it into two right-angled triangles[5] by dropping a line segment from B perpendicular to AC. Let D be the point where it hits AC. If you have trouble visualizing this, see Figure 2.8. Since $\triangle ADB$ is a right-angled triangle, $\|BD\| = c\sin\alpha$, $\|AD\| = c\cos\alpha$, and therefore, $\|AC\| - \|AD\| = b - c\cos\alpha$, as shown. Furthermore, since $\triangle BDC$ is a right-angled triangle,

$$a^2 = (c\sin\alpha)^2 + (b - c\cos\alpha)^2$$
$$= b^2 + c^2(\sin^2\alpha + \cos^2\alpha) - 2bc\cos\alpha$$
$$= b^2 + c^2 - 2bc\cos\alpha.$$

....

[5]Two right-angled triangles are, by their very nature, twice as good as one.

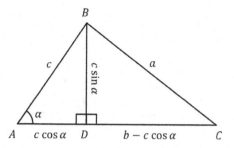

Figure 2.8 • Proof of the Law of Cosines.

The first step uses the Theorem of Pythagoras, and the last step uses the Pythagorean Identity, so we're double-dipping on things Pythagorean here.[6]

2.1.4 Orientation

Given two vectors $\vec{u}$ and $\vec{v}$, the *orientation* from $\vec{u}$ to $\vec{v}$ is the angle in the range $-\pi$ to π that $\vec{u}$ must be rotated counterclockwise[7] to make it parallel to and pointing in the same direction as $\vec{v}$. The orientation of a single vector $\vec{v}$ is defined to be the orientation from $[1, 0]$ to $\vec{v}$. Trigonometric functions (known as *trig functions* to their friends) are useful for figuring out orientations. For example, if we rotate the vector $\vec{u} = [1, 0]$ by angle θ to get a new vector $\vec{v} = [v_x, v_y]$, Figure 2.9 shows that $\cos\theta = v_x/1$ and $\sin\theta = v_y/1$; therefore, $v_x = \cos\theta$ and $v_y = \sin\theta$; that is, $\vec{v} = [\cos\theta, \sin\theta]$.

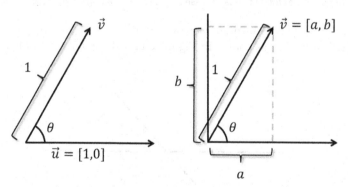

Figure 2.9 • Given a vector $\vec{u} = [1, 0]$, rotate it by angle θ to get vector $\vec{v} = [v_x, v_y]$. Find v_x and v_y.

....

[6]But as they say, when you've got a hammer, everything looks like a nail.
[7]Also known as *widdershins*.

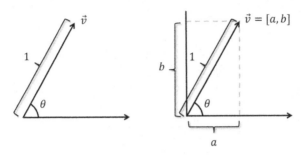

Figure 2.10 • Find the orientation θ of $\vec{v} = [v_x, v_y]$.

Conversely, to find the orientation θ of $\vec{v} = [v_x, v_y]$, Figure 2.10 shows that $\cos\theta = v_x/1$, $\sin\theta = v_y/1$, and $\tan\theta = v_y/v_x$; therefore, $\theta = \arccos v_x = \arcsin v_y = \arctan(v_y/v_x)$.

The best way to compute θ is by calling the two-argument function `atan2(u.y, u.x)`. The one-argument arctangent function `atan` is only good in the first quadrant. For example, the horizontal angle to the vector $[1, 1]$, calculated by `arctan(1/1)`, is 45°, as expected. But the horizontal angle to the vector $[-1, -1]$ calculated by `arctan(-1/-1)` = `arctan(1)` is 45° too, even though the correct answer should be $-135°$ as shown by Figure 2.11. The `atan2` function takes into account the signs of both parameters and gives the correct answer.

• IMPORTANT POINT •

Use `sin` and `cos` to rotate things, but use `atan2` to find the angle they were rotated by.

Now, let's try to rotate an arbitrary vector $\vec{u} = [u_x, u_y]$ by some angle β to get $\vec{v} = [v_x, v_y]$, as shown in Figure 2.12. All we have to do is find $\vec{u}$'s

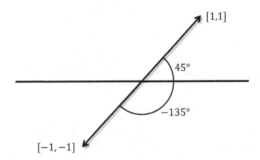

Figure 2.11 • The angle from the horizontal to $[1, 1]$ in a counterclockwise direction is 45°, and the angle to $[-1, -1]$ is $-135°$.

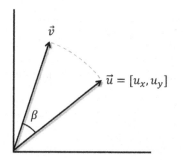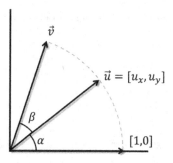

Figure 2.12 • Rotating $\vec{u}$ by angle β counterclockwise to get $\vec{v}$ and rotating $[1,0]$ by angle $\alpha + \beta$ counterclockwise to get $\vec{v}$.

orientation α because $\vec{v}$ is just $[1,0]$ rotated by angle $\alpha+\beta$, and we already know how to rotate $[1,0]$ by an arbitrary angle. Clearly,

$$\vec{v} = [v_x, v_y] = [\cos(\alpha + \beta), \sin(\alpha + \beta)].$$

Since we have the value of β and we know that $\alpha = \arctan(u_y/u_x)$, we're good to go. The code for rotating vector u by angle beta to give vector v should look something like this:

```
void Rotate(const D3DXVECTOR2& u,
D3DXVECTOR2& v, float beta){
  float alpha = atan2(u.y, u.x);
  v.x = cos(alpha + beta);
  v.y = sin(alpha + beta);
} //Rotate
```

This uses an arctangent, a sine, and a cosine. The arctangent is actually unnecessary. Fortunately for us, there are two useful trig identities:

$$\cos(\alpha + \beta) = \cos\alpha\cos\beta - \sin\alpha\sin\beta$$
$$\sin(\alpha + \beta) = \sin\alpha\cos\beta + \cos\alpha\sin\beta.$$

They're not difficult to prove, but the proofs are a little more complicated than you might expect. If you're a math geek, you can read them in Appendix A. Regardless, let's take them for granted now and push on. Since $\alpha = \arctan(u_y/u_x)$, $\sin\alpha = \sin\arctan(u_y/u_x) = u_y$ and $\cos\alpha =$

$\cos \arctan(u_y/u_x) = u_x$. Therefore,

$$\begin{aligned}
\cos(\alpha + \beta) &= \cos \alpha \cos \beta - \sin \alpha \sin \beta \\
&= \cos \left(\arctan \frac{u_y}{u_x} \right) \cos \beta - \sin \left(\arctan \frac{u_y}{u_x} \right) \sin \beta \\
&= u_x \cos \beta - u_y \sin \beta;
\end{aligned}$$

$$\begin{aligned}
\sin(\alpha + \beta) &= \sin \alpha \cos \beta + \cos \alpha \sin \beta \\
&= \sin \left(\arctan \frac{u_y}{u_x} \right) \cos \beta + \cos \left(\arctan \frac{u_y}{u_x} \right) \sin \beta \\
&= u_y \cos \beta + u_x \sin \beta.
\end{aligned}$$

Notice that the need for arctangents has disappeared. The code for rotating vector **u** by angle **beta** to give vector **v** becomes

```
void Rotate(const D3DXVECTOR2& u,
D3DXVECTOR2& v, float beta){
    v.x = u.x * cos(beta) - u.y * sin(beta);
    v.y = u.x * sin(beta) + u.y * cos(beta);
} //Rotate
```

We've replaced an arctangent with four floating-point multiplications, which in practice is much faster. On the graphics card this is done in hardware with a matrix multiplication:

$$[u_x, u_y] \begin{bmatrix} \cos \beta & \sin \beta \\ -\sin \beta & \cos \beta \end{bmatrix}.$$

See Chapters 4–6 of [Dunn and Parberry 11] for more details.

● 2.2 Reflections on Reflection

A video game is kind of like a movie except that each animation frame is computed on the fly before it is shown. Each object's position $\vec{s}$ is recomputed by adding to it $\Delta_t \vec{v}$, where Δ_t is the time since the last frame and $\vec{v}$ is its current velocity. When two objects collide, the collision most likely happens *between frames*. For example, in Figure 2.13 (top) the ball is not colliding with the wall in frame $t = 1$, but in frame $t = 2$ they have interpenetrated. Even worse, an object that moves fast can appear to pass right though another object without overlapping it. This is called *tunneling*.

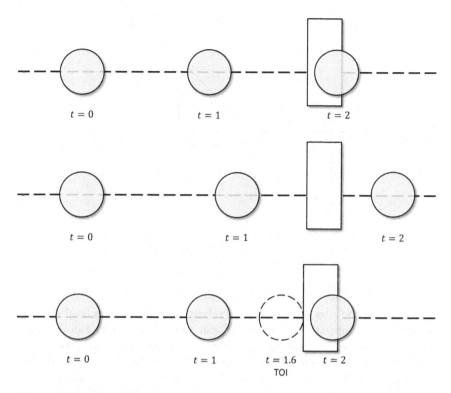

Figure 2.13 ● The ball moving right along the dotted line overlaps the wall on frame 2 (top). If it's moving fast enough, it can tunnel completely through the wall (middle). We need to interpolate the time of impact between frames (bottom).

Figure 2.13 (middle) shows a ball tunneling through a wall between frames $t = 1$ and $t = 2$. We need to interpolate between frames to find the *time of impact*, abbreviated TOI, as shown in Figure 2.13 (bottom).

When objects collide, they rebound in a different direction. You hopefully remember the "angle of incidence equals angle of reflection" rule that you learned in school. Putting that into code is harder than you might think because the angle isn't always obvious. I'll explain it in three stages. In Section 2.2.1, I'll bounce balls off the walls; that is, I'll reflect them in lines that are parallel to the edge of the screen. Once we've mastered that, I'll move to balls bouncing off arbitrary lines in Section 2.2.2. We'll need to learn a new concept along the way, the vector operation *dot product*. Finally, we'll tackle balls bouncing off each other in Section 2.2.3.

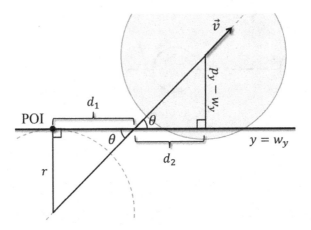

Figure 2.14 • POI for a ball hitting the ceiling.

● 2.2.1   Bouncing Off the Walls

Reflecting off the edge of the screen is relatively easy. All you need to do is negate the appropriate component of your velocity vector and do a scalar multiplication by a restitution coefficient between 0 and 1. The problem is, unless you make a special effort, you're not going to know that your object has collided with the wall until just before or just after it collides. The actual contact occurs between frames. Let's see if we can find the *point of impact*, abbreviated POI, for a ball with velocity vector $\vec{v} = [v_x, v_y]$ bouncing off the ceiling at height w_y. We've been happily moving it by a fixed distance in every frame, but we've found that since the last frame, it has moved to a point $[p_x, p_y]$ for which $p_y > w_y$.

The angle θ that $\vec{v}$ makes with the horizontal is $\arctan(v_y/v_x)$. Clearly the y-coordinate of the POI is going to be w_y. The x-coordinate of the POI will be distance d to the left of the x-coordinate of the ball, where $d = d_1 + d_2$ as shown in Figure 2.14. You can see on the left that $\tan\theta = r/d_1$, so

$$d_1 = r/\tan\theta = r v_x/v_y,$$

and on the right, $\tan\theta = (p_y - w_y)/d_2$, so

$$d_2 = (p_y - w_y)/\tan\theta = (p_y - w_y)v_x/v_y.$$

Therefore,

$$d = d_1 + d_2 = (r + p_y - w_y)v_x/v_y,$$

so the POI is

$$[p_x - (r + p_y - w_y)v_x/v_y, w_y].$$

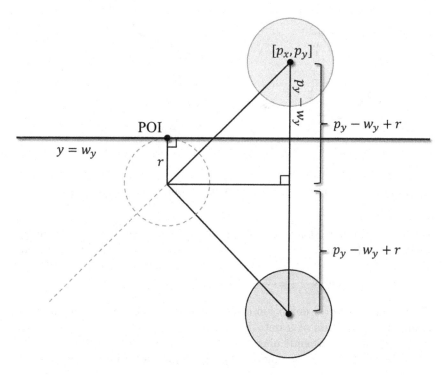

Figure 2.15 • Corrected position for a ball bouncing off the ceiling.

Finding the new position for the ball doesn't require any trig functions. Its x-coordinate doesn't change because it's bouncing off a horizontal line, but its y-coordinate needs to change to what it would have been if the ball had bounced off the ceiling at the POI. Examining Figure 2.15, we see that the vertical distance from the current center of the ball at $[p_x, p_y]$ is $p_y - w_y + r$, and it needs to go twice that distance down to get to where it needs to be, that is, to y-coordinate $p_y - 2(p_y - w_y + r) = 2(w_y - r) - p_y$. Its new position is, therefore,

$$[p_x, 2(w_y - r) - p_y],$$

and its new velocity is $c_r[v_x, -v_y]$, where c_r is the coefficient of restitution.

2.2.2 Bouncing Off a Line

Now, suppose we want to reflect a vector in a line placed at any old angle in 2D space using the "angle of incidence equals angle of reflection" rule. Before we get to reflections, though, we're going to need the concept of the *dot product*. The dot product of two vectors is a scalar. The Linear

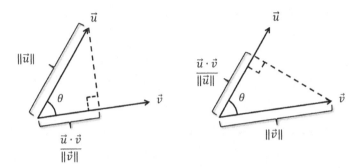

Figure 2.16 • The Geometry World definition of vector dot product.

Algebra World definition is that you multiply them together component by component, then add the results. So, if $\vec{u} = [u_x, u_y]$ and $\vec{v} = [v_x, v_y]$, then

$$\vec{u} \cdot \vec{v} = [u_x, u_y] \cdot [v_x, v_y] = u_x v_x + u_y v_y.$$

The Geometry World definition of $\vec{u} \cdot \vec{v}$ is that it is the length of the perpendicular projection of $\vec{u}$ onto $\vec{v}$ times the length of $\vec{v}$, and equivalently, the length of the perpendicular projection of $\vec{v}$ onto $\vec{u}$ times the length of $\vec{u}$ (see Figure 2.16). If the angle between $\vec{u}$ and $\vec{v}$ is θ, then

$$\cos \theta = \frac{\vec{u} \cdot \vec{v}}{\|u\| \|v\|},$$

as you can see by looking at either side of Figure 2.16. This gives us a cool way of computing θ:

$$\theta = \arccos \frac{\vec{u} \cdot \vec{v}}{\|u\| \|v\|}.$$

We can implement this in code as follows. **D3DXVec2Dot** is the vector dot product function in **D3DX**.

```
float Angle(
  const D3DXVECTOR2& u, const D3DXVECTOR2& v)
{
  return acos(D3DXVec2Dot(&u, &v)/
    (D3DXVec2Length(u) * D3DXVec2Length(v)));
} //Angle
```

Now, we can get down to the business at hand: figuring out how to reflect the vector $\vec{u}$ in a line placed at any orientation. Suppose the line is specified by giving its unit normal vector $\hat{n}$, as shown in Figure 2.17. Let's

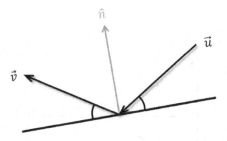

Figure 2.17 • Reflecting $\vec{u}$ in a line specified by its normal $\hat{n}$ to get $\vec{v}$.

call the resulting vector $\vec{v}$. The perpendicular projection of $\vec{u}$ onto $\hat{n}$ has length

$$\frac{\vec{u} \cdot \hat{n}}{\|\hat{n}\|} = \vec{u} \cdot \hat{n}.$$

Looking at Figure 2.18 we see that the vector projection of $\vec{u}$ onto $\hat{n}$ is $(\vec{u} \cdot \hat{n})\hat{n}$. Therefore, as shown in Figure 2.19,

$$\vec{v} = \vec{u} - 2(\vec{u} \cdot \hat{n})\hat{n}.$$

This equation has a short and very sweet implementation in code that uses just five scalar multiplications and three scalar additions:

```
void Reflect(const D3DXVECTOR2& u,
  const D3DXVECTOR2& n, D3DXVECTOR2& v)
{
  v = u - 2.0f * D3DXVec2Dot(&u, &n) * n;
} //Reflect
```

You will find a variant of this method buried in Section 10.6 of [Dunn and Parberry 11], where it finds a use in the standard lighting model. My

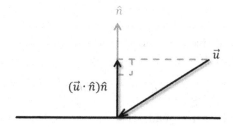

Figure 2.18 • The vector projection of $\vec{u}$ onto $\hat{n}$ is $(\vec{u} \cdot \hat{n})\hat{n}$.

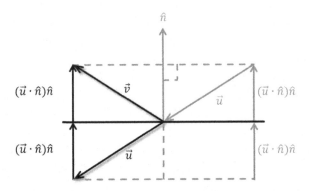

Figure 2.19 • $\vec{v} = \vec{u} - 2(\vec{u} \cdot \hat{n})\hat{n}$.

coauthor Fletcher Dunn observes that it is a popular job interview question for aspiring game programmers, so pay attention.

2.2.3 Bouncing Balls

Now for ball-to-ball collision response. Let's start with the case in which ball B_1 is stationary and ball B_2 is moving with velocity vector $\vec{v}$: they've collided and we want to move B_2 back to the point of impact. What follows is adapted from Appendix A.13 of [Dunn and Parberry 11].

Let δ be the sum of the balls' radii, so that the point of impact is when their centers are distance δ apart. If B_1 is at position $\vec{p}_1$ and B_2 is at position $\vec{p}_2$, let $\vec{c} = \vec{p}_1 - \vec{p}_2$ be the vector from the center of the B_2 to the center of B_1. Let θ be the angle between $-\vec{v}$ and $\vec{c}$. We want to find d, the distance that B_2 has to travel in direction $-\vec{v}$ to the point of impact. All of this is shown in Figure 2.20. By the Law of Cosines,

$$\delta^2 = d^2 + \|\vec{c}\|^2 - 2d\|\vec{c}\| \cos\theta.$$

By the geometric interpretation of dot product,

$$\|\vec{c}\| \cos\theta = -\hat{v} \cdot \vec{c},$$

where $\hat{v}$ is the normalized version of $\vec{v}$. Putting these two things together with the fact that $\|\vec{c}\|^2 = \vec{c} \cdot \vec{c}$,

$$\delta^2 = d^2 + \vec{c} \cdot \vec{c} + 2d\hat{v} \cdot \vec{c}.$$

Rearranging this, we get a quadratic equation in d:

$$d^2 + 2d\hat{v} \cdot \vec{c} + \vec{c} \cdot \vec{c} - \delta^2 = 0.$$

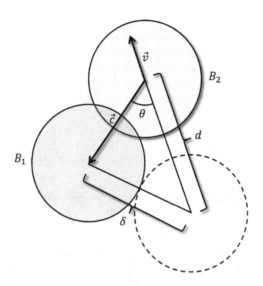

Figure 2.20 • Ball to ball collision. Solve for d.

Solving for d as one of the roots of this quadratic equation,

$$d = \frac{-2\hat{v}\cdot\vec{c} \pm \sqrt{4(\hat{v}\cdot\vec{c})^2 - 4(\vec{c}\cdot\vec{c} - \delta^2)}}{2}$$

$$= -\hat{v}\cdot\vec{c} \pm \sqrt{(\hat{v}\cdot\vec{c})^2 - \vec{c}\cdot\vec{c} + \delta^2}.$$

The two roots correspond to the distance at which the collision starts and the distance at which the collision ends. We want the former one, corresponding to the smaller root ($\hat{v}\cdot\vec{c}$ is a negative number so that $-\hat{v}\cdot\vec{c}$ is positive):

$$d = -\hat{v}\cdot\vec{c} + \sqrt{(\hat{v}\cdot\vec{c})^2 - \vec{c}\cdot\vec{c} + \delta^2}.$$

We'd better be careful of the number inside that square root. It might be negative, which can only happen if Figure 2.20 is actually wrong and the balls miss.

What do we do if both balls are moving? Actually, we've done all the hard work already. We can view things from the perspective of a bug sitting on B_1. From his frame of reference, B_1 is stationary and B_2 is moving at velocity $\vec{v}_2 - \vec{v}_1$ (see Figure 2.21). So, set $\vec{v} = \vec{v}_2 - \vec{v}_1$ in the above, and you are good to go,[8] except that the above procedure will give you only d_2, the distance moved back by B_2. B_1 will need to move back d_1, the same distance scaled by their relative velocity, $d_1 = d_2\|v_1\|/\|v_2\|$.

....

[8] This only works for nonaccelerating frames of reference.

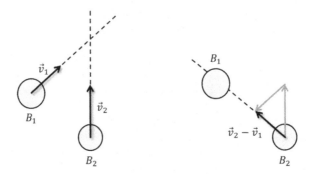

Figure 2.21 • If both balls are moving (left), we can reduce it to the case of one ball moving by using vector subtraction (right).

Now that we can move the balls back to their point of impact, we have to make them bounce. The approach taken is similar to that of bouncing a ball off the tangent between them using the techniques of Section 2.2.2, except that in a perfectly elastic collision, the balls will share the components of velocity along a line between their centers.

Suppose ball B_1 has velocity vector $\vec{u}$. If $\vec{u}'$ and $\vec{v}'$ are the respective velocity vectors of the balls after collision, one would be tempted to apply Figure 2.19 to both balls independently, giving

$$\vec{u}' = \vec{u} - 2(\vec{u} \cdot \hat{n})\hat{n},$$
$$\vec{v}' = \vec{v} - 2(\vec{v} \cdot \hat{n})\hat{n}.$$

The vectors $(\vec{u} \cdot \hat{n})\hat{n}$ and $(\vec{v} \cdot \hat{n})\hat{n}$ are the components of $\vec{u}$ and $\vec{v}$ orthogonal to the tangent, respectively. The sum of the absolute value of the magnitudes of these gets shared evenly between the two balls in the appropriate directions. That is, each ball gets magnitude:

$$\frac{2(\vec{u} \cdot \hat{n}) - 2(\vec{v} \cdot \hat{n})}{2} = \vec{u} \cdot \hat{n} - \vec{v} \cdot \hat{n} = (\vec{u} - \vec{v}) \cdot \hat{n}.$$

Therefore, the proper way to calculate $\vec{u}'$ and $\vec{v}'$ is

$$\vec{u}' = \vec{u} - ((\vec{u} - \vec{v}) \cdot \hat{n})\hat{n},$$
$$\vec{v}' = \vec{v} + ((\vec{u} - \vec{v}) \cdot \hat{n})\hat{n}.$$

The following function to update u and v, given the tangent normal vector n, assumes that n has already been normalized:

```
void Reflect(D3DXVECTOR2& u,
    D3DXVECTOR2& v, const D3DXVECTOR2& n)
```

```
{
  D3DXVECTOR2 dv = u - v;
  float m = D3DXVec2Dot(&dv, &n);
  u -= m * n;
  v += m * n;
} //Reflect
```

Putting everything in this section together, once we discover that two balls have collided (that is, their centers are closer than the sum of their radii), here's what we have to do:

1. Move the balls back to the point of impact.
2. Reflect their velocity vectors in the tangent between them at the point of impact, sharing the perpendicular components equally.
3. Move the balls forward in that direction a distance equal to that moved back in Step 1.

We start by declaring some useful local variables and initializing those that can be initialized.

```
BOOL BallBounce(
  D3DXVECTOR2& p1, D3DXVECTOR2& v1, float r1,
  D3DXVECTOR2& p2, D3DXVECTOR2& v2, float r2)
{
  D3DXVECTOR2 rv, vhat, c, n, v1hat, v2hat;
  float cdotvhat, r, s, d, m, rs;

  D3DXVec2Normalize(&v1hat, &v1);
  D3DXVec2Normalize(&v2hat, &v2);
  rs = D3DXVec2Length(&v1)/D3DXVec2Length(&v2);

  rv = v1 - v2;
  D3DXVec2Normalize(&vhat, &rv);

  c = p2 - p1;
  cdotvhat = D3DXVec2Dot(&c, &vhat);
  D3DXVec2Normalize(&n, &c);
  m = D3DXVec2Dot(&rv, &n);

  r = r1 + r2;
```

Step 1. We move p1 and p2 back to the point of impact. We could do this after Step 2, but it's better to bail out as early as possible if there's really no collision.

```
s = cdotvhat*cdotvhat - D3DXVec2LengthSq(&c) + r*r;
if(s >= 0.0f)
  d = -cdotvhat + sqrt(s);
else return FALSE;

p1 -= d * v1hat;
p2 -= d * (v2hat + v1hat);
```

Step 2. Now we compute the change in velocities.

```
v1 -= m * n;
v2 += m * n;
```

Step 3. We need to recompute v1hat and v2hat because v1 and v2 just changed in Step 2. Then we can move p1 and p2 to where they should be.

```
D3DXVec2Normalize(&v1hat, &v1);
D3DXVec2Normalize(&v2hat, &v2);
p1 += d * v1hat;
p2 += d * v2hat;

return TRUE
} //BallBounce
```

● 2.3 Digital Calculus

Remember your high school physics class? I suppose they talked about things like a particle starting at position $s = 0$ at time $t = 0$ moving at velocity u under constant acceleration a. Hopefully, you remember from class that the particle's position s and velocity v at time t are given by the equations

$$s = ut + at^2/2, \tag{2.1}$$

$$v = u + at. \tag{2.2}$$

Perhaps you were taught that these equations work with vectors too. The vector version talks about a particle starting at position $\vec{s} = [0,0]$ at time $t = 0$ moving at velocity $\vec{u}$ under constant acceleration $\vec{a}$. Its position $\vec{s}$ and velocity $\vec{v}$ at time t are given by

$$\vec{s} = \vec{u}t + \vec{a}t^2/2,$$

$$\vec{v} = \vec{u} + \vec{a}t.$$

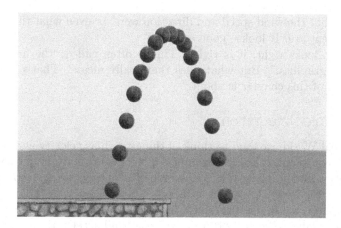

Figure 2.22 • The path followed by a cannonball launched at an orientation of about 75°.

The vector version is not so much of a big deal when you stop to think about it. For example, in two dimensions, just do the high-school thing in each dimension and slam the results into a 2D vector. Simple.

You may also have learned in your calculus class that Equation (2.2) is the *derivative* or *differential* of Equation (2.1), and that Equation (2.1) is the *integral* of Equation (2.2). This is an application of the Fundamental Theorem of Calculus, which states that differentiation and integration are the same but backwards.

All of this may be but a vague and hazy memory that for the sake of your mental health you are actively trying to suppress, but perhaps that's just as well. The physics you learned in high school was *continuous physics*. You are about to learn *discrete physics*, which is a very different animal. It looks similar, and mathematicians would agree that discrete physics converges to continuous physics in the limit, but there is no pressing need for us to obsess about reality.[9] All we want to do is make a game where the physics looks right, and we know that when we see it, right?

For example, suppose we threw a ball into the air at about 75° to the horizontal. If we had a high-speed camera and took a bunch of images of the ball flying through the air and superimposed them, we'd expect to see something like Figure 2.22. The horizontal speed of the ball appears to be constant, its vertical speed seems to slow as it gets higher, and its path looks like a parabola. Figure 2.22 actually shows the discrete simulation of a ball. Is it right? Who cares! We don't know how hard the ball was

....

[9]Indeed, there are indications that both time and space are discrete at the quantum level, so continuous physics is probably the approximation and discrete physics the reality.

thrown, what the wind speed and direction were, or even what the units of measurement are. It looks "good enough."

So if it looks right, it is right. This is often called "the first law of computer graphics." But what does that really mean? That's what the remainder of this chapter is about.

2.3.1   Euler Integration

In the Real World, we tend to think of things such as velocity and position as being continuous. So, for example, if we take a body under constant acceleration and graph its velocity as a function of time, we get a continuous graph like Figure 2.23. But in a discrete universe, such as the one inside our computer, we divide time into discrete units or *frames*. During each frame we compute the new position, velocity, and acceleration of the body and compose a frame of animation to display on the screen.

Let's take a closer look at what's going on here. Suppose we know an object's position, velocity, and acceleration in frame i (see Figure 2.24). Let's call them s_i, v_i, and a_i, respectively. Let Δt be the duration of the previous animation frame. Then Δt is our best guess for the duration of the current frame (which isn't over yet). We can compute s_{i+1} and v_{i+1} as follows:

$$s_{i+1} = s_i + v_i \Delta t,$$
$$v_{i+1} = v_i + a_i \Delta t.$$

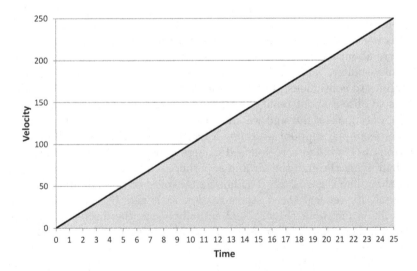

Figure 2.23 • Velocity versus time in a continuous universe.

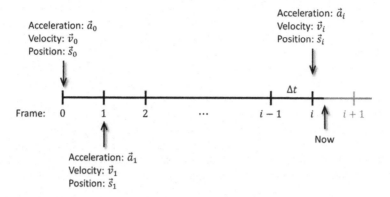

Figure 2.24 • Timeline for a moving object.

This corresponds to the classic *Euler integration*, named after the German mathematician Leonhard Euler[10] (1701–1783) that you probably learned in calculus class in school. Instead of integrating the curve, we sum over discrete time slices (see Figure 2.25).

Objects will need to store their position, velocity, acceleration, and time since the last move like so:

```
D3DXVECTOR2 m_vPos;
D3DXVECTOR2 m_vVelocity;
D3DXVECTOR2 m_vAcceleration;
int m_nLastMoveTime;
```

Code for a **move** function that updates an object's position, velocity, and time since the last move should look something like this:

```
void move(){
  const float SCALE = 20.0f;
  const float SCALE2 = 42.0f;
  int time=g_cTimer.time();
  int dt = time - m_nLastMoveTime;
  m_vPos += m_vVelocity*(float)dt/SCALE;
  m_vVelocity += m_vAcceleration*(float)dt/SCALE2;
  m_nLastMoveTime = time;
} //move
```

....

[10]Euler is pronounced "oiler," not "yooler." If you want to see a mathematician cringe, pronounce it "yooler."

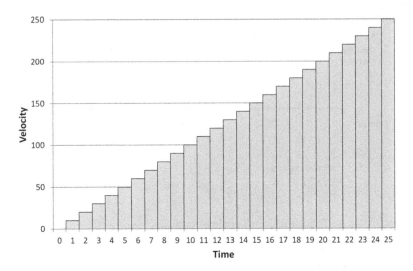

Figure 2.25 • Velocity versus time in a discrete universe.

Suppose that an object starts at rest and accelerates at 10 m/s for 14 s. Where does it end up after 14 s? To get the answer, we use Equation (2.1):

$$s = ut + at^2/2$$
$$= 0 + 5 \times 14^2 \text{ m}$$
$$= 980 \text{ m.}$$

Inside the computer, we compute the distance moved in each frame and accumulate all those distances to get the total distance. We have to assume that the velocity is constant within each frame. We end up with the set of distances in Table 2.1, which is too small. The final distance traveled is 910 m instead of 980.

Of course, we can always change the code so that the velocity is updated first:

```
m_vVelocity += m_vAcceleration*(float)dt/SCALE2;
m_vPos += m_vVelocity*(float)dt/SCALE;
```

However, Table 2.2 shows that this makes the final distance too large, 1050 m instead of 980. Clearly, we're never going to be able to get it exactly right. The gray area in Figure 2.23 is always going to be slightly different from that in Figure 2.25. The point is that it doesn't really matter.

t	a	v	s	Δs	$\sum \Delta s$
0	10	0	0	0	0
1	10	10	5	0	0
2	10	20	20	10	10
3	10	30	45	20	30
4	10	40	80	30	60
5	10	50	125	40	100
6	10	60	180	50	150
7	10	70	245	60	210
8	10	80	320	70	280
9	10	90	405	80	360
10	10	100	500	90	450
11	10	110	605	100	550
12	10	120	720	110	660
13	10	130	845	120	780
14	10	140	980	130	910

Table 2.1 • Distances using Euler integration, updating position before velocity. Column 1 is the frame number, Column 2 is acceleration, which remains constant, Column 3 is velocity, Column 4 is expected distance traveled, Column 5 is the distance traveled in the current frame, and Column 6 is the sum of Column 5 up to the current frame.

t	a	v	s	Δs	$\sum \Delta s$
0	10	0	0	0	0
1	10	10	5	10	10
2	10	20	20	20	30
3	10	30	45	30	60
4	10	40	80	40	100
5	10	50	125	50	150
6	10	60	180	60	210
7	10	70	245	70	280
8	10	80	320	80	360
9	10	90	405	90	450
10	10	100	500	100	550
11	10	110	605	110	660
12	10	120	720	120	780
13	10	130	845	130	910
14	10	140	980	140	1050

Table 2.2 • Distances using Euler integration, updating position before velocity. Column 1 is the frame number, Column 2 is acceleration, which remains constant, Column 3 is velocity, Column 4 is expected distance traveled, Column 5 is the distance traveled in the current frame, and Column 6 is the sum of Column 5 up to the current frame.

2.3.2   Verlet Integration

Loup Verlet (1951–) developed the concept that is now called *Verlet integration* for use in particle physics simulation. There are mathematical reasons for using Verlet integration instead of Euler integration when simulating real particle systems. But what about in games? Game programmers don't care as much about reality. One useful feature of Verlet integration is that it is easy to incorporate constraints, for example, to fix lengths and angles. This means that Verlet integration makes it easier to code soft body animation including cloth and ragdoll physics.

Verlet's thinking goes like this. Suppose we know a_i, s_i, and s_{i-1} and want to compute s_{i+1}. Let $\Delta s_i = s_i - s_{i-1}$ be the distance moved in the previous animation frame. Let's try to compute Δs_{i+1}, the distance to be moved in the current frame. We know that

$$\Delta s_{i+1} = v_i \Delta t + a_i \Delta t^2 / 2.$$

Now, Δs_i is a good approximation for $v_i \Delta t$. Therefore, substituting for $v_i \Delta t$ in the above equation,

$$\Delta s_{i+1} = \Delta s_i + a_i \Delta t^2 / 2.$$

Since $s_{i+1} = s_i + \Delta s_{i+1}$, substituting for Δs_{i+1},

$$s_{i+1} = s_i + \Delta s_i + a_i \Delta t^2 / 2.$$

Substituting for Δs_i, we get

$$s_{i+1} = s_i + (s_i - s_{i-1}) + a_i \Delta t^2 / 2$$
$$= 2s_i - s_{i-1} + a_i \cdot \delta t^2 / 2.$$

This last equation is the key to Verlet integration. It shows how to compute s_{i+1} from s_i, s_{i-1}, a_i, and Δt. There is no need to store velocity at all. We can even fake a type of friction by using the following equation instead:

$$s_{i+1} = 1.99 s_i - 0.99 s_{i-1} + a_i \cdot \Delta t^2 / 2.$$

We implement this by storing each object's position, last position, acceleration, and last move time.[11]

```
D3DXVECTOR2 m_vPos;
D3DXVECTOR2 m_vOldPos;
D3DXVECTOR2 m_vAccel;
int m_nLastMoveTime;
```

. . . .

[11] That's right, we don't store velocity.

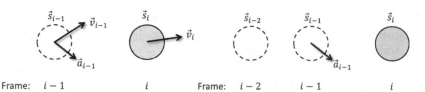

Frame: $i-1$ i Frame: $i-2$ $i-1$ i

Figure 2.26 • Discrete motion   **Figure 2.27** • Discrete motion with Verlet
with Euler integration.   integration.

We then update position once per frame:

```
int time = g_cTimer.time();
int dt = time - m_nLastMoveTime;
D3DXVECTOR2 vTemp = m_vPos; //this will be old
m_vPos += m_vPos - m_vOldPos
 + m_vAccel*dt*dt/2.0f; //update
m_vOldPos = vTemp; //what was current is now old
m_nLastMoveTime = time; //update time
```

Figures 2.26 and 2.27 summarize the difference between Euler and Verlet
integration for computing the motion of a body under acceleration. Our
code can be optimized slightly by assuming that dt is constant. In fact,
we can make it equal to 1. There's no need to store time:

```
D3DXVECTOR2 m_vPos;
D3DXVECTOR2 m_vOldPos;
D3DXVECTOR2 m_vAccel;
```

The code becomes simpler too.

```
D3DXVECTOR2 vTemp = m_vPos; //this will be old
m_vPos +=
 m_vPos - m_vOldPos + m_vAccel/2.0f;
m_vOldPos = vTemp; //what was current is now old
```

Even better, we can ignore the division by 2 and ramp the acceleration
down to compensate if the resulting motion looks too fast.

```
D3DXVECTOR2 vTemp = m_vPos; //this will be old
m_vPos += m_vPos - m_vOldPos + m_vAccel;
m_vOldPos = vTemp; //what was current is now old
```

The astute reader will be asking themselves how we can assume dt == 1 when in fact it is highly unlikely to be the case. However, we can repeat this code many times per frame. For example,

```
const int ITERATIONS = 7; //Why 7? Why not.
D3DXVECTOR2 vTemp;
for(int i=0; i<ITERATIONS; i++){
 vTemp = m_vPos;
 m_vPos += m_vPos - m_vOldPos + m_vAccel;
 m_vOldPos = vTemp;
} //for
```

In practice we should do as many ITERATIONS as we can fit into a frame, that is, ITERATIONS == dt.[12]

```
int time = g_cTimer.time();
int dt = time - m_nLastMoveTime;
D3DXVECTOR2 vTemp;
for(int i=0; i<dt; i++){
 vTemp = m_vPos;
 m_vPos += m_vPos - m_vOldPos + m_vAccel;
 m_vOldPos = vTemp;
} //for
m_nLastMoveTime = time;
```

How do we do collision response with Verlet integration? Let's take the example of bouncing off the right-hand wall. Once we've detected a collision, here's what we do. To simplify things a little, lets suppose the ball is touching the right-hand wall, either because we're lucky or we've detected a penetration and backed off the ball's current position m_vPos and old position m_vOldPos to keep it that way. The situation looks like Figure 2.28 (left). The ball is coming in from the bottom left corner along the dotted line and will reflect to the top left corner along the other dotted line with the angle of incidence equal to the angle of reflection. It's just a matter of moving m_vOldPos to the right to make it that way. That is, if dx is the difference in the x-coordinates of the current and old positions, then we want to move m_vOldPos to the right by 2 times dx as shown in Figure 2.28 (right).

```
float dx = m_vPos.x - m_vOldPos.x;
m_vOldPos.x += 2.0f * dx;
```

....

[12]Usually, dt is in the range of tens of milliseconds.

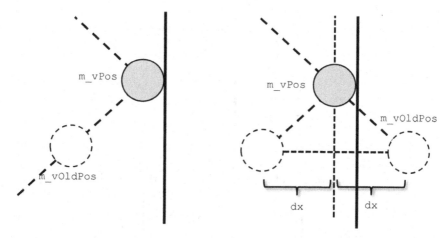

Figure 2.28 ● The Verlet bounce. Bouncing off the right-hand wall using Verlet integration.

That can be simplified slightly to

```
m_vOldPos.x = 2.0f * m_vPos.x - m_vOldPos.x;
```

But where does the coefficient of restitution fit in? How can we move m_vOldPos to scale back the speed of the reflected ball? As we can see in Figure 2.29, it needs to move in the direction of m_vPos. Here's how to do it with a coefficient of restitution r. To compute the new value of m_vOldPos, we compute the vector vDelta from m_vOldPos to m_vPos, negate its y-component, scale it by r, and add it to m_vPos (see Figure 2.30):

```
const float r = 0.8f; //for example
D3DXVECTOR2 vDelta = m_vPos - m_vOldPos;
vDelta.y = -vDelta.y;
m_vOldPos = m_vPos + r * vDelta
```

Replacing the vector operations with component-wise operations makes the code slightly less readable and slightly more efficient:[13]

```
m_vOldPos.x = m_vPos.x + r*(m_vPos.x - m_vOldPos.x);
m_vOldPos.y += r*(m_vOldPos.y - m_vPos.y);
```

....

[13]But one can argue that any optimizing compiler worth its salt ought to be able to perform the optimization for you.

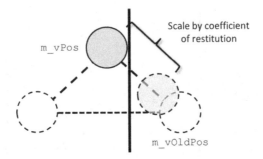

Figure 2.29 • Trying to fit a coefficient of restitution into Figure 2.28.

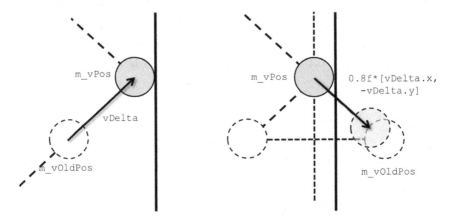

Figure 2.30 • The Verlet bounce using vectors.

● 2.4 Relaxation

I mentioned earlier that Verlet integration makes it easy to enforce constraints on the particles. It's about time I backed up that claim. For
example, let's model a stick by applying Verlet integration to two particles
at the ends of the stick. (See Figure 2.31.) The constraint is that the distance between the particles must remain constant. We move the particles
at the ends of the stick independently, then try to correct their positions
before rendering if they are the wrong distance apart. Suppose its ends are
at positions m_vP1 and m_vP2, and it is supposed to have length LEN.

```
const float LEN = 42.0f
D3DXVECTOR2 m_vP1, m_vP2;
```

First we get a vector vStick along the stick and find its length fLen.

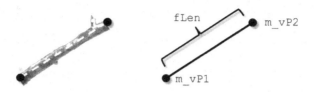

Figure 2.31 • Modeling a stick as two particles.

```
D3DXVECTOR2 vStick = m_vP1 - m_vP2;
float fLen = D3DXVec2Length(&vStick);
```

Then we find the difference between the stick now and what it should be.

```
vStick *= 1.0f - LEN/fLen;
```

We split the difference between the two ends.

```
m_vP1 += 0.5f * vStick;
m_vP2 -= 0.5f * vStick;
```

Putting it all together and simplifying the code a little, we get the following useful function.[14]

```
void StickRelax(VECTOR& p1, VECTOR& p2){
  D3DXVECTOR2 vStick = p1 - p2;
  vStick *= 1.0f - LEN/D3DXVec2Length(&vStick);
  p1 += 0.5f * vStick;
  p2 -= 0.5f * vStick;
}; //StickRelax
```

So far, so good. But what if we've got two sticks joined together at one end? We can model them using three particles as shown in Figure 2.32. But in satisfying the length constraint on one stick, we may move the shared m_vP2, violating the length constraint on the other stick (see Figure 2.33). Here's what we do.

Given these declarations,

```
const float LEN = 42.0f
VECTOR m_vP1, m_vP2, m_vP3;
```

....

[14]It's "useful" in the sense that we'll use it again in a moment.

Figure 2.32 • Modeling a pair of sticks using three particles.

Figure 2.33 • The shared point m_vP2 cannot move in both directions simultaneously.

we treat the sticks independently:

```
StickRelax(m_vP1, m_vP2);
StickRelax(m_vP2, m_vP3);
```

Notice that this code is not exactly as we drew it in Figure 2.33. When we move m_vP2 the second time, it's not starting from its original position (see Figure 2.34), but it's making progress towards where it needs to be. All we need to do is to repeat the process, which is called *relaxation*.

```
const int ITERATIONS = 7; //Why 7? Why not
for(int i=0; i<ITERATIONS; i++){
   StickRelax(m_vP1, m_vP2);
   StickRelax(m_vP2, m_vP3);
} //for
```

This is what is known as *Jacobi* or *Gauss-Seidel* relaxation.[15] It is a general method for satisfying multiple constraints that works quite well, which means that if the conditions are right, it will converge. The number of **ITERATIONS** will depend on the physical system being modeled and details such as the speeds and the floating-point precision. If **ITERATIONS** is small, the stick acts like a spring. As **ITERATIONS** gets larger, the spring becomes more stick-like.

....

[15]I'll probably get flamed by at least one mathematician for glossing over the subtle differences between Jacobi and Gauss-Seidel relaxation. Gandalf would probably have said this about mathematicians: "Meddle not in the affairs of mathematicians, for they are subtle and quick to anger."

Figure 2.34 • Instead of taking the two forces at m_vP2 together (left), treat them consecutively (center and right).

• 2.5 Exercises

1. Prove that the angles of a triangle add up to $180°$.

2. You are in a gun emplacement at world space coordinates $[365, 99]$, and your gun turret is at angle $42°$ widdershins[16] from the horizontal. What angle must you rotate it in order to point to an adversary at $[836, 999]$?

3. Prove the two parts of the Law of Cosines that we didn't prove in Section 2.1.3:

$$b^2 = a^2 + c^2 - 2ac\cos\beta,$$
$$c^2 = a^2 + b^2 - 2ab\cos\gamma.$$

4. Prove that $\sin(\alpha + \beta) = \sin\alpha\cos\beta + \cos\alpha\sin\beta$. (Hint: See Appendix A.)

5. Suppose you are animating a ball of radius 75 that starts out below the top of the screen rolling at angle θ counterclockwise from the horizontal. You want it to bounce off the top of the screen, which has y-coordinate 768. Suppose that it ends up at point $\vec{p}_0$ after the first animation frame. For each of the values of θ and $\vec{p}_0$ below, find the coordinates of the POI and the corrected position $\vec{p}_1$ of the ball after bouncing off the top of the screen. Show all of your work.

   (a) $\theta = 1.855$, $\vec{p}_0 = [141, 881]$. I'm going to help you get started by giving you the answer this time. Please verify for me[17] that the POI is $[141, 881]$ and $\vec{p}_1 = [141, 505]$.
   (b) $\theta = 1.064$, $\vec{p}_0 = [632, 914]$.
   (c) $\theta = 0.896$, $\vec{p}_0 = [698, 816]$.
   (d) $\theta = 0.756$, $\vec{p}_0 = [762, 756]$.
   (e) $\theta = 0.695$, $\vec{p}_0 = [892, 814]$.

....

[16]Well? What do you think the index at the back of the book is for?
[17]I've been known to make mitsakes.

6. Suppose you are animating a scene in which a green ball of radius 128 has been firmly bolted to the floor at position $[680, 450]$, and a blue ball of radius 75 is rolling towards it. In frame 0, the blue ball is at $[280, 250]$. In frame 1, our animation has unfortunately allowed the balls to overlap, and the blue ball is at the position $\vec{g}_0$ given below. Find the distance d that the blue ball must be moved back along its path to the TOI and its corrected position $\vec{g}_1$ after bouncing off the green ball. Show all of your work.

   (a) $\vec{g}_0 = [564, 599]$. I'm going to help you get started by giving you the answer this time. Please verify for me that $d = 148.03$ and $\vec{g}_1 = [415, 611]$.
   (b) $\vec{g}_0 = [576, 589]$. I'll do it a second time, but then I'm going to cut you loose. Verify for me that $d = 127.22$ and $\vec{g}_1 = [461, 626]$.
   (c) $\vec{g}_0 = [618, 547]$. (You are on your own now. Go for it.)
   (d) $\vec{g}_0 = [640, 520]$.
   (e) $\vec{g}_0 = [714, 367]$.
   (f) $\vec{g}_0 = [725, 315]$.

3

A Rigid Body Physics Game

Let's apply the math and physics from Chapter 2 to make a rigid body dynamics game, one in which things are rigid in the sense that they can't be deformed by the forces that act on them. I'll show you the source code in detail, describing what it does and how it does it. Just as importantly, I'll describe the design decisions that made it look the way it does. You can download the source code from the website for this book [Parberry 12] and experiment with it yourself. My favorite rigid body dynamics game in real life is eight-ball pool, but let's simplify things a little bit and restrict it to the end game, in which you have to sink the eight ball without sinking the cue ball.

This chapter is divided into six sections. Section 3.1 contains an overview of the Eight-Ball Pool End Game, including how to play it, what physics we will need, and the code structure. Section 3.2 begins our journey through the code file-by-file. Section 3.3 is on Render World, and Section 3.4 is on Object World (see Section 1.4.1). Section 3.5 is on the objects in the game, which are obviously pool balls. We end in Section 3.6 with some exercises for the reader.

3.1 The Eight-Ball Pool End Game

This section describes our Eight-Ball Pool End Game in more detail than you probably want (to be on the safe side). It is divided into two parts. Section 3.1.1 describes how to play, which is pretty obvious: Just mash the space bar and the arrow keys until you get the hang of it. Section 3.1.2 talks about how the code is organized.

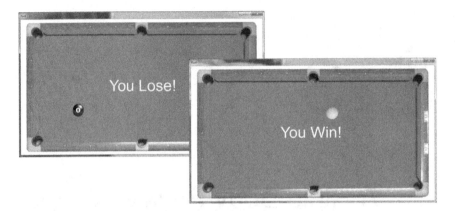

Figure 3.1 • Winning and losing the Eight-Ball Pool End Game.

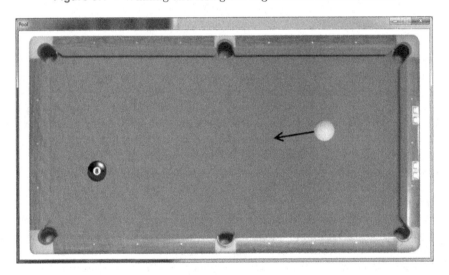

Figure 3.2 • The Eight-Ball Pool End Game in play.

3.1.1 How to Play

In the Eight-Ball Pool End Game, you have only a cue ball and an eight ball
on the table, as shown in Figure 3.2. Your aim is to sink the eight-ball into
a pocket before the cue ball. If you sink the cue ball, you lose (Figure 3.1,
left). Otherwise, if you sink the eight ball, you win[1] (Figure 3.1, right). At
the start, the cue ball is on the baseline, and you can move it along that

....

[1]In real life you also lose if you completely miss the eight ball, but we'll ignore that
rule.

Files	Class	Description
GameObject.cpp, h	CGameObject	Base object class
BallObject.cpp, h	CBallObject	Derived ball object class
ObjectManager.cpp, h	CObjectManager	Base object manager class
BallManager.cpp, h	CBallManager	Derived ball manager class
ObjectWorld.cpp, h	CObjectWorld	Object world
RenderWorld.cpp, h	CRenderWorld	Render world
MyGame.cpp	–	Game main
SndList.h	–	Sound list
GameDefines.h	–	Game defines

Table 3.1 • Files and classes in project My Game.

line with the up and down arrow keys. An arrow on the screen shows the direction that the cue ball will travel. To fire it, hit the space bar. You can change the direction vector with the left and right arrow keys before you fire. Once the balls come to rest after each shot (assuming both balls are still on the table), you will see the arrow for your next shot (see Figure 3.2). When the game is over, the space bar will reset the game back to the initial conditions.

3.1.2 Code Structure

The code is organized into a Visual Studio 10 solution that has three projects called Engine, Tools, and My Game. Engine and Tools contain code that is outside the scope of this book, including details of the care and feeding of DirectX and Windows programming. Tools also contains code from TinyXML, an Open Source XML reader. We will use it to read settings from an XML file named GameSettings.xml. I want you to ignore those details, so I haven't given you the source code. Engine in particular contains classes CRenderer, C3DSprite, CSpriteManager, and CTextManager, whose tasks you can guess from their names.

Project My Game consists of seven code files and eight header files containing declarations and definitions for the six classes shown in Table 3.1.

1. The Render World class CRenderWorld implements the Render World shown in Figure 3.3, top right.

2. The Object World class CObjectWorld implements the Object World shown in Figure 3.3, top left. The Object World class also makes use of the following classes.

3. The Game Object class CGameObject is a generic object in the Object World responsible primarily for knowing where it is and where it is going.

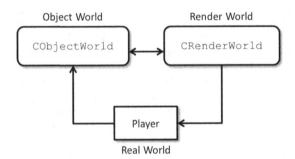

Figure 3.3 • The organization of our code using the two Game Engine Worlds of Figure 1.1.

4. The Ball Object class `CBallObject` is derived from `CGameObject`. It adds ball-specific things and is also in the Object World.

5. The Object Manager class `CObjectManager` is responsible for managing a collection of objects and the interactions between them. It is also in the Object World.

6. The Ball Manager class `CBallManager` is derived from `CObjectManager` and adds ball-specific things. It is also in the Object World.

The main control structure in our game code is the `ProcessFrame` loop. Each iteration of the `ProcessFrame` loop consists of asking the Object World to move all of the objects and then to draw them. The Object World is obviously responsible for the former since only it knows about their locations and velocities, but it will clearly need to ask the Render World for help with the latter.

First, let's see what happens when `ProcessFrame` asks the Object World to move all of the balls. The process is illustrated in Figure 3.4. The Object World's **move** function calls the Ball Manager's **move** function. The Ball Manager's **move** function calls the Object Manager's **move** function, then does ball-to-ball collision detection and response. The Object Manager's **move** function loops through all of the objects in its Object List and asks them to move themselves by calling the Ball Object **move** function. This in turn calls the Game Object **move** function and performs ball-to-rail and ball-to-pocket collision detection and response.

Next, `ProcessFrame` asks the Object World to draw the game objects. It assumes that the objects themselves are healthy and mentally well-adjusted in the sense that they know where they are and where they are going in Object World. The process is again illustrated in Figure 3.4. The Object World's **draw** function calls the Ball Manager's **draw** function, which inherits the Object Manager's **draw** function, which loops through its Object List and asks the Render World to draw each object listed there.

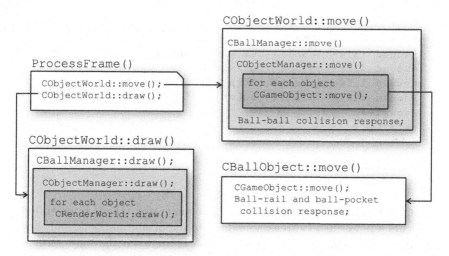

Figure 3.4 • Flow of control for the **ProcessFrame** loop.

● 3.2 Code Run-Through

Project My Game has an XML file and, as we mentioned above, seven source files and eight header files. Let's hit the high points.

● 3.2.1 File GameSettings.xml

```
<settings>
 <game name="Pool End Game" />
 <renderer width="1024" height="531" />

 <!-- image file names -->
 <images>
  <image src="Images\\pooltable1024x531.png" />
 </images>

 <!-- sprites -->
 <sprites>
  <sprite name="vector" file="Images\\vector.png"/>
  <sprite name="cueball" file="Images\\cueball.png"/>
  <sprite name="eightball" file="Images\\8ball.png"/>
 </sprites>

 <!-- sound -->
 <sound cps="1" bps="8" rate="22050"/>
```

```
<sounds level="0">
 <sound file="Sounds\\cue.wav" copies="1"/>
 <sound file="Sounds\\ballclick.wav" copies="4"/>
 <sound file="Sounds\\thump.wav" copies="4"/>
 <sound file="Sounds\\pocket.wav" copies="2"/>
</sounds>
</settings>
```

3.2.2   File GameDefines.h

File GameDefines.h contains a couple of enumerated types. Enumerated types are a powerful way to assign names to important numbers, and they let you assign a meaningful type name to them when they are used in declarations. If you're unfamiliar with them, get familiar fast.

GameObjectType describes the three kinds of game object; the arrow for drawing the impulse vector to be applied to the cue ball (see Figure 3.2), the cue-ball object, and the eight-ball object.

```
enum GameObjectType{
 ARROW_OBJECT, CUEBALL_OBJECT, EIGHTBALL_OBJECT
};
```

GameStateType describes the possible game states; the first is the initial game state when the balls are in their initial positions, the second is when the balls are actually in motion, the third is when setting up the next shot as shown in Figure 3.2, the fourth and fifth are when the player has won and lost, respectively.

```
enum GameStateType{
 INITIAL_GAMESTATE, BALLSMOVING_GAMESTATE,
 SETTINGUPSHOT_GAMESTATE, WON_GAMESTATE,
 LOST_GAMESTATE
};
```

3.2.3   File MyGame.cpp

Think of the file MyGame.cpp as being the main for your game. It starts with declarations of some global variables. The character array g_szGameName is a place to store the game's name. This will automatically be read from GameSettings.xml and displayed in the window's title bar as shown at the top left of Figure 3.2. Global variable g_nGameState will record the current game state (refer back to Section 3.2.2 for the definition of GameStateType).

```
char  g_szGameName [256];
GameStateType  g_nGameState  =  INITIAL_GAMESTATE ;
```

Next, we declare some useful singleton class instances. The timer g_cTimer takes care of measuring time for you. The Sound Manager g_pSoundManager manages the game sounds for you automatically, taking input from Game Settings.xml. Finally, we'll declare the Render World g_cRenderWorld and the Object World g_cObjectWorld.

```
CTimer  g_cTimer ;
CSoundManager * g_pSoundManager ;

CRenderWorld  g_cRenderWorld ;
CObjectWorld  g_cObjectWorld ;
```

That ends the list of global variables. The first function is CreateObjects, which creates the cue-ball and eight-ball objects. It asks the Ball Manager to create them at certain places and squirrels away pointers to them in global variables g_pCueBallObject and g_p8BallObject for later use.

```
void  CreateObjects (){
  D3DXVECTOR2  v;

  // create eight ball
  v.x = 750.0f; v.y = (float) g_nScreenHeight /2.0f;
  g_cObjectWorld . create (EIGHTBALL_OBJECT , v);

  // create cue ball
  v.x = 295.0f; v.y = (float) g_nScreenHeight /2.0f;
  g_cObjectWorld . create (CUEBALL_OBJECT , v);
  g_cObjectWorld . ResetImpulseVector ();
} // CreateObjects
```

Function BeginGame starts the game by setting the initial game state, starting the level timer, clearing the Object World of objects, then calling function CreateObjects above to create new ones.

```
void  BeginGame (){
  g_nGameState  =  INITIAL_GAMESTATE ;
  g_cTimer . StartLevelTimer ();
```

```
  g_cObjectWorld.clear();
  CreateObjects();
} //BeginGame
```

Function `InitGame` initializes your game for you. It asks the Render World
to initialize Direct3D, then to load images from disk. The image files are
specified in `gamesettings.xml`.

```
void InitGame(){
  g_cRenderWorld.Initialize();
  g_cRenderWorld.LoadImages();
  BeginGame();
} //InitGame
```

Function `EndGame` cleans things up at the end of the game. The only thing
that really can't clean up after itself is the Render World since DirectX is
a little picky about the order in which things get cleaned up.

```
void EndGame(){
  g_cRenderWorld.End();
} //EndGame
```

Function `RenderFrame` renders a frame of animation. The Render World
does the heavy lifting here. We ask the Render World to start up the
graphics pipeline, and if that fails, we simply leave. Otherwise, we ask the
Render World to draw the background, then the Object World to draw the
objects. It will figure out where the objects should be in Render World and
will ask Render World to draw them there. Finally, it asks Render World to
draw the win-loss message, if any, then to close down the graphics pipeline.

```
void RenderFrame(){
  if(g_cRenderWorld.BeginScene()){
    g_cRenderWorld.DrawBackground();
    g_cObjectWorld.draw();
    g_cRenderWorld.DrawWinLoseMessage(g_nGameState);
    g_cRenderWorld.EndScene();
  } //if
} //RenderFrame
```

Function `ProcessFrame` is called once per frame of animation. It starts
by telling the Sound Manager that it is starting a new frame. This is to
prevent two identical sounds being played during the same animation frame
since two identical sounds played simultaneously equals one sound played

twice as loud. It then calls on the Object World to move the balls, then calls function RenderFrame above to draw them in their new positions.

```
void ProcessFrame (){
  g_pSoundManager ->beginframe ();
  g_cObjectWorld.move ();
  RenderFrame ();
```

Finally, ProcessFrame checks to see whether the player has won or lost, and if neither, checks whether the conditions are right for the player to take another shot (the balls were moving, none have been pocketed, yet they've all stopped), and if they are, it takes the appropriate action.

```
  if (g_cObjectWorld . CueBallDown ())
    g_nGameState = LOST_GAMESTATE ;
  else if (g_cObjectWorld.BallDown ())
    g_nGameState = WON_GAMESTATE ;
  else if (g_nGameState == BALLSMOVING_GAMESTATE &&
  !g_cObjectWorld.BallDown () &&
  g_cObjectWorld . AllBallsStopped ()){
    g_nGameState = SETTINGUPSHOT_GAMESTATE;
    g_cObjectWorld . ResetImpulseVector ();
  }
} //ProcessFrame
```

Function KeyboardHandler is your keyboard handler. Windows encodes the key as a member of an enumerated type starting with VK_. If the player hits the ESC key, then the function returns TRUE, indicating that the player wants to quit.

```
BOOL KeyboardHandler (WPARAM keystroke ){
  switch(keystroke){
    case VK_ESCAPE: return TRUE; //quit
```

The up and down arrow keys move the cue ball vertically if we are in game state INITIAL_GAMESTATE. It calls the Object World's AdjustCueBall function to move the cue ball up or down, then calls its ResetImpulse Vector function to make sure that the arrow remains pointing to the eight ball.

```
  case VK_UP:
    if (g_nGameState == INITIAL_GAMESTATE ){
      g_cObjectWorld . AdjustCueBall (MOVEDELTA );
```

```
      g_cObjectWorld.ResetImpulseVector();
   } //if
 break;

 case VK_DOWN:
   if(g_nGameState == INITIAL_GAMESTATE){
     g_cObjectWorld.AdjustCueBall(-MOVEDELTA);
     g_cObjectWorld.ResetImpulseVector();
   } //if
 break;
```

The left and right arrow keys control the impulse vector to be applied to the cue ball. If we are in game states INITIAL_GAMESTATE or SETTINGUPSHOT_ GAMESTATE, then the Object World's AdjustImpulseVector is called to add or subtract a small value from the impulse angle.

```
 case VK_LEFT:
   if(g_nGameState == SETTINGUPSHOT_GAMESTATE ||
   g_nGameState == INITIAL_GAMESTATE)
     g_cObjectWorld.AdjustImpulseVector(ANGLEDELTA);
   break;

 case VK_RIGHT:
   if(g_nGameState == SETTINGUPSHOT_GAMESTATE ||
   g_nGameState == INITIAL_GAMESTATE)
     g_cObjectWorld.AdjustImpulseVector(-ANGLEDELTA);
   break;
```

The final case is the space bar. If the player has won or lost and the balls have stopped moving, then it restarts the game by calling function BeginGame described above. It needs to wait for the balls to stop moving because the player might have sunk the eight ball (which is, albeit temporarily, a win), but the cue ball may continue rolling into a pocket (which is a lose). Otherwise it shoots.

```
 case VK_SPACE:
   if((g_nGameState == WON_GAMESTATE ||
   g_nGameState == LOST_GAMESTATE) &&
   g_cObjectWorld.AllBallsStopped())
     BeginGame();
   else
     if(g_nGameState==SETTINGUPSHOT_GAMESTATE ||
     g_nGameState == INITIAL_GAMESTATE){
       g_nGameState = BALLSMOVING_GAMESTATE;
       g_cObjectWorld.shoot();
```

```
      g_pSoundManager ->play(CUE_SOUND);
    } //else if
    break;
```

This ends the switch statement and the keyboard handler.

```
  } //switch
  return FALSE;
} //KeyboardHandler
```

Finally, we have the Window Procedure, WindowProc, and WinMain. I strongly advise you not to mess with these unless you know what you're doing. The hard work is handled by my functions DefaultWindowProc and DefaultWinMain hidden in the Engine code.

```
LRESULT CALLBACK WindowProc(HWND h, UINT m,
WPARAM w, LPARAM l){
  return DefaultWindowProc(h, m, w, l);
} //WindowProc

int WINAPI WinMain(HINSTANCE hI, HINSTANCE hP,
LPSTR lpC, int nCS){
  return DefaultWinMain(hI, hP, lpC, nCS);
} //WinMain
```

• 3.3 Render World

The Render World takes care of the rendering tasks that are particular to your game. It is derived from CRenderer, which does the heavy lifting of interacting with DirectX. It's a small class with two public member functions.

```
class CRenderWorld: public CRenderer{
  public:
    void DrawWinLoseMessage(GameStateType state);
    void LoadImages();
}; //CRenderWorld
```

Function DrawWinLossMessage draws a "You lose" or "You win" message to the screen depending on whether the parameter state indicates that the player has won or lost. CRenderer's TextWrite function takes care of the details of writing text to the screen.[2] Nothing is written if neither ball is in a pocket.

```
void CRenderWorld::DrawWinLoseMessage(
  GameStateType state)
{
 switch(state){
   case WON_GAMESTATE:
     TextWrite("You Win!");
     break;
   case LOST_GAMESTATE:
     TextWrite("Loser!");
     break;
 } //switch
} //DrawWinLoseMessage
```

Function LoadImages loads the images for Render World, again using CRenderer to do the heavy lifting.

```
void CRenderWorld::LoadImages(){
 LoadBackground();
 Load(ARROW_OBJECT, "arrow");
 Load(CUEBALL_OBJECT, "cueball");
 Load(EIGHTBALL_OBJECT, "eightball");
} //LoadImages
```

Note that the second parameter to the Load calls is the value of the name field in the <sprite> tag in gamesettings.html.

```
<images>
 <image name="background"
   src="Images\\pooltable1024x531.png" />
</images>

<sprites>
 <sprite name="arrow" file="Images\\vector.png"/>
 <sprite name="cueball" file="Images\\cueball.png"/>
 <sprite name="eightball" file="Images\\8ball.png"/>
</sprites>
```

....

[2]The details of which are truly horrendous. Amongst other things, they involve calling a Windows API function with 14 parameters, 12 of which are zero. Be thankful that I've taken care of it for you.

3.4   Object World

The Object World is where objects live. In this game, they are the pool balls that live under the care of a Ball Manager derived from a base Object Manager class.

3.4.1   Class CObjectWorld

Class CObjectWorld implements our abstract Object World. Its task is to keep track of all the game objects, including the player object. Its private member variables include a pointer to a Ball Manager, which it will create at runtime to help keep track of the ball objects.

```
class CObjectWorld{
  private:
    CBallManager* m_pBallManager;
```

Next, we have some useful member variables that represent the player's state: m_fCueBallImpulseAngle is the angle that the cue ball will be fired at, m_pCueBallObject and m_p8BallObject are handy pointers to the cueball and eight-ball objects, which are otherwise hidden deep in the bowels of the Object World, as we will see later, and m_bDrawImpulseVector records whether we want to draw the cue ball's impulse vector arrow on the screen.

```
    float m_fCueBallImpulseAngle;
    CBallObject* m_pCueBallObject;
    CBallObject* m_p8BallObject;
    BOOL m_bDrawImpulseVector;
```

Public member functions include a constructor and a create function. The latter creates a game object at a particular place in the Object World.

```
  public:
    CObjectWorld();
    void create(GameObjectType t,
      D3DXVECTOR2 position);
```

Next, function clear clears the Object World of all objects, move moves all objects, and draw asks the Render World to draw all objects at their current positions.

```
    void clear();
    void move();
    void draw();
```

The next set of functions are to be used by the player to communicate with
the game, or used by the game to communicate with the player. Their
names are descriptive of their functions, so you can read them for yourself.

```
    void ResetImpulseVector ();
    void AdjustImpulseVector (float amount);
    void AdjustCueBall (float amount);
    void shoot ();
    BOOL BallDown ();
    BOOL CueBallDown ();
    BOOL AllBallsStopped ();
}; //CObjectWorld
```

We start with the Object World constructor which makes a tiny Ball
Manager and sets some member variables to sensible initial values.

```
CObjectWorld :: CObjectWorld (){
  m_pBallManager = new CBallManager (4);
  m_fCueBallImpulseAngle = 0.0f;
  m_pCueBallObject = m_p8BallObject = NULL;
  m_bDrawImpulseVector = TRUE;
} //constructor
```

The create function creates a ball object and squirrels away a pointer to it
in the correct private member variable. These pointers will be useful later.

```
 void CObjectWorld :: create (
GameObjectType t, D3DXVECTOR2 position){
  CGameObject* b;
  b = m_pBallManager ->create(t, position);
  if (t == CUEBALL_OBJECT)
    m_pCueBallObject = (CBallObject*)b;
  else if (t == EIGHTBALL_OBJECT)
    m_p8BallObject = (CBallObject*)b;
} //create
```

To clear the Object World we need only to clear the Ball Manager. The
rest of the values can take care of themselves.

```
 void CObjectWorld :: clear (){
  m_pBallManager ->clear();
} //clear
```

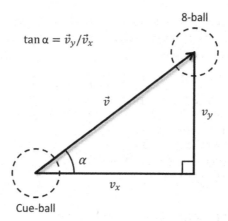

Figure 3.5 • Computing the impulse angle α from the impulse vector $\vec{v}$.

The draw function draws all of the objects in the Object World, first drawing the impulse vector if appropriate, then asking the Ball Manager to draw the balls.

```
void CObjectWorld::draw(){
  if(m_pCueBallObject){ //draw impulse vector
    D3DXVECTOR2 v = m_pCueBallObject->m_vPosition;
    if(m_bDrawImpulseVector)
      g_cRenderWorld.draw(ARROW_OBJECT,
        v.x, v.y, m_fCueBallImpulseAngle);
  } //if
  m_pBallManager->draw();
} //draw
```

The move function asks the Ball Manager to move the balls, then perform collision response.

```
void CObjectWorld::move(){
  m_pBallManager->move();
  m_pBallManager->CollisionResponse();
} //move
```

ResetImpulseVector makes the impulse vector point from the cue ball to the eight ball. This involves computing a new value for m_fCueBallIm pulseAngle. First we compute a vector v from the cue ball to the eight ball by computing the difference of their position vectors (see Section 2.7.3 of [Dunn and Parberry 11]). As shown in Figure 3.5, if $\vec{v} = (\vec{v}_x, \vec{v}_y)$, then the impulse angle α is given by $\tan \alpha = \vec{v}_y / \vec{v}_x$; that is, $\alpha = \arctan \vec{v}_y / \vec{v}_x$. We use the handy math function `atan2` that performs the division and the arctangent for us at the same time.

```
void CObjectWorld :: ResetImpulseVector (){
 m_bDrawImpulseVector = TRUE;
 D3DXVECTOR2 v =
   m_p8BallObject ->m_vPosition -
   m_pCueBallObject ->m_vPosition;
 m_fCueBallImpulseAngle = atan2(v.y, v.x);
} // ResetImpulseVector
```

Function `AdjustImpulseVector` is a no-brainer:

```
void CObjectWorld :: AdjustImpulseVector (float amount){
 m_fCueBallImpulseAngle += amount;
} // AdjustImpulseVector
```

Function `AdjustCueBall` moves the cue ball up or down. It's almost a no-brainer. We just have to make sure that the cue ball stays inside the rails. Fortunately `CBallObject` will provide us a handy-dandy function `RailCollision` to do that.

```
void CObjectWorld :: AdjustCueBall (float amount){
 if(m_pCueBallObject){
   m_pCueBallObject ->m_vPosition.y += amount;
   m_pCueBallObject ->RailCollision ();
 } // if
} // AdjustCueBall
```

Function `shoot` applies the impulse vector to the cue ball. That means we should stop drawing the impulse vector for a start. Fortunately, `CBallObject` once again rides to the rescue by providing a function `DeliverImpulse`. The impulse magnitude of `40.0f` is a kluge.

```
void CObjectWorld :: shoot (){
 m_bDrawImpulseVector = FALSE;
 if(m_pCueBallObject)
   m_pCueBallObject ->
     DeliverImpulse (m_fCueBallImpulseAngle , 40.0f);
} // shoot
```

Function `BallDown` returns TRUE if one of the balls is in a pocket. We just check *m_pCueBallObject and *m_p8BallObject to see whether one of them has their m_bInPocket variable set to TRUE.

```
BOOL CObjectWorld::BallDown(){
 return m_pCueBallObject->m_bInPocket ||
   m_p8BallObject->m_bInPocket;
} //BallDown
```

`CueBallDown` does the same thing but just for the cue ball. Since the game has only an eight ball and a cue ball, there's no need to write a similar function for the eight ball.

```
BOOL CObjectWorld::CueBallDown(){
 return m_pCueBallObject->m_bInPocket;
} //CueBallDown
```

Function `AllBallsStopped` checks whether all of the balls have stopped. That's the signal for the player to shoot again. We just check *m_pCueBall Object and *m_p8BallObject to see whether both of them have their m_bAtRest variable set to TRUE.

```
BOOL CObjectWorld::AllBallsStopped(){
 return m_pCueBallObject->m_bAtRest &&
   m_p8BallObject->m_bAtRest;
} //AllBallsStopped
```

3.4.2 Class CBallManager

`CBallManager` is derived from `CObjectManager` and adds to it some specifically ball-related member variables and functions.

```
class CBallManager: public CObjectManager{
 private:
   void CollisionResponse(int i);
 public:
   CBallManager(int size);
   CGameObject* create(GameObjectType object,
     D3DXVECTOR2 position);
   void CollisionResponse();
}; //CBallManager
```

The constructor simply passes a work order on to the CObjectManager constructor.

```
CBallManager :: CBallManager (int size ):
  CObjectManager (size ){
} //constructor
```

Function create is essentially the same as CObjectManager::create except that it creates a CBallObject instead of a CGameObject. I suppose I could have used templates here.

```
CGameObject * CBallManager :: create (
GameObjectType object , D3DXVECTOR2 position )
{
  if(m_nCount < m_nSize ){
    int i=0; while(m_pObjectList [i])i++;
    m_pObjectList [i] =
     new CBallObject (object , position );
    m_nCount ++;
    return m_pObjectList [i];
  } //if
  else return NULL ;
} //create
```

Function CollisionResponse(i) checks for collisions of all balls with the ball at index i in the Object List. First, we get a handy pointer b1 that points to the ball at index i, and we check that it makes sense.

```
void CBallManager :: CollisionResponse (int i){
  CBallObject * b1 = (CBallObject *)m_pObjectList [i];
  if(!b1 || !(b1->m_nObjectType == CUEBALL_OBJECT ||
  b1->m_nObjectType == EIGHTBALL_OBJECT ))return ;
```

Next, we have a for loop that compares b1 against only higher-indexed objects (to avoid processing each collision twice). We get a handy-dandy pointer b2 to the other ball and check that it makes sense too.

```
  for(int j=i+1; j<m_nSize; j++){
    CBallObject * b2 = (CBallObject *)m_pObjectList [j];
    if(b2){
```

Let vDeltaS be the vector difference of the ball's positions and distance be the distance between their centers when they collide, which is the sum of their radii.

```
D3DXVECTOR2 vDeltaS =
  b1->m_vPosition - b2->m_vPosition;
float distance = (b1->m_nSize + b2->m_nSize)/2.0f;
```

If the magnitude of vDeltaS is less than the collision distance distance, then they collide, so start by making the right sound. We flag both balls as moving under the assumption that this will be corrected in the next frame if we get it wrong. Note the use of D3DXVec2LengthSq instead of D3DXVec2Length to save doing a square root.

```
if(D3DXVec2LengthSq(&vDeltaS) < distance*distance
&& !(b1->m_bAtRest && b2->m_bAtRest)){
  g_pSoundManager->play(BALLCLICK_SOUND);
  b1->m_bAtRest = b2->m_bAtRest = FALSE;
```

Finally, we do the collision response by calling an implementation of the BallBounce function from Section 2.2.3.

```
    BallBounce(b1, b2);
  } //if close enough
  } //if object exists
 } //for all objects
} //CollisionResponse
```

Finally, function CollisionResponse applies CollisionResponse(i) to all balls in the Object List.

```
void CBallManager::CollisionResponse(){
  for(int i=0; i < m_nSize; i++)
    CollisionResponse(i);
} //CollisionResponse
```

3.4.3 Class CObjectManager

Class CObjectManager manages a collection of CObjects. It will have an array m_pObjectList of pointers to Game Objects created at runtime, a count m_nCount of how many objects are currently in the array,[3] and another counter m_nSize that will be set to the size of the Object List once we have one.

....

[3]There will be only two in our game of pool, but as the MythBusters say, "Anything worth doing is worth overdoing."

```
class CObjectManager{
 protected:
  CGameObject* m_pObjectList[MAX_OBJECTS];
  int m_nCount;
  int m_nSize;
```

Public member functions begin with a constructor and a destructor. Function create creates a new Game Object of type objecttype and returns a pointer to it. Functions move and clear do the obvious things to all of the objects in the Object List.

```
 public:
  CObjectManager(int size);
  ~CObjectManager();
  CGameObject* create(GameObjectType objecttype);
  void move();
  void clear();
}; //CObjectManager
```

The constructor creates and initializes an array that it will be using for the Object List.

```
CObjectManager::CObjectManager(int size){
 m_pObjectList = new CGameObject*[size];
 m_nCount = 0;
 for(int i=0; i<size; i++)
   m_pObjectList[i] = NULL;
   m_nSize = size;
 } //for
} //constructor
```

The destructor riffles through the object array and deletes any Game Objects that it points to. These will have been created by member function create below. Then, it destroys the Object List array.

```
CObjectManager::~CObjectManager(){
 for(int i=0; i<MAX_OBJECTS; i++)
   delete m_pObjectList[i];
 delete [] m_pObjectList;
} //destructor
```

Speaking of function create, here it is. It finds the next empty place in m_pObjectList (if any), creates a new Game Object there, increments m_nCount, then returns a pointer to the Game Object created, if any.

```
CGameObject* CObjectManager::create(
GameObjectType objecttype){
  if(m_nCount < MAX_OBJECTS){
    int i=0; while(m_pObjectList[i])i++;
    m_pObjectList[i] = new CGameObject(objecttype);
    m_nCount++;
    return m_pObjectList[i];
  } //if
  else return NULL;
} //create
```

The move function moves all of the objects in the Object List using their own personal move functions.

```
void CObjectManager::move(){
  CGameObject* p;
  GameObjectType t;
  for(int i=0; i<m_nSize; i++){
    p = m_pObjectList[i];
    if(p){
      t = p->m_nObjectType;
      if(t == CUEBALL_OBJECT || t == EIGHTBALL_OBJECT)
        p->move();
    } //if p
  } //for
} //move
```

Function clear NULLs out the Object List without destroying it.

```
void CObjectManager::clear(){
  m_nCount = 0;
  for(int i=0; i<m_nSize; i++){
    delete m_pObjectList[i];
    m_pObjectList[i] = NULL;
  } //for
} //clear
```

● 3.5 Objects

The objects in this game are the pool balls. We have a class that implements an abstract ball object that does ball-like things and has ball-related interests, derived from a base game object class that can, in principle, be used to derive all kinds of useful objects and is designed to encapsulate all of the things that they are likely to have in common.

3.5.1 Class CBallObject

CBallObject is derived from CGameObject and contains specifically ball-related member variables and functions. It has three friend classes, the same ones as CGameObject for the same reasons.

```
class CBallObject : public CGameObject {
friend class CBallManager ;
friend class CObjectWorld ;
friend class CObjectManager ;
```

Private member variable m_nSize indicates the ball's size in the Object World, and m_bInPocket records whether the ball is in a pocket. Private member functions PocketCollision and RailCollision are collision-response functions for the pockets and rails, respectively. Function SetVelocity sets the ball's velocity to a specified vector.

```
private :
   int m_nSize ;
   BOOL m_bInPocket ;

   BOOL PocketCollision ();
   BOOL RailCollision ();
   void SetVelocity (D3DXVECTOR2 velocity );
```

Public member functions include a constructor, a move function that overrides the corresponding CGameEngine function with specifically ball-related moving activities, and a DeliverImpulse function.

```
public :
  CBallObject (
   ObjectType object , D3DXVECTOR2 position );
   void ToggleDrawImpulseVector ();
   void move ();
   void draw ();
   void DeliverImpulse (float angle , float magnitude );
}; //CBallObject
```

The CBallObject constructor passes its parameters over to the CGameObject constructor, then sets its ball-related private member variables to sensible initial values.

```
CBallObject::CBallObject(
GameObjectType object, D3DXVECTOR2 position):
CGameObject(object){
  m_nSize = 50;
  m_vPosition = position;
  m_bAtRest = TRUE;
  m_bInPocket = FALSE;
} //constructor
```

Function PocketCollision begins with three kluged-up constants HMAR
GIN, CMARGIN, and VMARGIN. These are, respectively, the distance from
the top and bottom edge of the world to the closest pockets, the diameter
of the center pocket, and the distance from the left and right edge of the
world to the closest pockets. Boolean local variable bVertical determines
if the ball object is close enough to the top or bottom rail to fall into a
pocket, should one be handily nearby (which may not necessarily be the
case).

```
BOOL CBallObject::PocketCollision(){
  const float HMARGIN = 103.0f;
  const float CMARGIN = 10.0f;
  const float VMARGIN = 95.0f;
  BOOL bVertical = m_vPosition.y < VMARGIN ||
   m_vPosition.y > g_nScreenHeight - VMARGIN;
```

If the ball is close enough to the left or right rails, then it is in a corner
pocket, provided bVertical says it is also close enough to the top or bottom
rails.

```
  if(m_vPosition.x < HMARGIN)
    m_bInPocket = bVertical;
  else if(m_vPosition.x > g_nScreenWidth - HMARGIN)
    m_bInPocket = bVertical;
```

That leaves the center pockets. This is similar, except that you need to be
close to the center of the screen instead of the left or right rails.

```
  else
   if(fabs(m_vPosition.x-g_nScreenWidth/2) < CMARGIN)
    m_bInPocket = bVertical;
```

Finally, some housekeeping. Balls in pockets are at rest.

```
 if(m_bInPocket)
   m_bAtRest = TRUE;

 return m_bInPocket;
} //PocketCollision
```

Function `RailCollision` performs collision response between the ball and the rails.[4] It has two parameters `oldx` and `oldy` that come in with the ball's previous position. It also has horizontal and vertical margins similar to those in function `PocketCollision` above. They are kluged except that they are smaller than the latter. Constant `fRailRestitution` is another kluged value that represents the springiness (or lack thereof) of the rails. Boolean variable `result` is going to record whether we've detected a rail collision.

```
BOOL CBallObject::RailCollision(
 float oldx, float oldy)
{
 const float HMARGIN = 98.0f;
 const float VMARGIN = 90.0f;
 const float fRailRestitution = 0.75f;
 BOOL result=FALSE;
```

The left and right rails reflect the x component of the ball's velocity, scaled by `fRailRestitution`. Notice that the ball is stepped back to prevent it not quite making it off the rail due to `fRailRestitution` being less than unity, which would result in a double reflection back onto the rail.

```
  if(m_vPosition.x < HMARGIN){ //left
    m_vPosition.x = oldx;
    m_vVelocity.x = -fRailRestitution*m_vVelocity.x;
    result = TRUE;
  }

  if(m_vPosition.x > g_nScreenWidth - HMARGIN){ //right
    m_vPosition.x = oldx;
    m_vVelocity.x = -fRailRestitution*m_vVelocity.x;
    result = TRUE;
  }
```

....

[4]The edges of the table that the balls (ideally) bonk off.

The top and bottom rails reflect the x component of the ball's velocity, scaled by fRailRestitution. Notice that the ball is stepped back for the same reason as before.

```
//bottom rail
if(m_vPosition.y < VMARGIN){
  m_vPosition.y = oldy;
  m_vVelocity.y = -fRailRestitution*m_vVelocity.y;
  result = TRUE;
}

//top rail
if(m_vPosition.y > g_nScreenHeight - VMARGIN){
  m_vPosition.y = oldy;
  m_vVelocity.y = -fRailRestitution*m_vVelocity.y;
  result = TRUE;
}

return result;
} //RailCollision
```

The virtual move function bails out if the ball is in a pocket; otherwise, it begins by letting the CGameObject move function do its stuff.

```
void CBallObject::move(){
 if(m_bInPocket)return;

 CGameObject::move();
```

Next, it does collision response with rails and pockets, playing the appropriate sounds and taking the appropriate actions.

```
 if(PocketCollision()){ //pocket collision
   g_pSoundManager->play(POCKET_SOUND);
   m_vPosition = D3DXVECTOR2(9999, 9999, 9999);
   m_bInPocket = TRUE;
   m_bAtRest = TRUE; // so it stays undrawn
 }
 if(RailCollision()) //rail collision
   g_pSoundManager->play(THUMP_SOUND);
} //move
```

Function draw draws all of the balls in the Object List by calling their draw functions.

```
void CBallManager :: draw (){
  CBallObject * p;
  for (int i=0; i<m_nSize; i++){
    p = (CBallObject *) m_pObjectList [i];
    if (p && !p->m_bInPocket){
      D3DXVECTOR2 v = p->m_vPosition ;
      g_cRenderWorld . draw (p->m_nObjectType , v.x, v.y);
    } //if
  } //for
} //draw
```

Next, we see the code for function DeliverImpulse. We need to use some trig here to convert an orientation angle into a vector pointing in that direction.

```
void CBallObject :: DeliverImpulse (
float angle , float magnitude ){
  m_bAtRest = FALSE;
  m_vVelocity = magnitude *
    D3DXVECTOR2 (cos (angle), sin (angle), 0.0f);
} // DeliverImpulse
```

Function SetVelocity is not just deceptively simple, it *is* simple. You might quibble at the first line because velocity might equal zero, but even so, the value of m_bAtRest will be corrected in the next frame. Put an if statement on the first line if you insist.

```
void CBallObject :: SetVelocity (D3DXVECTOR2 velocity){
  m_bAtRest = FALSE;
  m_vVelocity = velocity;
} // SetVelocity
```

● 3.5.2 Class CGameObject

Class CGameObject is a generic game object. It has three friend classes, the Object Manager and the Ball Manager because they need to manage it and the Render World because it needs to draw it.

```
class CGameObject {
friend class CObjectManager ;
friend class CObjectWorld ;
friend class CRenderWorld ;
```

It has protected member variables m_nObjectType (its type), m_vPosition
(its current position), m_vVelocity (its velocity, a vector encoding both
speed and direction), m_nLastMoveTime (the last time the object moved,
probably in the previous animation frame), m_bAtRest (TRUE if and only if
it is at rest), and m_nFrictionTime (a timer for applying friction).

```
protected :
  GameObjectType m_nObjectType ;
  D3DXVECTOR2 m_vPosition ;
  D3DXVECTOR2 m_vVelocity ;
  int m_nLastMoveTime ;
  BOOL m_bAtRest ;
  int m_nFrictionTime ;
```

CGameObject also has two public member functions. The first is a constructor that specifies the object's type. Second, we have virtual function move,
to be overridden in later derived object classes such as CBallObject.

```
  public :
    CGameObject (GameObjectType objecttype );
    virtual void move ();
}; // CGameObject
```

The constructor squirrels away the object type and sets member variables
to sensible initial values.

```
CGameObject :: CGameObject (GameObjectType objecttype ){
  m_nObjectType = objecttype ;
  m_vPosition = m_vVelocity = D3DXVECTOR2 (0, 0, 0);
  m_nFrictionTime = g_cTimer .time ();
} // constructor
```

The Game Object move function begins by computing tfactor, the time
since the object last moved. It then adds to its position m_vPosition the
distance moved since the last frame, assuming it is moving at constant
velocity m_vVelocity, which is m_vVelocity * tfactor scaled back by
an amount SCALE that is kluged up to make the motion look right.

```
void CGameObject :: move (){
  const float SCALE = 20.0f ;
  int time=g_cTimer .time ();
  int dt = time - m_nLastMoveTime ;
  m_vPosition += m_vVelocity * (float)dt / SCALE ;
  m_nLastMoveTime = time ;
```

Friction is then applied by reducing velocity by 5%, but not on each frame, just 10 times a second. If speed is less than 1.0, the object is stopped. The numbers 0.95, 10, and 1.0 are kluged to make it look right.

```
if(g_cTimer.elapsed(m_nFrictionTime, 100))
  m_vVelocity *= 0.95f;
if(D3DXVec2LengthSq(&m_vVelocity) < 1.0f)
  stop();
} //move
```

● 3.6 Exercises

1. Replace the pool table artwork with some of your own. It can look as bad as that in Figure 3.6. Which constants might you need to change in the code to make it work?

2. Make a list of places in the code where I've put kluged numbers just to make the code work. Discuss each of them, explaining what they are for, what range of values can they be allowed to take, which values are affected by the choice of others, and what I should have done instead.

3. Explain why the code !(b1->m_bAtRest && b2->m_bAtRest) is needed in function CBallManager::CollisionResponse(i) on p. 69. How can two nonmoving objects collide?

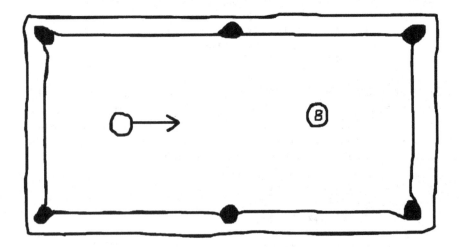

Figure 3.6 • Hand-drawn artwork.

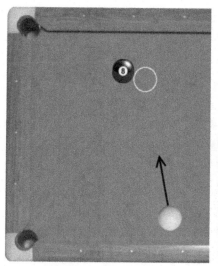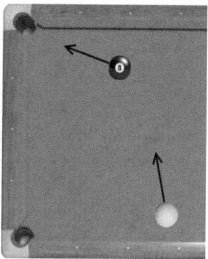

Figure 3.7 • Exercise 5: A circle (left) and an arrow (right) showing where the cue ball will hit and the direction that the eight ball will take, respectively.

4. Our ball-ball collisions are *perfectly elastic*, which means that momentum is conserved. Our ball-rail collisions are *inelastic*, which means that it is not. Where would you put code to make ball-ball collisions inelastic? Go ahead and do it.

5. Use the techniques of Chapter 2.2.3 to add a circle that shows where the cue ball is going to hit the eight ball (turn it on and off with the C key) and the direction that the eight ball will take (turn it on and off with the V key). See Figure 3.7 for how it should look. The circle and arrow should move as you move the cue ball's impulse vector, and of course, they should only appear when both balls are at rest and the cue ball will actually hit the eight ball.

4

A Soft Body Physics Toy

Let's take a look at some code for Gauss-Seidel relaxation on a chain of springs joined together to make a soft body. We'll start with our Pool End Game code from Chapter 3 with all of the pool game-specific code removed. Technically what I'm about to show you is a toy, not a game, because while you can play with it, there is no concept of winning or losing or even a score. Let's call it the Ball and Spring Toy.

The Ball and Spring Toy lets you play with a body made up of a bunch of balls connected by constraints. The constraints can be either stick-like (with no springiness) or spring-like (with lots of springiness). You can cycle through various types of bodies and you can apply impulses to them to see how they react. The toy starts with the body in the air, from which position it drops under gravity to rest at the bottom of the screen.

The controls are very basic. The space bar applies an impulse in a random direction, the enter key restarts with the current body type, and the back key advances to the next body type. The escape key, as always, quits. These are summarized in Table 4.1.

The primary classes of interest are shown in Table 4.2. The basic objects are particles and springs, represented by the classes CParticle and

Key	Action
ESC	Quit
Enter	Restart with current body
Back	Restart with next body
Space	Apply impulse

Table 4.1 • The keys used in the Ball and Spring Toy.

Files	Class	Description
AbstractList.h	CAbstractList<>	Abstract list template
Particle.cpp, h ParticleMan.cpp, h	CParticle CParticleManager	Particle Particle manager
Spring.cpp, h SpringMan.cpp, h	CSpring CSpringManager	Spring Spring manager
Body.cpp, h	CBody	Physics body

Table 4.2 • The primary classes of interest in the Ball and Spring Toy.

CSpring, respectively. Both have their own managers, CParticleManager and CSpringManager, respectively, that are tasked with maintaining a list of particles and springs. The class CBody represents a body made up of particles and springs. The class instances that go into a body that is made up of two particles joined by a spring are shown in Figure 4.1.

In order to make the creation of Manager classes more seamless, I've started with a templated Abstract List class CAbstractList whose template specifies what kind of thing it is to manage. CParticleManager will be declared as being derived from CAbstractList <CParticle>, and CSpringManager will be declared as being derived from CAbstractList <CSpring>.

CAbstractList uses templates[1] to abstract away the list maintenance aspects of the CObjectManager class that we saw in Section 3.4.3. One queer thing about templated classes is that both the definition and the code must appear in the same header file, in our case AbstractList.h. If you ignore this, you are in for a whole world of pain and abstruse compiler error messages, which is the same thing really.

Let's suppose we are making a list of things. CAbstractList<thing> is defined as follows. It has a base m_pList for an array of pointers to things, a member variable m_nCount for the number of things in the list, and a member variable m_nSize for the maximum number of things allowed in the list.

```
template <class thing>
class CAbstractList{
 protected:
   thing** m_pList;
   int m_nCount;
   int m_nSize;
```

· ·

[1]If you are unfamiliar with templates, I recommend going back to the source [Stroustrup 97] for more information.

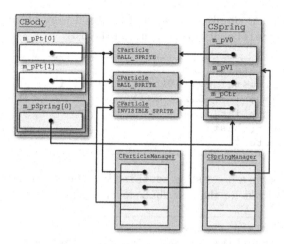

Figure 4.1 • How the classes in the Ball and Spring Toy relate to each other.

It has a constructor that has a single parameter, the desired list size, and a destructor. Function `Insert` inserts a preexisting `thing` into the list, while `create` creates one and inserts it for you. Function `clear` clears out the list, `delete`-ing all of the `things` in it.

```
public:
  CAbstractList(int size);
  CAbstractList();
   BOOL Insert(thing* newthing);
  thing* create();
  void clear();
}; //CAbstractList
```

The constructor is pretty basic, creating an array of pointers to `things` and setting `m_nSize` to its size and `m_nCount` to zero. The list is nulled out for safety.

```
template <class thing>
CAbstractList<thing>::CAbstractList(int size){
  m_pList = new thing* [size];
  m_nCount = 0; //no things
  for(int i=0; i<size; i++)
    m_pList[i] = NULL;
  m_nSize = size;
} //constructor
```

The destructor simply undoes all of the good work of the constructor, taking care to delete all of the things in the list.

```
template <class thing>
CAbstractList<thing>::~CAbstractList(){
  for(int i=0; i<m_nSize; i++)
    delete m_pList[i];
  delete [] m_pList;
} //destructor
```

Insert inserts a preexisting newthing into the list, returning TRUE if it succeeded. It looks for the first NULL slot in the list and puts it there.

```
template <class thing>
BOOL CAbstractList<thing>::Insert(thing* newthing){
  if(m_nCount < m_nSize){
    int i=0; while(m_pList[i])i++;
    m_pList[i] = newthing;
    m_nCount++;
    return TRUE;
  } //if
  else return FALSE;
} //Insert
```

Function create makes a new thing and Inserts it into the list, returning a pointer to the new thing (NULL if it failed).

```
template <class thing>
thing* CAbstractList<thing>::create(){
  thing* p = new thing();
  if(Insert(p))
    return p;
  else{
    delete p; return NULL;
  } //else
} //create
```

Function clear goes through the whole list and deletes all of the things in it, setting all the pointers to NULL again.

```
template <class thing>
void CAbstractList<thing>::clear(){
  m_nCount = 0;
  for(int i=0; i<m_nSize; i++){
```

```
      delete m_pList[i];
      m_pList[i] = NULL;
   } //for
} //clear
```

● 4.1 Particles

CParticle represents a particle or moving point in space. It has a lot of friends because it is a very basic object.

```
class CParticle{
  friend class CParticleManager;
  friend class CSpring;
  friend class CSpringManager;
  friend class CObjectWorld;
  friend class CBody;
```

Private member variables include the sprite type m_nSpriteType, which represents how the particle looks in Render World, its position m_vPos, and its old position m_vOldPos for Verlet integration. The remaining private member variables represent its radius, orientation, and the horizontal and vertical scale factors for its sprite in Render World. Function EdgeCollision detects and responds to the particle's collision with the edges of the screen.

```
  private:
    SpriteType m_nSpriteType;
    D3DXVECTOR2 m_vPos;
    D3DXVECTOR2 m_vOldPos;
    float m_fRadius;
    float m_fAngle;
    float m_fXScale;
    float m_fYScale;

    BOOL EdgeCollision();
```

Public member functions include two constructors, one that specifies the sprite and initial position, and one that doesn't. The move function moves the particle using Verlet integration, while DeliverImpulse delivers an impulse of a given angle and magnitude to the particle.

```
public:
  CParticle(SpriteType sprite, D3DXVECTOR2 position);
  CParticle();
  void move();
  void DeliverImpulse(float angle, float magnitude);
}; //CParticle
```

The constructors are fairly basic. The one without parameters sets the particle's m_nSpriteType to INVISIBLE_SPRITE, meaning that it doesn't have one and won't be drawn. This will be used to create the invisible springs.

```
CParticle::CParticle(SpriteType sprite,
D3DXVECTOR2 position)
{
  m_nSpriteType = sprite;
  m_fAngle = 0.0f; m_fXScale = m_fYScale = 1.0f;
  m_fRadius = 32.0f;
  m_vPos = m_vOldPos = position;
} //constructor

CParticle::CParticle(){
  m_nSpriteType = INVISIBLE_SPRITE;
  m_vPos = m_vOldPos = D3DXVECTOR2(0, 0);
  m_fAngle = 0.0f; m_fXScale = m_fYScale = 1.0f;
  m_fRadius = 32.0f;
} //constructor
```

Function EdgeCollision detects whether the particle has hit the edge of the screen, and if so, it responds by making the particle bounce off it. It returns a Boolean that represents whether an edge collision has occurred. It starts by declaring local variables rebound for the return value, fRestitution for the coefficient of restitution of the edges (arbitrarily set to 0.8f), vDelta for the vector difference between the current and old positions, and MINCOLLISION for the slowest speed at which a bounce occurs.

```
BOOL CParticle::EdgeCollision(){
  BOOL rebound = FALSE;
  const float fRestitution = 0.8f;
  D3DXVECTOR2 vDelta = m_vPos - m_vOldPos;
  const float MINCOLLISIONSPEED = 2.0f;
```

The next set of local variables are the `left`, `right`, `top`, and `bottom` of the screen minus a margin of size `m_nRadius`.

```
float left, right, top, bottom;
left = bottom = m_fRadius;
right = g_nScreenWidth - m_fRadius;
top = g_nScreenHeight - m_fRadius;
```

If the particle has hit the left or right wall, then move it to the wall to prevent interpenetration, reflect the old position in the wall to make the particle bounce off (see Section 2.2), and set the return value `rebound` to TRUE if the particle is moving fast enough to make a noise.

```
if(m_vPos.x < left || m_vPos.x > right){
  m_vPos.x = m_vPos.x < left? left: right;
  vDelta.y = -vDelta.y;
  m_vOldPos = m_vPos + fRestitution * vDelta;
  rebound = rebound ||
   fabs(vDelta.x) > MINCOLLISIONSPEED;
} //if
```

Horizontal walls are similar. Having checked for both vertical and horizontal walls, we can return the result.

```
if(m_vPos.y < bottom || m_vPos.y > top){
  m_vPos.y = m_vPos.y < bottom? bottom: top;
  vDelta.x = -vDelta.x;
  m_vOldPos = m_vPos + fRestitution * vDelta;
  rebound = rebound ||
   fabs(vDelta.y) > MINCOLLISIONSPEED;
} //if

 return rebound;
} //EdgeCollision
```

The `move` function moves using Verlet integration (see Section 2.3.2), checks for an edge collision, and makes the appropriate sound if the collision was fast enough. The speed test is necessary because the collision detection will deliver low-velocity collisions that result in an undetectable less than one pixel bounce. The gravity value of `0.2f` is a kluge.

```
void CParticle::move(){
 D3DXVECTOR2 vTemp = m_vPos;
 m_vPos += m_vPos - m_vOldPos;
```

```
m_vOldPos = vTemp;
m_vPos.y -= 0.2f; //gravity

if(EdgeCollision()){
  if(g_nCurrentBody == RAGDOLL_BODY)
    g_pSoundManager->play(OW_SOUND);
  else if(m_nSpriteType == BALL_SPRITE)
    g_pSoundManager->play(BOING_SOUND);
  else if(m_nSpriteType == WOODCIRCLE_SPRITE)
    g_pSoundManager->play(THUMP_SOUND);
} //if
} //move
```

Function `DeliverImpulse` delivers an impulse of a given `magnitude` at a given `angle` by using the same trick we used in function `DeliverImpulse` in Section 3.5.1 to find the vector impulse; it then subtracts it from `m_vPos` to get the appropriate `m_vOldPos`.

```
void CParticle::DeliverImpulse(
float angle, float magnitude)
{
  m_vOldPos = m_vPos - magnitude *
  D3DXVECTOR2(cos(angle), sin(angle));
} //DeliverImpulse
```

Class `CParticleManager` is in charge of managing all of the particles in our game. It is an instance of the templated class `CAbstractList`, so it has all of its useful functionality. It has a boring constructor, a function `create` that creates a particle, a `move` function that asks all particles to move, and a `draw` function that asks Render World to draw all of the particles. Note that only particles get drawn since the springs are represented by their center particles.

```
class CParticleManager:
public CAbstractList<CParticle>
{
  public:
    CParticleManager(int size);
    CParticle* create(SpriteType sprite,
      D3DXVECTOR2 position);
    void move();
    void draw();
}; //CParticleManager
```

The constructor is, as I've said, boring (but essential).

```
CParticleManager :: CParticleManager (int size):
CAbstractList (size){} //constructor
```

Function create creates a particle of a given SpriteType and places it at rest at a given initial position.

```
CParticle* CParticleManager :: create(
SpriteType sprite, D3DXVECTOR2 position)
{
  CParticle* p = CAbstractList :: create();
  if(p){
    p->m_nSpriteType = sprite;
    p->m_vPos = p->m_vOldPos = position;
  } //if
  return p;
} //create
```

Function move asks all particles to move, being careful to check for NULL pointers in case any of the particles have been deleted.

```
void CParticleManager :: move (){
  CParticle* p; //a particle
  for(int i=0; i<m_nSize; i++){
    p = m_pList[i]; //handy particle pointer
    if(p)p->move(); //make it move
  } //for
} //move
```

Finally, draw asks the Render World to draw all of the particles in the list at their respective positions, orientations, and scales.

```
void CParticleManager :: draw (){
  CParticle* p;
  for(int i=0; i<m_nSize; i++){
    p = m_pList[i]; //handy particle pointer
    if(p){ //if there's a particle there
      D3DXVECTOR2 v = p->m_vPos;
      g_cRenderWorld.draw(p->m_nSpriteType, v.x, v.y,
        p->m_fAngle, p->m_fXScale, p->m_fYScale);
    } //if
  } //for
} //draw
```

● 4.2 Springs

Class CSpring represents a spring, which will be managed by a Spring Manager class CSpringManager and used to make a body class CBody. Both of these are declared to be friends of CSpring because they will need access to CSpring's private member variables. CAbstractList<CSpring> needs to be a friend too because CSpringManager is an instance of it.

```
class CSpring{
  friend class CAbstractList <CSpring >;
  friend class CSpringManager ;
  friend class CBody;
```

CSpring has three private member variables that point to the particles that make up the spring, m_pV0 and m_pV1 at the ends (drawn as balls in Render World) and m_pCenter at the center (drawn as a spring in Render World). Notice that the use of pointers will enable us to share particles at the end of springs and thus connect them together to make bodies.

```
private :
  CParticle * m_pV0;
  CParticle * m_pV1;
  CParticle * m_pCenter ;
```

Its rest length m_fRestLength is the natural length of the spring when it is not being acted on by longitudinal forces. This will be computed from the initial positions of m_pV0 and m_pV1. The spring's coefficient of restitution m_fRestitution is a measure of its springiness. This should be between 0.0f and 0.5f with smaller values indicating spring-like behavior and larger values indicating stick-like tendencies.

```
    float m_fRestLength ;
    float m_fRestitution ;
```

It has two public member functions in addition to a constructor, Relax, which performs one round of Gauss-Seidel relaxation, and ComputeCenter, which computes the position of the particle pointed to by m_pCenter from the positions of the object at the ends. The center gets dragged around by the endpoints and does not otherwise participate in any motion or velocity computations.

```
  public :
    CSpring ();
```

```
    void Relax ();
    void ComputeCenter ();
}; // CSpring
```

CSpring's `Relax` function begins by computing a vector `vDelta` from one end of the spring to the other (the direction doesn't matter), which is needed to be able to compute the current length `fLength` of the spring. If the spring's current length `fLength` is significantly different from its rest length `m_fRestLength` (which I've chosen to mean less than half a pixel different in Render World), then we are to perform relaxation; otherwise, it's hardly worth bothering.

```
void CSpring::Relax(){
  D3DXVECTOR2 vDelta =
    m_pV0->m_vPosition - m_pV1->m_vPosition;
  float fLength = D3DXVec2Length(&vDelta);

  if(fabs(fLength - m_fRestLength) > 0.5f){
```

Next, the actual relaxation code. Impressive, isn't it? It should be familiar to you from function `StickRelax` in Section 2.4, with the addition of scaling the change in position by the coefficient of restitution.

```
    vDelta *= 1.0f - m_fRestLength/fLength;
    vDelta *= m_fRestitution;
    m_pV0->m_vPosition -= vDelta;
    m_pV1->m_vPosition += vDelta;
```

Naturally, we don't want the balls to go off the edge of the screen, so we slam in a little edge-collision code.

```
    float r = m_pV0->m_fRadius;
    m_pV0->m_vPos.x =
      clip(r, m_pV0->m_vPos.x, g_nScreenWidth-r-1);
    m_pV0->m_vPos.y =
      clip(r, m_pV0->m_vPos.y, g_nScreenHeight-r-1);
    r = m_pV1->m_fRadius;
    m_pV1->m_vPos.x =
      clip(r, m_pV1->m_vPos.x, g_nScreenWidth-r-1);
    m_pV1->m_vPos.y =
      clip(r, m_pV1->m_vPos.y, g_nScreenHeight-r-1);
  } //if
} //Relax
```

You may not have seen a clip function before, but all it does is clip the middle parameter to be between the outside two.

```
inline float clip(float a, float b, float c){
  return max(a, min(b, c));
} //clip
```

CSpring's ComputeCenter function begins by storing away the positions of its endpoints in two handy local variables p0 and p1.

```
void CSpring::ComputeCenter(){
  D3DXVECTOR2 p0 = m_pV0->m_vPosition;
  D3DXVECTOR2 p1 = m_pV1->m_vPosition;
```

Next, it finds the orientation m_fAngle of the center object, which is the arctangent of v.y/v.x where v is the vector displacement from one end to the other. If you've forgotten about atan2, the principle is the same as in the Object World's ResetImpulseVector function in the Pool End Game, (see Section 3.4.1), so I won't belabor the point.

```
  D3DXVECTOR2 v = p0 - p1;
  m_fAngle = m_pCenter->m_fAngle = atan2(v.y, v.x);
```

The position of the spring's center is the average of the positions of its ends, and its horizontal scale is apparent size, the length of v, divided by its image size, which I've hard-coded to 256 because it is.

```
  m_pCenter->m_vPosition = (p0 + p1)/2.0f;
  m_pCenter->m_fXScale = D3DXVec2Length(&v)/256.0f;
} //ComputeCenter
```

Class CSpringManager is in charge of managing all of the springs in our game. It is an instance of the templated class CAbstractList, so it has all of its useful functionality. It has a boring constructor, a function ConnectSpring that creates a spring and connects it to end and center particles, a Relax function that basically tells all of its springs to chill out and Relax themselves, and a move function that makes the center points catch up with where the centers of their springs should be.

```
class CSpringManager: public CAbstractList<CSpring>{
  public:
    CSpringManager(int size);
```

```
    CSpring* ConnectSpring(
      CParticle* v0, CParticle* v1,
      CParticle* cntr, float restitution);
    void Relax(int iterations);
    void move();
}; //CSpringManager
```

The constructor is, as I've said, boring (but essential).

```
CSpringManager::CSpringManager(int size):
CAbstractList(size){} //constructor
```

ConnectSpring does the obvious squirreling away of values into spring
member variables. Rest length is just the magnitude of the difference between the end particle positions since we assume that the end particles are
already in their rest positions.

```
CSpring* CSpringManager::ConnectSpring(CParticle* v0,
CParticle* v1, CParticle* cntr, float restitution)
{
  if(m_nCount >= m_nSize)return NULL;
  CSpring* p = create();
  p->m_pV0 = v0;
  p->m_pV1 = v1;
  p->m_pCenter = cntr;

  D3DXVECTOR2 vDelta = v0->m_vPos - v1->m_vPos;
  p->m_fRestLength = D3DXVec2Length(&vDelta);

  p->m_fRestitution = restitution;
  return p;
} //ConnectSpring
```

Relax tells all of the springs in the list to Relax, Gauss-Seidel style.

```
void CSpringManager::Relax(int iterations){
  for(int i=0; i<iterations; i++)
    for(int j=0; j<m_nSize; j++){
      CSpring* p = m_pObjectList[j];
      if(p)p->Relax();
    } //for
} //Relax
```

Finally, move tells all of the springs in the list to compute the positions of their center particles.

```
void CSpringManager::move(){
  for(int i=0; i<m_nSize; i++){
    CSpring* p = m_pObjectList[i];
    if(p)p->ComputeCenter();
  } //for
} //move
```

4.3 Soft Bodies

Class CBody represents a body made up of particles and springs. It's going to keep a list of its particles and springs in case the programmer wants to provide extra functionality such as modifying or destroying particles or springs dynamically. The tedious work of managing the particles and spring is taken care of by the Particle Manager and the Spring Manager, respectively. GameDefines.h contains an enumerated type for the different kinds of bodies that are available to play with.

```
enum BodyType{
  CHAIN2_BODY, CHAIN3_BODY, CHAIN4_BODY,
  TRIANGLE_BODY, SQUARE_BODY, WHEEL5_BODY,
  WHEEL6_BODY, RAGDOLL_BODY,
  NUM_BODIES //must be last
}; //BodyType
```

The bodies that these types describe are as follows:

1. CHAIN2_BODY describes a chain of two balls connected by a constraint, more of a dumbbell than a chain, really. See Figures 4.2 and 4.4, top.

2. CHAIN3_BODY describes a chain of three balls connected by two constraints. See Figures 4.2 and 4.4, second from top.

3. CHAIN4_BODY describes a chain of four balls connected by three constraints. See Figures 4.2 and 4.4, third from top.

4. TRIANGLE_BODY describes an equilateral triangle made from three balls and three constraints. See Figures 4.2 and 4.4, bottom left.

5. SQUARE_BODY describes a square made from four balls and six constraints. The extra constraints are cross braces that prevent the whole thing from collapsing in on itself. See Figures 4.2 and 4.4, bottom right.

Figure 4.2 • Some simple bodies made from up to four balls and six springs.

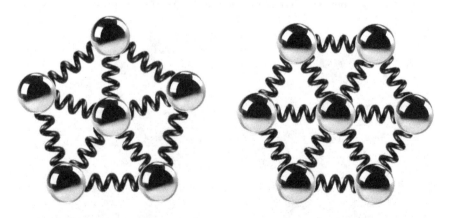

Figure 4.3 • Some bodies made from six balls with ten springs (left) and seven balls with twelve springs (right).

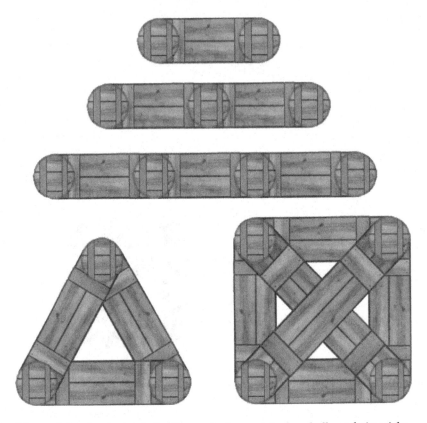

Figure 4.4 • Some simple bodies made from up to four balls and six sticks.

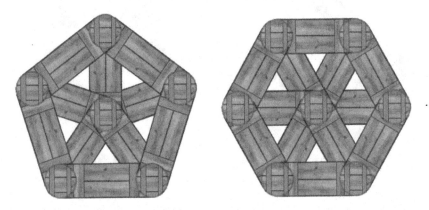

Figure 4.5 • Some bodies made from six balls with ten sticks (left) and seven balls with twelve sticks (right).

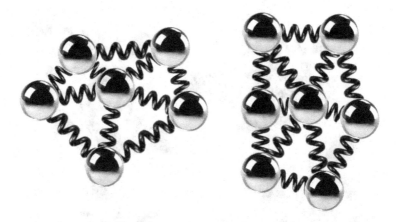

Figure 4.6 • Acceptable level of distortion from small impulses.

6. WHEEL5_BODY describes a wheel-like shape with a hub and five balls around the periphery, or equivalently, a pentagon with a ball at the center and spokes radiating out from it. See Figures 4.3 and 4.5, left.

7. WHEEL6_BODY describes a wheel-like shape with a hub and six balls around the periphery, or equivalently, a hexagon with a ball at the center and spokes radiating out from it. See Figures 4.3 and 4.5, right.

8. RAGDOLL_BODY describes a ragdoll that is complicated enough to need a subsection of its own, Section 4.4.

As you experiment with the bodies in the Ball and Spring Toy, you will see that the soft bodies distort quite a bit under impulse and on collision with the walls, as shown, for example, in Figure 4.6. The bodies spring more or less quickly back to their original shape over the space of a few seconds of animation. Unfortunately, however, by repeatedly mashing on the space bar you may be able to get the bodies to distort unnaturally as shown in Figure 4.7, left. At the extreme, you may be able to jump the body into an alternate stable state as shown in Figure 4.7, right. The spring forces all balance out, but the body is all tied up in a knot, which mirrors what is prone to happen in real life if a young child gets hold of your bouncy toy. There is really no way to prevent this from happening other than setting the magnitudes of the constraints and impulses so that there is insufficient force to turn a body inside out.

• IMPORTANT POINT •

You will inevitably need to fine-tune the magnitudes of your forces and constraints to prevent soft bodies from reaching an unintended stable state.

Figure 4.7 • Unacceptable level of distortion from large impulses.

First, the private member variables. CBody begins with a particle pointer array m_pPt , the number of particles in it m_nParticleCount, and the maximum number allowed m_nParticleMax.

```
class CBody{
 private:
   CParticle** m_pPt;
   int m_nParticleCount;
   int m_nParticleMax;
```

It also has a spring pointer array m_pSpring, the number of springs in it m_nSpringCount, and the maximum number allowed m_nSpringMax. There is another array m_pCtr of pointers to particles at the spring centers, but this is more in the way of a temporary array to be used while constructing the body.

```
   CSpring** m_pSpring;
   CParticle** m_pCtr;
   int m_nSpringCount;
   int m_nSpringMax;
```

There is a special particle pointer m_pEdgeParticle that we are going to make sure points to a particle on the edge of the body. Delivering an impulse to this point will make the body rotate.

```
CParticle* m_pEdgeParticle;
```

Since it is going to be interacting with the Particle Manager and the Spring Manager a lot (where "interacting with" means "begging them to do all the hard work"), it's useful for a body to have direct pointers to them.

```
CParticleManager* m_pPMan;
CSpringManager* m_pSMan;
```

Function ChooseSprites chooses whether to draw balls and springs or circles and sticks, ConnectSpring connects up a spring between two particles, CreateEdgeCenter creates a center point for a spring, and Create Point creates a new particle.

```
void ChooseSprites(
   SpriteType& ball, SpriteType& spring, float r);
void ConnectSpring(
   int p0, int p1, int s, float r=0.5f);
void CreateEdgeCenter(int edge,
   SpriteType sprite);
CParticle* CreatePoint(
   int point, SpriteType sprite, D3DXVECTOR2 v);
```

Next, the public member functions. There is a constructor, a destructor, various Make functions that make different kinds of bodies, Deliver Impulse and ApplyTorque functions that do what their names imply, a Teleport function that magically shifts the body to a new location without disturbing the springs or particles, and a move function that handles the only detail of body motion not already covered elsewhere, which is setting the orientation of the springs' end particles correctly.

```
public:
  CBody(CParticleManager* p, CSpringManager* s);
  ~CBody();

  CParticle* MakeChain(
   int count, int radius, float r, float angle);
  CParticle* MakeTriangle(int radius, float r);
```

```
    CParticle* MakeSquare(int radius, float r);
    CParticle* MakeWheel(int sides,
      int radius, float r);
    CParticle* MakeRagdoll();

    void DeliverImpulse(float angle, float magnitude);
    void ApplyTorque(float angle, float magnitude);
    void Teleport(float xdelta, float ydelta);
    void move();
}; //CBody
```

The constructor and destructor behave completely as expected.

```
CBody::CBody(CParticleManager* p, CSpringManager* s){
  m_pPMan = p; m_pSMan = s;
  m_pPt = NULL; m_nParticleCount = m_nParticleMax = 0;
  m_pSpring = NULL; m_nSpringCount = m_nSpringMax = 0;
  m_pEdgeParticle = NULL;
} //constructor

CBody::~CBody(){
  delete [] m_pPt;
  delete [] m_pSpring;
} //destructor
```

Function `ChooseSprites` uses a restitution value `r` provided as a parameter to set the call-by-reference parameters `ball` and `spring` to the appropriate sprite type.

```
void CBody::ChooseSprites(
SpriteType& ball, SpriteType& spring, float r)
{
  if(r > 0.49f){
    ball = WOODCIRCLE_SPRITE; spring = STICK_SPRITE;
  } //if
  else{ //springs and balls
    ball = BALL_SPRITE; spring = SPRING_SPRITE;
  } //else
} //ChooseSprites
```

Function `ConnectSpring` gives us a readable shorthand for connecting a spring.

```
void CBody::ConnectSpring(
int p0, int p1, int s, float r)
{
  m_pSpring[s] = m_pSMan->
    ConnectSpring(m_pPt[p0], m_pPt[p1], m_pCtr[s], r);
} //ConnectSpring
```

Function CreateEdgeCenter gives us a readable shorthand for creating a spring's center particle.

```
void CBody::CreateEdgeCenter(
int edge, SpriteType sprite)
{
  m_pCtr[edge] =
    m_pPMan->create(sprite, D3DXVECTOR2());
} //CreateEdgeCenter
```

Function CreatePoint gives us a readable shorthand for creating a general body particle.

```
CParticle* CBody::CreatePoint(
int point, SpriteType sprite, D3DXVECTOR2 v)
{
  m_pPt[point] = m_pPMan->create(sprite, v);
  return m_pPt[point];
} //CreatePoint
```

Function DeliverImpulse delivers an impulse to all of the body's particles at once, so that the springs are neither compressed nor expanded.

```
void CBody::DeliverImpulse(
float angle, float magnitude)
{
  for(int i=0; i<m_nParticleCount; i++)
    if(m_pPt[i])
      m_pPt[i]->DeliverImpulse(angle, magnitude);
} //DeliverImpulse
```

Function ApplyTorque applies a torque by delivering an impulse to an edge particle, assuming that whatever Make function made the body assigned this value correctly.

```
void CBody::ApplyTorque(float angle, float magnitude){
  if(m_nParticleCount > 0 && m_pPt[1])
    m_pPt[1]->DeliverImpulse(angle, magnitude);
} //ApplyTorque
```

Function `Teleport` adds a delta value to each particle's current and old positions so that it is moved without disturbing the springs.

```
void CBody::Teleport(float xdelta, float ydelta){
  for(int i=0; i<m_nParticleCount; i++){
    m_pPt[i]->m_vPos.x += xdelta;
    m_pPt[i]->m_vPos.y += ydelta;
    m_pPt[i]->m_vOldPos.x += xdelta;
    m_pPt[i]->m_vOldPos.y += ydelta;
  } //for
} //Teleport
```

Function `move` handles the only detail of body motion not already covered elsewhere, that is, setting the orientation of the springs' end particles correctly so that the springs are oriented from one endpoint to the other. Of course, we don't apply this to shiny particles such as the ones at the end of `SPRING_SPRITE`s, because these look the same however they are oriented, simply reflecting their faux surroundings.

```
void CBody::move(){
  for(int i=0; i<m_nSpringCount; i++)
    if(m_pSpring[i] && m_pSpring[i]->m_pCenter &&
    m_pSpring[i]->m_pCenter->
    m_nSpriteType == STICK_SPRITE)
      m_pSpring[i]->m_pV0->m_fAngle =
        m_pSpring[i]->m_pV1->m_fAngle =
          m_pSpring[i]->m_pCenter->m_fAngle;
} //move
```

Since the functions to make various kinds of bodies look remarkably similar, I'll just describe one here and leave you to read the rest yourself in the code. Function `MakeTriangle` has two parameters, the `radius`, which we've taken to be half of the length of the sides, and the coefficient of restitution `r`. A triangle has three springs, three particles for the vertices at the corners, and three particles for the centers of the springs. We start by making space for them.

```
CParticle* CBody::MakeTriangle(int radius, float r){
  m_nParticleCount = m_nParticleMax = 3;
  m_pPt = new CParticle* [m_nParticleMax];
  m_nSpringCount = m_nSpringMax = 3;
  m_pCtr = new CParticle* [m_nSpringMax];
  m_pSpring = new CSpring* [m_nSpringMax];
```

Next, we decide what kind of sprites to use, springs and balls or sticks and circles, and we pick a vector v position as a starting point for the first vertex of the triangle.

```
  SpriteType nVertexObject, nEdgeObject;
  ChooseSprites(nVertexObject, nEdgeObject, r);

  D3DXVECTOR2 v = D3DXVECTOR2(
    g_nScreenWidth/2.0f,
    g_nScreenHeight/2.0f + radius);
```

Next, we create the particles for the centers of the springs.

```
  for(int i=0; i<3; i++)
    CreateEdgeCenter(i, nEdgeObject);
```

Now for the three particles at the corners of the triangle.

```
  CreatePoint(0, nVertexObject, v);
  v.x +=   radius;
  v.y -= radius * tan(D3DX_PI/3.0f);
  CreatePoint(1, nVertexObject, v);
  v.x -= 2.0f * radius;
  CreatePoint(2, nVertexObject, v);
```

The last act of creation is to hook up the springs to the corner particles using the convenient ConnectSpring function that I talked about earlier.

```
  ConnectSpring(0, 1, 0, r);
  ConnectSpring(1, 2, 1, r);
  ConnectSpring(2, 0, 2, r);
```

Now, we just need to clean up and exit. We reclaim the space for the m_pCtr array since we're no longer going to need it, but we keep the m_pPt and m_pSpring arrays in case we need them for things like applying forces to

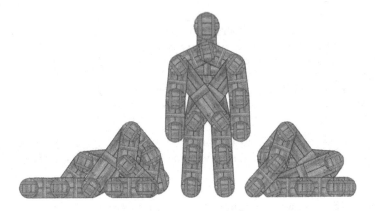

Figure 4.8 • Woodie the Zen Master with yoga disciples at his feet.

particles or destroying springs. We reclaim the memory in the destructor, naturally.

```
m_pEdgeParticle = m_pPt[0];
delete [] m_pCtr;
return m_pPt[0];
} //MakeTriangle
```

• 4.4 Ragdoll Physics

Let's construct a wooden ragdoll robot named, appropriately, Woodie. There's nothing to prevent us from hooking up a few chains from the previous section and calling them a "ragdoll." In a sense, it is a perfectly good ragdoll but it would be a little more impressive if it didn't flop about *quite* so much. Take a look at Figure 4.8. The two Woodies huddled in heaps on the floor may in fact be advanced yoga disciples or they may, like Marvin the Paranoid Android, be terminally depressed. Let's see if we can make Woodie more human-like. If you apply various impulses to him, you should see him strike various vaguely humanoid poses in flight in Figure 4.9. That's what we are aiming for.

We're going to create Woodie out of sticks, springs, and balls.[2] His skeleton will be made of balls and sticks (Figure 4.10, left), and a judicious placement of cross-braced springs will keep his limbs constrained (Figure 4.10, right). We start by defining 14 points on Woodie's skeleton

....
[2]Would it were so easy in real life.

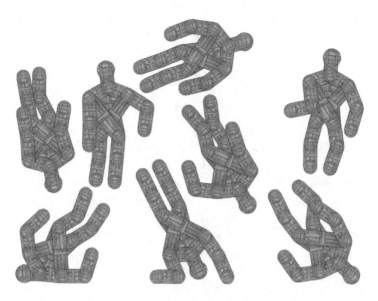

Figure 4.9 • Woodie the ragdoll robot falling with style.

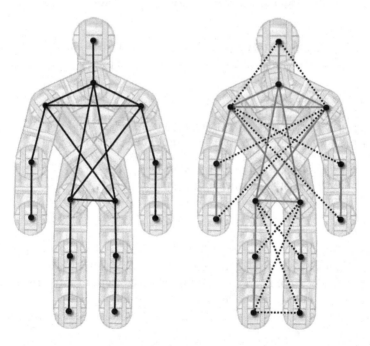

Figure 4.10 • Woodie's basic skeleton (left), with springs to restrain flopping limbs (right).

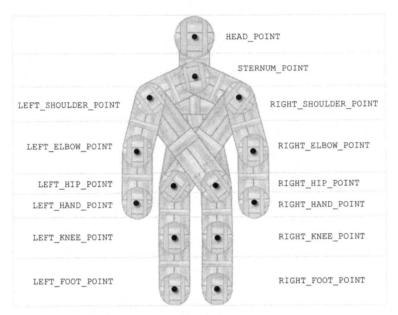

Figure 4.11 • Points on Woodie's skeleton.

using an enumerated type `PointType` where balls are going to be placed. These points correspond to the dots in Figure 4.11.

```
enum PointType{
  HEAD_POINT, STERNUM_POINT,
  LEFT_HIP_POINT, RIGHT_HIP_POINT,
  LEFT_SHOULDER_POINT, RIGHT_SHOULDER_POINT,
  LEFT_ELBOW_POINT, RIGHT_ELBOW_POINT,
  LEFT_HAND_POINT, RIGHT_HAND_POINT,
  LEFT_KNEE_POINT, RIGHT_KNEE_POINT,
  LEFT_FOOT_POINT, RIGHT_FOOT_POINT,
  NUM_POINTS
}; //PointType
```

The enumerated type `EdgeType` represents the sticks and springs that join up Woodie's points. First, we have 11 edge types that correspond in a vague way to bones in the human body (see Figure 4.12).

```
enum EdgeType{
  NECK_BONE,
  LEFT_COLLAR_BONE, RIGHT_COLLAR_BONE,
  LEFT_HUMERUS_BONE, RIGHT_HUMERUS_BONE,
```

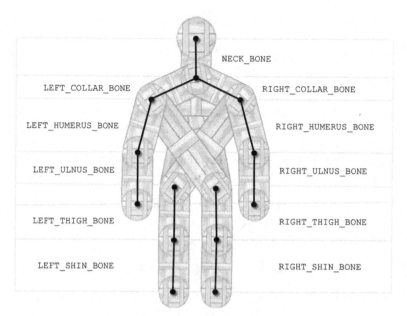

Figure 4.12 • Woodie's bones, the sticks that correspond roughly to human bones.

```
LEFT_ULNUS_BONE , RIGHT_ULNUS_BONE ,
LEFT_THIGH_BONE , RIGHT_THIGH_BONE ,
LEFT_SHIN_BONE , RIGHT_SHIN_BONE ,
```

Bracers don't actually correspond to human bones, but they serve to brace Woodie's torso to prevent it collapsing in on itself (see Figure 4.13). We need six of those.

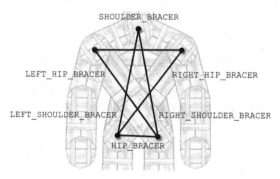

Figure 4.13 • Woodie's bracers, the sticks that serve to brace his torso internally.

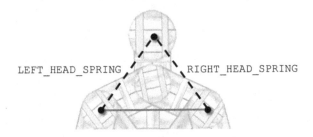

Figure 4.14 • The dotted lines are springs that prop up Woodie's head.

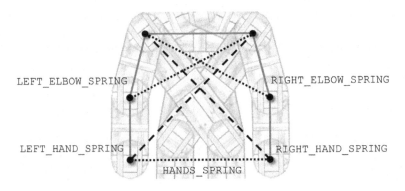

Figure 4.15 • The dotted lines are springs keep Woodie's arms from flopping around.

```
HIP_BRACER , SHOULDER_BRACER ,
LEFT_SHOULDER_BRACER , RIGHT_SHOULDER_BRACER ,
LEFT_NECK_BRACER , RIGHT_NECK_BRACER ,
```

Finally, we need 12 springs to enforce constraints that keep Woodie in some semblance of a basic humanoid form (see Figures 4.14–4.16).

```
LEFT_HEAD_SPRING , RIGHT_HEAD_SPRING ,
FEET_SPRING , LEFT_FOOT_SPRING , RIGHT_FOOT_SPRING ,
LEFT_KNEE_SPRING , RIGHT_KNEE_SPRING ,
HANDS_SPRING , LEFT_ELBOW_SPRING , RIGHT_ELBOW_SPRING ,
LEFT_HAND_SPRING , RIGHT_HAND_SPRING ,
NUM_EDGES
}; //EdgeType
```

Now, it's just a matter of creating the particles in the right places and hooking them up with springs and sticks. The details are in function

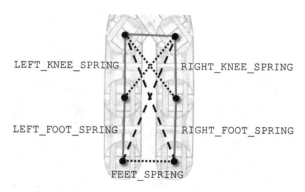

LEFT_KNEE_SPRING   RIGHT_KNEE_SPRING

LEFT_FOOT_SPRING   RIGHT_FOOT_SPRING

FEET_SPRING

Figure 4.16 • The dotted lines are springs keep Woodie's legs from flopping around.

MakeRagdoll. It's just a more complicated version of the function MakeTri angle that we saw in the previous subsection, so I won't bore you with the details here. Make sure that you read the code yourself, though.

4.5 Exercises

1. The code in this chapter assumes that particles have unit mass. Start by adding an m_nMass private member variable to CParticle. What parts of the code should change? Go ahead and code it up. Create a body that shows off your new effect.

2. Add functionality for springs that only expand (they never get shorter than their rest length) and springs that only contract (they never get longer than their rest length). Create a body that shows off your new effect.

3. Add functionality for springs to have a minimum compressed length m_fMinCompressedLength that they never get compressed beyond. Create a body that shows off your new effect.

4. Make a Body Manager CBodyManager from the Abstract List CAb stractList<CBody>, and use it to create a toy with more than two bodies to play with at a time.

5. Customize Woodie so that he looks like a different robot. Reskinning him with different images doesn't require any coding (Figure 4.17, center). Try changing the code so that his proportions are different, and add functionality to allow different sprites for different parts of his body (for example, Figure 4.17, right).

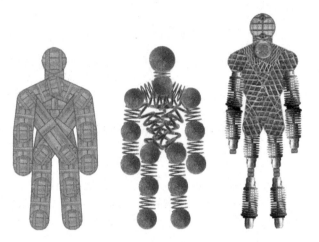

Figure 4.17 • Woodie and his family.

* 6. Implement particle-particle collision detection and response. One way to do this is to reorient so that the tangent between the two colliding particles is vertical, then reuse or recycle the code from `CParticle`'s `EdgeCollision` function.

Part II

Game Physics with Box2D

5

Getting Started

This chapter is divided into three sections that help you get started with Box2D. Section 5.1 describes how to download and install Box2D for use with Visual Studio 10. Section 5.2 gives you an overview of the structure and parts of Box2D. Section 5.4 starts you off with a simple Box2D application to whet your appetite for what Box2D can do. We end in Section 5.5 with some exercises for the reader.

Whether you read this chapter or not is up to you. If you're a beginner, you should definitely read it. If you're advanced, perhaps you should at least skim through it.

● 5.1 Download and Set Up Box2D

The four steps that you need to go through to use Box2D in your game are

1. download Box2D,
2. install the Box2D header files,
3. change the Visual Studio code generation settings,
4. build and install the Box2D library file `Box2D.lib`.

In more detail:

1. Download Box2D. Go to the Box2D website [Catto 12], click on the downloads link, then click on the `Box2D_v2.2.1.zip` link.[1] This will download the `Box2D_v2.2.1.zip` folder to your computer.

....

[1]The details will probably have changed since I wrote this. In particular I expect the 2.2.1 to be larger. I expect you can figure it out for yourself.

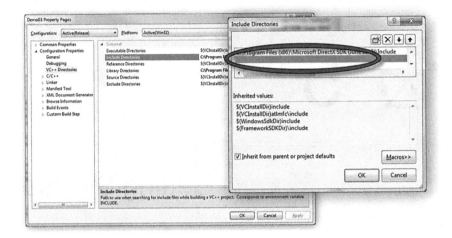

Figure 5.1 • Adding your dev folder to Visual Studio's list of Includes. Type your dev folder's name into the circled text box.

2. Install the Box2D header files.

   (a) Inside `Box2D_v2.2.1.zip`, you will find a folder called Box2D. Copy it into your dev folder. (While you are there, grab the Box2D Manual [Catto 11], which will also be useful to you in understanding Box2D.)

   (b) Add your dev folder to your Visual Studio project Include directories.[2] (See Figure 5.1.)

   (c) In your source code, `#include <Box2D\Box2D.h>`.

3. Change the Visual Studio code generation settings. If you haven't done so already, you need to change Visual Studio's code generation settings to Multi-Threaded DLL. Right-click on your project and select Properties. In the Property Pages dialog box (shown in Figure 5.2), select Configuration Properties\C/C++\Code Generation in the left-hand pane. In the right-hand pane, select Runtime library and change it to Multi-threaded DLL(MD). You should do this for both release and debug configurations, which you select using the drop-down menu at top left of the Property Pages dialog box.

4. Build and install the Box2D library file `Box2D.lib`.

   (a) Inside `Box2D_v2.2.1.zip` you will find a folder called Build. Copy it out of the zip file if you haven't done so already. Open `Box2D.sln` in the Build folder with Visual Studio.

....

[2]I know this sounds weird, but it's true.

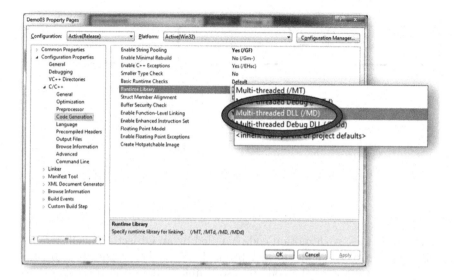

Figure 5.2 • Setting the code generation settings in Visual Studio's Property Pages dialog box.

    (b) Build in Release mode, then close Visual Studio.

    (c) Copy `Box2D.lib` from Build\vs10\bin\Release, and paste it into a new folder called lib in your dev folder.

    (d) Add the new lib folder to Visual Studio's library directories. In the Property Pages dialog box (shown in Figure 5.2), select Configuration Properties\VC++ Directories in the left-hand pane. In the right-hand pane, select Library Directories and add your new lib folder to the list. You should again do this for both release and debug configurations.

    (e) Add `Box2D.lib` to your dev project. This time, in the left-hand pane of the Property Pages dialog box (shown in Figure 5.2), select Configuration Properties\Linker\Input. Then select Additional Dependencies in the right-hand pane, and add `Box2D.lib` to the list of library files. You should again do this for both release and debug configurations.

• 5.2 Overview of Box2D

In Chapter 3, we saw how to write code for some simple physics into a rudimentary game engine. The code ended up being scattered between several

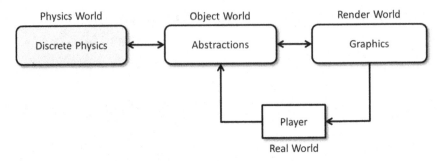

Figure 5.3 • Adding the Physics World to Figure 1.1.

source-code files, with motion code handled by an Object and collision detection and response code in the Object Manager. This wasn't too onerous in Chapter 3, because the code was so simple, but by the time we got to Chapter 2, the code started to get complicated enough to be a world of its own, which we will call *Physics World* (see Figure 5.3). Box2D provides you with a Physics World that handles physics calculations for your Object World.

Let's look at a quick run-through of how Physics World, Object World, and Render World interact in Figure 5.4. It begins with the game loop in `MyGame.cpp`. Within that loop, your code calls `RenderFrame` to render a frame of animation to the video screen. `RenderFrame` asks Object World to draw the objects in the game, which include a pirate. `RenderFrame` can't ask Render World to draw the pirate yet, because while Render World contains the pirate's sprite image read in from a file, it doesn't know the pirate's location in the world. Object World gets this from Physics World, then tells it to Render World, which now has all of the information that it needs to know to draw the pirate to the screen.

Before we start looking at code in Section 5.4, we need definitions for some of the terms used in Box2D. A *shape* is a two-dimensional geometric object such as a circle or a polygon. A *fixture* consists of a shape plus some additional physical coefficients such as density, friction, and coefficient of restitution. A *body* is the abstract representation of a physical object in 2D space. It consists of a fixture plus some other physical properties such as position and orientation. A *joint* is a constraint used to hold two or more bodies together. It consists of a joint type, various coefficients depending on the type of joint (for example, an *anchor point* that specifies the point at which two bodies are connected by the joint), and pointers to the bodies that it constrains. Figure 5.5 shows how these concepts work together to represent a pair of objects connected by a joint.

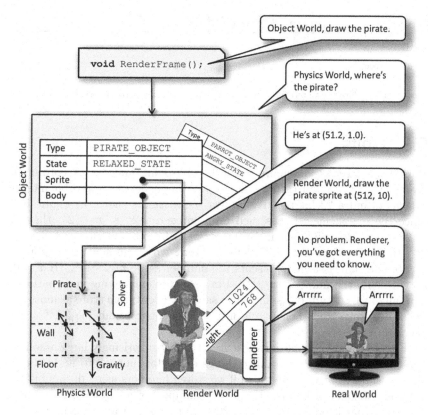

Figure 5.4 • How Physics World fits into Figure 1.2.

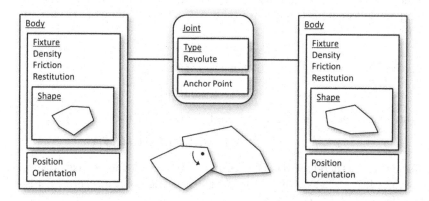

Figure 5.5 • How the Box2D core concepts of bodies, fixtures, shapes, and joints are used to represent the compound object at top.

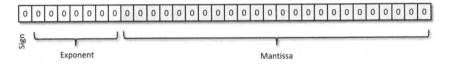

Figure 5.6 • How a **float** is stored in binary according to the IEEE 754 Standard.

5.3 Units

Box2D uses **floats**, which are 32-bit floating-point numbers. According to the IEEE 754 Standard, they are stored using a sign bit, an 8-bit integer *exponent*, and a 23-bit positive integer *mantissa*, as shown in Figure 5.6. Since the exponent x is a signed 8-bit integer, $-2^7 \leq x < 2^7$; that is, $-128 \leq x < 128$. Since the mantissa m is a 24-bit positive integer, $0 \leq m < 2^{24}$; that is, $0 \leq m < 16,777,216$. A **float** with sign $s = \pm 1$, exponent $x \neq 0$, and mantissa m represents the number $s(1 + m/2^{23})2^x$. (If $x = 0$, it represents the number $m/2^{23}$.) I'm probably exhausting your patience with all of this detail, but suffice it to say that **floats** can store at most 2^{32} different values, and their precision is equivalent to about $\log_{10} 2^{24} \approx 7.2$ decimal digits.

Floating-point calculations can go astray by surprisingly large amounts due to round-off error. To make things easier for humans to understand, let's consider what would happen if we stored numbers using decimal floating point instead of binary. Here's an example[3] of a single floating point operation that is off by more than 20%. Suppose we want to compute

$$123457.1467 - 123456.659$$

in decimal floating point with six significant figures after the decimal point (and one before it), as shown in Figure 5.7. The first number, 123457.1467, is represented by

$$x = 5, \; m = 1.234571.$$

The second number, 123456.659, is represented by

$$x = 5, \; m = 1.234567.$$

Subtracting the second number from the first gives us

$$x = 5, \; m = 1.234571 - 1.234567 = 0.000004.$$

The result is therefore $0.000004 \times 10^5 = 0.4$. But the correct answer is $123457.1467 - 123456.659 = 0.4877$. The floating point answer of 0.4 is off by a factor of $0.887/0.4887 \approx 22\%$.

....

[3]I admit it, I got it from Wikipedia.

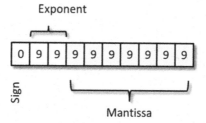

Figure 5.7 • How a `float` could be stored in decimal in our example.

As you can imagine, this error gets compounded and magnified during each sequence of floating-point operations. Fortunately for us, there is a rich area of mathematics called *numerical analysis* that studies numerical approximations such as these. There are well-studied methods for limiting the propagation of round-off errors caused by floating-point computations. The Box2D manual [Catto 11] is careful to explain that the use of these methods in Box2D requires judicious use of the precision offered by `float`s. It would be unwise, for example, to measure all distances as integer values. That would essentially be throwing away the exponent part, reducing `float`s to 23-bit integers, which is foolish when you compare that to the 32 bits available in `int`s.

More precisely, Box2D has been tuned to work well for distance units between 0.1 and 10.0. This means that you should measure things in Physics World in different units than you use for Render World.

• IMPORTANT POINT •

Box2D is tuned for distance units between 0.1 and 10. Do not use Render World coordinates in Physics World. If you ignore this advice, you may find that Box2D's numerical computations fail to stabilize. For example, if your bouncing balls seem to bounce forever, first check on your Physics World units.

• 5.4 Our First Box2D App

Let's go ahead and make a simple Box2D App. It won't be a game yet, but let's at least prove that we can wire up Box2D to a rendering engine. Even if you don't like the rendering engine in Chapter 3, at least it will serve as an example of how easy the process is. This is boring. Hit the space bar once and you'll see a falling object (Figure 5.8). Hold down the space bar for a couple of seconds and the autorepeat will get you many objects (Figure 5.9). Hold it down for longer and you'll see a continuous stream of objects (Figure 5.10) that will stop when the screen is about full

Figure 5.8 • Hit the space bar, and you'll get a ball or a book falling from the top of the screen.

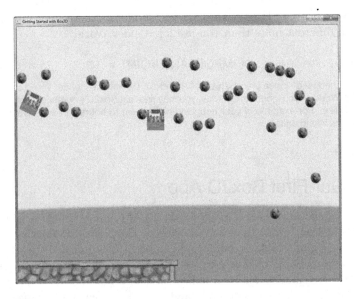

Figure 5.9 • Autorepeat gets more objects to fall from the sky.

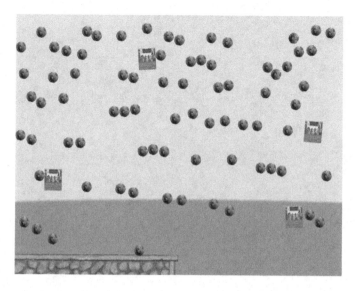

Figure 5.10 • After more time on the autorepeat, even more objects fall from the sky.

(Figure 5.11). At this point, hitting or holding down the space bar will do nothing, but hitting the backspace key will reset you back to the start conditions (Figure 5.10), and you can begin again.[4]

In summary, here's what we have to do. Take the code from the Pool End Game in Chapter 3 and rip out all pool-specific declarations and definitions. Make sure that you rip out all of the code for motion and collision response while you're in there. Then, do the following:

1. `MyGame.cpp`: Declare a `b2World` structure for the Physics World.
2. `NonPlayerObjects.cpp`: Delete everything and replace it with new functions that create objects in parallel in both Physics World and Object World.
3. `MyGame.cpp`: Call the functions from `NonPlayerObjects.cpp` as needed to create game objects.
4. `Object.cpp`: Make the destructor ask the Physics World to destroy the matching Physics body. Change the `draw` function to get the object's position and orientation from the Physics World.
5. `ObjectManager.cpp`: The `move` function now needs only to ask the Physics World to perform a simulation step.

....

[4]Particularly if you are easily entertained.

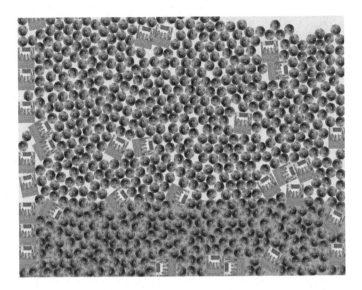

Figure 5.11 • Eventually, they stop falling no matter how much you abuse the space bar. The Object Manager is full. There are 720 objects here.

We're going to use function RW2PW defined in **gamedefines.h** along with its inverse PW2PRW. Remember the advice from Section 5.3 telling us to keep the size of Physics World objects coordinates between 0.1 and 10.0? The maximum size of our game objects in Render World is 128 × 128 pixels. Dividing this by 10.0 gives Physics World objects with maximum height and width 12.8, which is (by experiment) close enough to 10.0 to make everything converge properly.

```
const float fPRV = 10.0f;
inline float PW2RW(float x){return x*fPRV;};
inline float RW2PW(float x){return x/fPRV;};
inline float RW2PW(int x){return (float)x/fPRV;};
```

We start by creating a Box2D Physics World in global variable g_b2d PhysicsWorld in file MyGame.cpp. The b2World constructor takes a single parameter, a b2Vec2 that specifies the direction and magnitude of the force of gravity. I want it to be 100 pixels per second per second downwards in Render World, but of course, b2World expects things to be in Physics World units, so I'd better use my RW2PW function. Gravity in Physics World is therefore b2Vec2(0, RW2PW(-100)).

```
b2World g_b2dPhysicsWorld(b2Vec2(0, RW2PW(-100)));
```

Box2D makes the code for the creation of game objects a little longer than our old `CreateObjects` function on p. 57 in Chapter 3 because we need to go through the right incantations to create things in the new Box2D Physics World. I have `CreateObjects` call `CreateWorldEdges`, which I've put out of the way in `NonPlayerObjects.cpp`. It's a good idea to put all of your object-creation code into a separate file so that you don't have to scroll through it on the way to something else.

    `CreateWorldEdges` starts by getting the Object World width and height into local variables `w` and `h`, respectively. These are in Render World units, remember. We translate them into Physics World units using `RW2PW`, and double `h` so that the top of the Physics World extends off the top of the screen in Render World.

```
void CreateWorldEdges (){
 float w, h;
 g_cObjectWorld.GetWorldSize (w, h);
 w = RW2PW(w);
 h = RW2PW(2.0f * h);
```

To make things less confusing, let's define four vertices at the corners of Physics World. Figure 5.12 shows how the edges of Physics World defined by these vertices line up with the screen in Render World.

```
 const b2Vec2 vBottomLeft = b2Vec2(0, 0);
 const b2Vec2 vBottomRight = b2Vec2(w, 0);
 const b2Vec2 vTopLeft = b2Vec2(0, h);
 const b2Vec2 vTopRight = b2Vec2(w, h);
```

First, we need a ground object, which we will put at the bottom of Physics World by setting its y-coordinate equal to zero. Start by creating a default body definition `b2BodyDef` called `bd`. Box2D is great at having constructors for everything, so we won't actually have to change any of it default values. We then use `bd` to create a `b2Body` called `edge`.

```
 b2BodyDef bd;
 b2Body* edge = g_b2dPhysicsWorld.CreateBody (&bd);
```

Make a `b2EdgeShape` called `shape` and use its `Set` function to make it run across the whole of Physics World horizontally from (0, 0) to (RW2PW(w), 0). Create a fixture on `edge` with shape `shape` by using `edge`'s `CreateFixture` function.

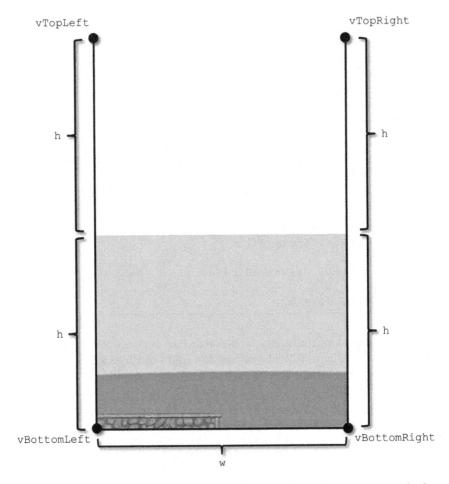

Figure 5.12 • The edges of the Physics World and how they line up with the screen in Render World.

```
b2EdgeShape shape;
shape.Set(vBottomLeft, vBottomRight);
edge->CreateFixture(&shape, 0);
```

Next, we adjust the shape to the left vertical side of Physics World and attach it to a fixture on **edge**. Notice that bodies can have multiple fixtures.

```
shape.Set(vBottomLeft, vTopLeft);
edge->CreateFixture(&shape, 0);
```

Finally, we attach a fixture for the right vertical side of Physics World to edge. That completes the definition of CreateWorldEdges in NonPlayer Objects.cpp.

```
   shape.Set(vBottomRight, vTopRight);
   edge->CreateFixture(&shape, 0);
} //CreateWorldEdges
```

Objects also are created in response to player input. You'll find these changes in function KeyboardHandler in file MyGame.cpp. Let's create a ball or a block in response to VK_SPACE. We've created two functions CreateBall and CreateBook in NonPlayerObjects.cpp to help us out. Both functions take two parameters specifying the coordinates of the created body in Physics World. CreateBook starts by creating a BOOK_OBJECT in Object World, bailing out if Object World is full. We'll save a pointer pGameObject for later to link the Object World body to the Physics body so that the Object World knows important things like its position in Physics World.

```
void CreateBook(float x, float y){
  CGameObject* pGameObject =
    g_cObjectWorld.create(BOOK_OBJECT);
  if(pGameObject == NULL)return;
```

The Physics World work begins with the declaration of a b2BodyDef structure called bd. We set bd to indicate that the book is a b2_dynamicBody, which means that the Box2D simulation engine will take care of moving it about in Physics World. We also set db to determine the book's initial position in Physics World.

```
b2BodyDef bd;
bd.type = b2_dynamicBody;
bd.position.Set(x, y);
```

We define its shape using a b2PolygonShape called bookshape and take advantage of its handy SetAsBox function to make it a box of the appropriate height and width. Pulling up cover.png from the Images folder, we see that the book image is 54 × 64 pixels. That means that it is 54 × 64 in Render World and RW2PW(54) × RW2PW(64) in Physics World. Perhaps counterintuitively,[5] function SetAsBox requires half-widths and

....

[5]Depending on your mindset.

half-heights, which is why you see `SetAsBox(RW2PW(27), RW2PW(32))`, not
`SetAsBox(RW2PW(54), RW2PW(64))` below.

```
b2PolygonShape bookshape;
bookshape.SetAsBox(RW2PW(27), RW2PW(32));
```

Next, a `b2FixtureDef` structure called `bookfd` is filled in with the book's
shape, density, and coefficient of restitution.

```
b2FixtureDef bookfd;
bookfd.shape = &bookshape;
bookfd.density = 1.0f;
bookfd.restitution = 0.3f;
```

Finally, we create a body pointed to by `pBook`, tell the Game Object pointed
to by `pGameObject` about it by calling its `SetPhysicsBody` function, and
we're done.

```
b2Body* pBook = g_b2dPhysicsWorld.CreateBody(&bd);
pGameObject->SetPhysicsBody(pBook);
pBook->CreateFixture(&bookfd);
} //CreateBook
```

Function `CreateBall` is similar, except it uses a `b2CircleShape` shape
called `ballshape`. In place of the `SetAsBox` function call used in function
`CreateBook`, we set `ballshape`'s `m_radius` field directly. The image in
`ball.png` in the Images folder is 32×32, which means that the ball has diameter 32 and radius 16 in Render World. Therefore, `ballshape.m_radius`
is set to `RW2PW(16)`. One may observe that given that the radius of a circle
is a kind of half-width-ish thing, the use of half-width and half-height in
`SetAsBox` now begins to make sense. It's probably that way for consistency.

```
b2CircleShape ballshape;
ballshape.m_radius = RW2PW(16);
```

I'll leave you to read the rest of function `CreateBall` in `NonPlayerOb
jects.cpp` yourself if you feel you need to. There's nothing exciting in it,
but if you must, you must, I suppose. Getting back to function `Keyboard
Handler` in `MyGame.cpp` for a moment, there's some fancy code to make
the balls and books appear in various places along the top of the screen,
but I won't bore you with the details. In response to `VK_BACK`, we call
the Object World's `clear` function to restart the game. More about that
function in a moment.

Descending from the highest level of the code in MyGame.cpp to the lowest level of the code for the lowly Game Object, we see in object.h that CGameObject retains only its m_nObjectType member variable and its constructor and destructor. Everything else has vanished. In return, it gets a b2Body pointer m_pBody and a SetPhysicsBody function that should be familiar from the description of function CreateBook a couple of paragraphs ago. The latter function sets the former member variable to the value of its parameter. Object.cpp should once again hold no surprises for you, with the one obvious exception being that its destructor calls g_b2dPhysicsWorld's DestroyBody function to release the Physics body pointed to by m_pBody.

```
CGameObject::~CGameObject(){
  if(m_pBody)
    g_b2dPhysicsWorld.DestroyBody(m_pBody);
} //destructor
```

Moving up a level from the Game Object to the Object Manager, we see in ObjectManager.cpp that CObjectManager's draw function used to have code to get the object's position from the Game Object directly like this:

```
if(p){
  D3DXVECTOR2 v = p->m_vPosition;
  g_cRenderWorld.draw(p->m_nObjectType, v.x, v.y);
} //if
```

Now, it has to get the object's position and orientation from the Physics World instead, as follows:

```
if(p){
  float a = p->m_pBody->GetAngle();
  b2Vec2 v = p->m_pBody->GetPosition();
  g_cRenderWorld.draw(p->m_nObjectType,
    PW2RW(v.x), PW2RW(v.y), a);
} //if
```

The Object Manager's move function is now only a single line of code. Instead of doing any kind of physics calculations itself, it asks the Physics World to perform a simulation step for it. What could be easier?

```
void CObjectManager::move(){
  g_b2dPhysicsWorld.Step(1.0f/60.0f, 6, 2);
} //move
```

Key	Ball Mass	Ball Rest.	Book Mass	Book Rest.
1	high	high	high	high
2	high	high	high	low
3	high	high	low	high
4	high	high	low	low
5	high	low	high	high
6	high	low	high	low
7	high	low	low	high
8	high	low	low	low
9	low	high	high	high
0	low	high	high	low
q	low	high	low	high
w	low	high	low	low
e	low	low	high	high
r	low	low	high	low
t	low	low	low	high
y	low	low	low	low

Table 5.1 • Keyboard bindings for Exercise 7.

● 5.5 Exercises

1. Follow the instructions in Section 5.1 to download and set up Box2D.

2. Download the code for the Box2D demo described in Section 5.4. Get it to compile. Those of you who installed Box2D without reading the instructions in Exercise 1 might want to go back and do it properly.[6]

3. Are 720 objects visible in Figure 5.11? If not, why not?

4. Assuming that you've completed Exercises 1 and 2 correctly, modify the code to generate both big books and small books.

5. In function CreateBook from file NonPlayerObjects.cpp, change the box size by replacing SetAsBox(RW2PW(27), RW2PW(32)) with SetAsBox(RW2PW(54), RW2PW(64)). Run your code, and take a screen shot after holding down the space bar for a while, then waiting for the objects to stop moving. Describe what happened and why.

6. If you keep increasing the force of gravity in this chapter's demo code, something very strange will happen. Determine what that strange behavior is, and find the smallest value at which the strange behavior seems to begin.

7. Experiment with changing the mass and restitution settings of the balls and books. Try, for example, creating books with high mass

....

[6]**Do not** message or email me asking how to get the demo to compile. Read. Think. Read. Think again. If you are totally lost then you might be tempted to message or email me in spite of this warning. Fair enough. But prepare to be mocked. It's small enough punishment for not being able to RTFM.

and high restitution, low mass and high restitution, high mass and low restitution, and low mass and low restitution. Now try each of the 16 combinations with the two kinds of objects. Tie them to the keyboard as shown in Table 5.1. Which do you prefer? Justify your answer.

8. Experiment with the parameters in the call to `g_b2dPhysicsWorld` `.Step` in the Object Manager's `move` function in `ObjectManager.cpp`. What happens if you change the first parameter? The second parameter? The third parameter? Try both higher values and lower values.

6

A Tale of Three Modules

Box2D has three modules, the *Common Module*, which contains some low-level code and data structures, the *Collision Module*, which contains code and data structures for collision detection and response, and the *Dynamics Module*, which contains code and data structures for the Physics World. The body of this chapter is divided into three sections, one per module. Section 6.1 will delve fairly deeply into the Common Module, since (in addition to its use throughout Box2D) it is a useful toolkit that can save you lots of programming time reinventing the wheel. Section 6.3 contains an introduction to the Collision Module at a deep enough level for you to get started writing a game. More details are available later in Chapter 8 if you need them. Section 6.5 introduces the Dynamics Module.

The `Box2D` source-code folder contains, among other things, three folders corresponding to the three modules, conveniently named `Common`, `Collision`, and `Dynamics`. After poking about for a while, you will find that the overall structure of the files and folders in Box2D is as shown in Figure 6.1. Fortunately, there is more structure here than meets the eye. Each module is made up of various components, as illustrated in Figure 6.2. This chapter and the next one will focus on the light gray components.

6.1 The Common Module

The Common Module contains code for some low-level things such as memory allocation and a math library. My first thought when I saw this was "Oh no! Not another math library!" but there is a good reason for this one. Box2D is designed to be cross-platform, spanning devices that are

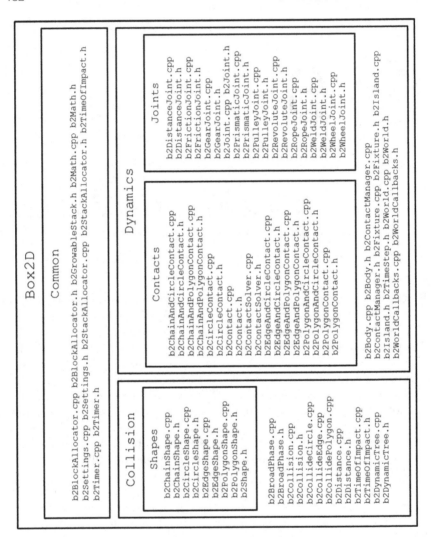

Figure 6.1 • The Box2D file structure. The boxes represent folders.

blindingly fast and provide a lot of hardware support (such as gamer PCs) to others that are less so, but are small and portable (cell phones). Writing your code to use the structures and functions that Box2D provides will enable your application to be cross-platform too.

Code and header files for the Common Module are found in folder Common. Table 6.1 lists them in three groups. The first group consists of files that are likely of no interest to you.

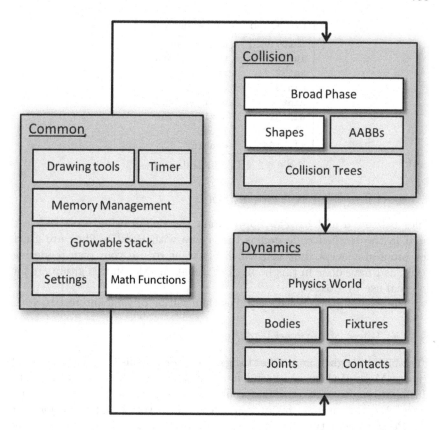

Figure 6.2 • The three Box2D modules with their dependencies and components. The darker components are the ones you probably don't need to know much about in order to make a game.

File	Description
`b2Draw.h, cpp`	Drawing tools for demos
`b2BlockAllocator.h, cpp`	For internal use
`b2GrowableStack.h, cpp`	For internal use
`b2StackAllocator.h, cpp`	For internal use
`b2Settings.h, cpp`	Constant definitions
`b2Timer.h, cpp`	Timer
`b2Math.h, cpp`	Math library

Table 6.1 • Common Module files.

Box2D Type	Typedeffed To
int8	signed char
int16	signed short
int32	signed int
uint8	unsigned char
uint16	unsigned short
uint32	unsigned int
float32	float
float64	double

Table 6.2 • Box2D scalar types.

6.1.1 Files Best Left Undisturbed

Files `b2Draw.h` and `b2Draw.cpp` contain the line-drawing tools that are used in the testbed code demos that come with Box2D. They are great for proof-of-concept, but you will likely want to use your own rendering tools, as I have done in this book. The remaining files in this group are for internal use by Box2D.

The second group consists of files that will be of some interest to you.

6.1.2 Files of Limited Interest

Files `b2Settings.h` and `b2Settings.cpp` largely consist of settings of all kinds. Most of them are best left alone, but some of them are relevant during tuning to make sure that your simulated physics looks and acts just right. For the curious, `b2Settings.h` is where you'll find definitions for the Box2D scalar types such as `float32` and `int32`. These are listed in Table 6.2.

Files `b2Timer.h` and `b2Timer.cpp` contain the Box2D timer class `b2Timer`. This class differs from the `CTimer` class in our codebase, used in Chapter 3 in that it is less functional but cross-platform.

6.2 The Math Library

The third group of files in the Common Module should be of great interest to you. Files `b2Math.h` and `b2Math.cpp` contain useful math structures such as vectors and matrices and code for operations on them. All of the functions are declared `inline` for speed. Table 6.3 lists some useful

Function	Description
`uint32 b2NextPowerOfTwo(uint32);`	Rounds up to next power of 2
`bool b2IsPowerOfTwo(uint32);`	true if a power of 2
`float32 b2InvSqrt(float32);`	Approximate but fast 1/sqrt

Table 6.3 • Scalar functions.

scalar functions. We'll spend most of this section going over them. We start with some useful[1] functions shown in Table 6.3. These functions deal with *scalars*, that is, things that are not vectors or matrices. Function b2NextPowerOfTwo rounds a number up to the next power of two, while b2IsPowerOfTwo returns true when its parameter is a power of 2 exactly. Function b2InvSqrt is a fast approximate inverse square root. That is, given n, it computes something close to $1/\sqrt{n}$, a function that often takes too long to compute exactly.

b2Vec2 is a 2D vector structure with member variables float32 x, y; and the functions shown in Table 6.4. Two of those functions, IsValid() and Skew(), deserve further comment. Function IsValid() returns true if b2IsValid(x) && b2IsValid(y), where

```
inline bool b2IsValid(float32 x){
 if(x != x)return false; // NaN
 float32 infinity =
  std::numeric_limits<float32>::infinity();
 return -infinity < x && x < infinity;
}
```

Suppose b2Vec2 v represents the vector $\vec{v}$. Then function v.Skew() returns the skew vector $\vec{s}$ such that there exists a vector $\vec{t}$ such that $\vec{s} \cdot \vec{t} = \vec{v} \times \vec{t}$. That is, if $\vec{v} = (x, y)$, then $\vec{s} = (-y, x)$.

b2Vec3 is a 3D vector structure (although I will confess that the comments call it a "2D column vector with 3 elements") with member variables float32 x, y, z; and the functions shown in Table 6.5. Note that it lacks many of the functions found in b2Vec2 (compare with Table 6.4).

b2Mat22 is a 2×2 matrix structure with member variables b2Vec2 ex, ey; and the functions shown in Table 6.6. The 2D vectors ex and ey store the columns of the matrix as follows:

$$[\text{ex}, \text{ey}] = \begin{bmatrix} \text{ex.x} & \text{ey.x} \\ \text{ex.y} & \text{ey.y} \end{bmatrix}.$$

Its GetInverse() function computes the multiplicative inverse in the usual way:

$$\begin{bmatrix} a & b \\ c & d \end{bmatrix}^{-1} = \frac{1}{ad - bc} \begin{bmatrix} d & -b \\ -c & a \end{bmatrix}.$$

....

[1] I admit that they look as if no sane person could ever find a rational use for them aside from printing them and using them as liner for their hamster cage. This is perfectly true until they actually need them, in which case they swear by them. Please bear with me. I am not *completely* insane.

Function	Description
b2Vec2();	Constructor
b2Vec2(float32, float32);	Constructor using coordinates
void SetZero();	Set to zero
void Set(float32, float32);	Set to value
b2Vec2 operator -() const;	Negate
float32 operator () (int32);	Read from indexed element
float32& operator () (int32);	Write to indexed element
void operator += (const b2Vec2&);	Add to
void operator -= (const b2Vec2&);	Subtract from
void operator *= (float32);	Multiply by scalar
float32 Length();	Vector norm
float32 LengthSquared();	Use to avoid square root
float32 Normalize();	Vector normalize
bool IsValid();	Is a valid vector
b2Vec2 Skew();	Skew vector

Table 6.4 • b2Vec2 functions.

Function	Description
b2Vec3();	Constructor
b2Vec3(float32, float32, float32);	Constructor using coordinates
void SetZero();	Set to zero
void Set(float32, float32, float32);	Set to value
b2Vec3 operator -() const;	Negate
void operator += (const b2Vec3&);	Add to
void operator -= (const b2Vec3&);	Subtract from
void operator *= (float32);	Multiply by scalar

Table 6.5 • b2Vec3 functions.

Function	Description
b2Mat22();	Constructor
b2Mat22(const b2Vec2&, const b2Vec2&);	Construct from columns
b2Mat22(float32, float32, float32, float32);	Construct from scalars
void Set(const b2Vec2&, const b2Vec2&);	Initialize from columns
void SetIdentity();	Set to identity matrix
void SetZero();	Set to zero matrix
b2Mat22 GetInverse() const;	Return inverse
b2Vec2 Solve(const b2Vec2&) const;	Solve $Ax = u$

Table 6.6 • b2Mat22 functions.

The code looks like the following. Notice that it returns the zero matrix if the matrix is singular.[2]

```
b2Mat22 GetInverse() const{
  float32 a = ex.x, b = ey.x, c = ex.y, d = ey.y;
  b2Mat22 B;
  float32 det = a*d - b*c;
  if(det != 0.0f) det = 1.0f/det;
  B.ex.x =  det*d;      B.ey.x = -det*b;
  B.ex.y = -det*c;      B.ey.y =  det*a;
  return B;
}
```

Suppose we have a 2×2 matrix M and we want to compute M^{-1} so that we can use it to multiply $M^{-1}\vec{u}$ for some 2D vector $\vec{u}$. Using GetInverse() followed by matrix-vector multiplication would cost us six scalar multiplications, a scalar addition,[3] and a scalar division for the GetInverse, four scalar multiplications and two scalar additions for the matrix-vector multiplication, a total of ten multiplications, three additions, and a division. It's slightly cheaper to instead solve for the vector $\vec{v}$ such that $M\vec{v} = \vec{u}$. The following code does this using eight multiplications, three additions, and a division, which saves two multiplications. Notice that this saves time only if we have only one vector $\vec{u}$ that we need to multiply by M^{-1}. If there is more than one, it's cheaper to compute M^{-1} once using GetInverse() and reuse it.

```
b2Vec2 Solve(const b2Vec2& u) const{
  float32 a = ex.x, b = ey.x, c = ex.y, d = ey.y;
  float32 det = a*d - b*c;
  if(det != 0.0f) det = 1.0f/det;
  b2Vec2 v;
  v.x = det * (d * u.x - b * u.y);
  v.y = det * (a * u.y - c * u.x);
  return v;
}
```

b2Mat33 is a 3×3 matrix structure with member variables b2Vec3 ex, ey, ez; and the functions shown in Table 6.7. Note that it lacks many of the functions found in b2Mat22 (compare with Table 6.6). The 3D vectors

....

[2]I hope that you recall from your linear algebra class that *singular* means "not invertible," which means determinant zero.
[3]Well OK, a subtraction. Same difference.

Function	Description
`b2Mat33();`	Constructor
`b2Mat33(const b2Vec3&, const b2Vec3&,` `const b2Vec3&);`	Construct from columns
`void SetZero();`	Set to zero matrix
`b2Vec3 Solve33(const b2Vec3&) const;`	Solve $Ax = b$
`b2Vec2 Solve22(const b2Vec2&) const;`	Same for upper 2×2
`void GetInverse22(b2Mat33*) const;`	Inverse of upper 2×2
`void GetSymInverse33(b2Mat33*) const;`	Symmetric inverse

Table 6.7 • `b2Mat33` functions.

Function	Description
`b2Rot();`	Constructor
`explicit b2Rot(float32);`	Initialize from an angle
`void Set(float32);`	Set from an angle
`void SetIdentity();`	Set to identity rotation
`float32 GetAngle() const;`	Get the angle
`b2Vec2 GetXAxis() const;`	Get the x-axis
`b2Vec2 GetYAxis() const;`	Get the y-axis

Table 6.8 • Rotation matrix `b2Rot` functions.

`ex`, `ey`, and `ez` store the columns of the matrix as follows:

$$[ex, ey, ez] = \begin{bmatrix} ex.x & ey.x & ez.x \\ ex.y & ey.y & ez.y \\ ex.z & ey.z & ez.z \end{bmatrix}.$$

`b2Mat33` has two functions that correspond to `b2Mat22`'s `Solve`. They are `Solve33`, which is the expected 3D version of `b2Mat22::Solve`, and `Solve22`, which is the same as `b2Mat22::Solve` performed on the top-left 2×2 submatrix of the `b2Mat33`. Also, `b2Mat33` has two functions that correspond to `b2Mat22`'s `GetInverse()`. `GetInverse22` is the same as `b2Mat22`'s `GetInverse()` performed on the top-left 2×2 submatrix of the `b2Mat33`, and `GetSymInverse33` computes the 3×3 inverse when the matrix is symmetrical, which it will often be for many physics applications.[4] Again, both return the zero matrix if singular.

`b2Rot` is a 2×2 rotation matrix structure with member variables `float 32 s, c;` and the functions shown in Table 6.8. Member variables `s` and `c` contain, respectively, the sine and the cosine of the rotation angle. This

....

[4]It does no checking for symmetry; If the matrix isn't symmetric, it simply returns the wrong value.

Function	Description

`b2Transform();`
`b2Transform(const b2Vec2&,`
`  const b2Rot&);`
`void SetIdentity();`
`void Set(const b2Vec2&, float32);`
	Constructor
	Init. from posn & rotn
	
	Set to identity transform
	Set from posn & angle

Table 6.9 • `b2Transform` functions. A transformation contains both translation and rotation.

is because the 2×2 matrix for rotating θ radians in 2D is[5]

$$\begin{bmatrix} \cos \theta & \sin \theta \\ -\sin \theta & \cos \theta \end{bmatrix}.$$

The two functions most worth commenting on are `GetXAxis()` and `GetYAxis()`, which return the basis vectors[6] of the space spanned by the matrix, the unit vectors $(1, 0)$ and $(0, 1)$ rotated by angle θ.

`b2Transform` is a 2×2 transformation structure with member variables `b2Vec2 p` and `b2Rot q`. The former represents a translation, and the latter a rotation. `b2Transform` functions are shown in Table 6.9.

Finally, the Common Module contains some useful math functions listed in Tables 6.10 and 6.11 and a class `b2Sweep` that is used internally for collision response.

• 6.3 The Collision Module

The Collision Module is contained in folder Collision. It includes definitions for shapes and functions that operate on them (see Section 6.4), broad-phase collision detection (Section 6.3.2), and a data structure called a *dynamic tree* (Section 8.4). Dynamic trees use the concept of an axially aligned bounding box, which we will cover first in Section 8.3. Normally, you won't need to interact with the broad-phase collision-detection code directly, but let's take a quick look under the hood to familiarize ourselves with what's going on there. Table 6.12 contains a list of the Collision Module files in folder Collision.

• 6.3.1 Contact Manifolds

A *contact manifold* is a discrete approximation to a continuous region of contact. When a circle collides with a polygon or another circle, they have

....

[5]See Section 5.1.1 of [Dunn and Parberry 11] if you're rusty.

[6]Basis vectors are useful for many things, including visualization of the effect of a matrix, see Section 3.3.3 of [Dunn and Parberry 11].

```
float32 b2Dot(const b2Vec2&, const b2Vec2&);
float32 b2Dot(const b2Vec3&, const b2Vec3&);
b2Vec2 b2Abs(const b2Vec2&);
```
```
float32 b2Cross(const b2Vec2&, const b2Vec2&);
b2Vec2 b2Cross(const b2Vec2&, float32);
b2Vec2 b2Cross(float32, const b2Vec2&);
b2Vec3 b2Cross(const b2Vec3&, const b2Vec3&);
```
```
b2Vec2 b2Min(const b2Vec2&, const b2Vec2&);
b2Vec2 b2Max(const b2Vec2&, const b2Vec2&);
b2Vec2 b2Clamp(const b2Vec2&, const b2Vec2&,
  const b2Vec2&);
b2Vec2 b2Mul(const b2Mat22&, const b2Vec2&);
b2Vec3 b2Mul(const b2Mat33&, const b2Vec3&);
b2Vec2 b2MulT(const b2Mat22&, const b2Vec2&);
b2Vec2 b2Mul22(const b2Mat33& A, const b2Vec2& v);
b2Vec2 b2Mul(const b2Rot&, const b2Vec2&);
b2Vec2 b2MulT(const b2Rot&, const b2Vec2&);
b2Vec2 b2Mul(const b2Transform&, const b2Vec2&);
b2Vec2 b2MulT(const b2Transform&, const b2Vec2&);
```
```
b2Vec2 operator*(float32, const b2Vec2&);
b2Vec3 operator*(float32, const b2Vec3&);
b2Vec2 operator+(const b2Vec2&, const b2Vec2&);
b2Vec3 operator+(const b2Vec3&, const b2Vec3&);
b2Vec2 operator-(const b2Vec2&, const b2Vec2&);
b2Vec2 operator-(const b2Vec3&, const b2Vec3&);
bool operator==(const b2Vec2&, const b2Vec2&);
```
```
float32 b2Distance(const b2Vec2&, const b2Vec2&);
float32 b2DistanceSquared(const b2Vec2&, const b2Vec2&);
```

Table 6.10 • Useful vector math functions.

```
b2Mat22 b2Abs(const b2Mat22&);
b2Mat22 operator+(const b2Mat22&, const b2Mat22&);
b2Mat22 b2Mul(const b2Mat22&, const b2Mat22&);
b2Mat22 b2MulT(const b2Mat22&, const b2Mat22&);
b2Rot b2Mul(const b2Rot&, const b2Rot&);
b2Rot b2MulT(const b2Rot&, const b2Rot&);
b2Transform b2Mul(const b2Transform&,
  const b2Transform&);
b2Transform b2MulT(const b2Transform&,
  const b2Transform&);
```

Table 6.11 • Useful matrix math functions.

File	Description
b2BroadPhase.h, cpp	Broad-phase collision detection
b2Collision.h, cpp	Contact points, distance, and TOI queries
b2CollideCircle.cpp	Contact manifolds for circles
b2CollideEdge.cpp	Contact manifolds for edges
b2CollidePolygon.cpp	Contact manifolds for polygons
b2Distance.h, cpp	Distance proxies
b2TimeOfImpact.h, cpp	Time of first impact, TOI
b2DynamicTree.h, cpp	Dynamic tree data structure

Table 6.12 • Collision Module files.

a single point of contact (called a *contact point* in Box2D), as shown in the first two collisions on the left of Figure 6.3. When two polygons collide, they may have one or two contact points, as shown in the last two collisions on the right of Figure 6.3. The *contact normal* is a unit vector that points from one shape to the other. Box2D makes the direction of this vector from the first shape to the second shape, where the terms "first" and "second" refer to the order in which they are stored. Contact normals are also shown in Figure 6.3.

If you go diving into the collision-detection code, you will undoubtedly see arrays and for loops making use of the value `b2_maxManifoldPoints` as the maximum number of contact points in a contact manifold, which may delude you into thinking that Box2D manifolds can have an arbitrary number of contact points. You will be disappointed to find that `b2settings.h` contains the following definition with a comment that says "Do not change this value":

```
#define b2_maxManifoldPoints 2
```

Box2D provides a simple contact manifold class `b2Manifold`, but while the comments state that it is strictly for internal use, it's often necessary to drill down into it if you want to do anything sophisticated with collision response. For example, while `b2Manifold` stores things like contact points in local coordinate space, programmers will more often than not need them in world space. Box2D provides a `b2WorldManifold` structure whose `Initialize` function will let you translate a `b2Manifold` from local coordinates to world coordinates. The logic behind this is probably that `b2Manifolds` are recomputed often and therefore need to be fast, whereas `b2WorldManifold` is slower and therefore should be recomputed only when explicitly requested by the programmer. Keep in mind that while `b2WorldManifold` knows things like the world-space coordinates of the contact points, the actual number of contact points (be it one or two)

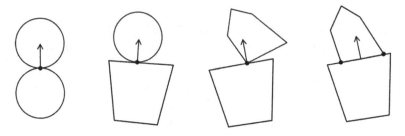

Figure 6.3 • A contact manifold consists of a contact normal and at most two contact points. From left to right, the contact manifolds for two circles, a circle and a polygon, two polygons with a single contact point, and two polygons with two contact points.

must be gotten from the corresponding `b2Manifold`. This means that you really can't avoid having to know at least *something* about the forbidden and mysterious `b2Manifold` structure. Since you don't need to know any more than this when writing your first game, we should postpone more details to Section 8.1.

6.3.2   Broad-Phase Collision Detection

Box2D uses the term *narrow-phase* collision detection to denote collision response between two objects, and the term *broad-phase* collision detection to denote collision response between all objects. Suppose our game has n objects. Algorithm 1 shows the obvious brute-force approach to broad-phase collision detection.

Algorithm 1 • Broad-phase collision detection

---

for $0 \leq i < n$ **do**
  for $i < j < n$ **do**
    Perform narrow-phase collision between object i and object j
  end for
end for

Algorithm 1 should be familiar from the `CObjectManager` collision code that we examined in Section 3.2. The `CObjectManager`'s `move()` function performed the outer loop on i, calling function `CollisionResponse` to perform the second loop and its body. As we did there, we compute collision response for both colliding objects together, and therefore need j, the index of the second loop, to be larger than i, the index of the first loop. The number of times that narrow-phase collision detection is performed is, therefore,

$$\sum_{i=0}^{n-1} \sum_{j=i+1}^{n-1} 1 = \sum_{i=0}^{n-1} n - i - 1$$

$$= \sum_{i=0}^{n-1} n - \sum_{i=0}^{n-1} i - \sum_{i=0}^{n-1} 1$$

$$= n^2 - (n-1)n/2 - n + 1$$

$$= n(n-1)/2 - 1.$$

This is quadratic in n, yet most of the narrow-phase collision tests will fail, because in most games, most of the time, most objects aren't colliding with a lot of other objects. It's a waste of time testing for quadratically many possible collision pairs when one might reasonably expect to find that at most a linear number of them are actual collisions. Box2D's b2BroadPhase class reduces this load by using a dynamic-tree data structure to organize the objects in such a way that we can iterate through collision pairs in time proportional to the number of collisions. Algorithm 1 is then replaced by Algorithm 2.

Algorithm 2 • Broad-phase collision detection with a dynamic tree

---

for each pair of objects i and j that the dynamic tree says may collide **do**

Perform narrow-phase collision between object i and object j

end for

6.4 Shapes

Box2D shapes are contained in a folder called Shapes in the Collision Module folder Collision. There, you will find the files listed in Table 6.13. File b2Shape.h contains the definition for the b2Shape base class, which has member functions to

- test a point for overlap with the shape,
- perform a ray cast against the shape,
- compute the shape's AABB,
- compute the mass properties of the shape.

The b2Shape base class has member variables for

- type (e.g., circle, polygon),
- radius.

File	Shape Class	Covered in
b2Shape.h, cpp	b2Shape	Section 6.4
b2CircleShape.h, cpp	b2CircleShape	Section 6.4.1
b2PolygonShape.h, cpp	b2PolygonShape	Section 6.4.1
b2EdgeShape.h, cpp	b2EdgeShape	Section 6.4.2
b2ChainShape.h, cpp	b2ChainShape	Section 6.4.2

Table 6.13 • The shape files in folder Shape.

6.4.1   Circles, Polygons, and Boxes

b2CircleShapes are derived from b2Shape and are defined in files b2Circle
Shape.h and b2CircleShape.cpp. Circle shapes have a position and radius. Circles are solid. You cannot make a hollow circle. However, you can
fake it with a chain of line segments using polygon shapes.

```
b2CircleShape circle;
circle.m_p.Set(2.0f, 3.0f); //position
circle.m_radius = 0.5f; //radius
```

b2PolygonShapes are derived from b2Shape and are defined in files
b2PolygonShape.h and b2PolygonShape.cpp. Polygon shapes must be
convex (meaning that all line segments connecting two points in the interior do not cross any edge, see Figure 6.4) and must have at least three
vertices. Like circles, they are solid, not hollow. Create polygons with a
counterclockwise winding (CCW) order. That is, vertices must be listed in
counterclockwise order as shown in Figure 6.5.

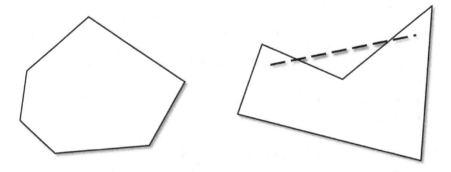

Figure 6.4 • The polygon on the left is convex. The one on the right is concave
since the dotted line connects two points in the interior of the polygon and crosses
two edges.

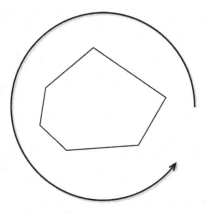

Figure 6.5 • Polygon vertices must be listed in counterclockwise order.

Although polygon member variables are public, it's best to use initialization functions to create polygons since the initialization functions automatically perform housekeeping tasks such as validation and creating normals, tasks that you would otherwise have to remember to do yourself. Polygon shapes are created by passing in a vertex array. The maximum size of the array is controlled by b2_maxPolygonVertices, which has a default value of 8. The following code creates a triangle with vertices at $(0,0)$, $(1,0)$, and $(0,1)$.

```
b2Vec2 vertices[3];
vertices[0].Set(0.0f, 0.0f);
vertices[1].Set(1.0f, 0.0f);
vertices[2].Set(0.0f, 1.0f);

int32 count = 3;

b2PolygonShape polygon;
polygon.Set(vertices, count);
```

The polygon shape has some custom initialization functions to create boxes.

```
void SetAsBox(float32 hx, float32 hy);
void SetAsBox(float32 hx, float32 hy,
   const b2Vec2& center, float32 angle);
```

Polygons inherit a value called the *radius* from b2Shape. The radius is used to create a thin buffer area called the *skin* around them, as shown

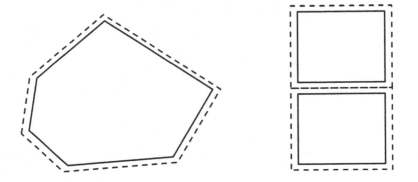

Figure 6.6 • Polygon skin shown as a dotted line (left). Stacked polygons are separated by their skins (right) in Physics World.

at left in Figure 6.6. The skin is used when stacking to keep polygons slightly separated and thus allow continuous collision to work against the core polygon. The polygon skin helps prevent tunneling by keeping the polygons separated, as shown at right in Figure 6.6.

6.4.2   Edges and Chains

Edge shapes are line segments. `b2EdgeShapes` are derived from `b2Shape` and are defined in files `b2EdgeShape.h` and `b2EdgeShape.cpp`. These are provided to assist in making a freeform static environment for your game. A major limitation of edge shapes is that they can collide with circles and polygons but not with each other. The collision algorithms used by Box2D require that at least one of two colliding shapes have volume. Edge shapes have no volume, so edge-edge collision is not possible. Edge shapes are created as follows:

```
b2Vec2 v1(0.0f, 0.0f);
b2Vec2 v2(1.0f, 0.0f);

b2EdgeShape edge;
edge.Set(v1, v2);
```

Suppose we connect some edge shapes end-to-end, and a polygon slides along it. A *ghost collision* is caused when the polygon collides with an internal vertex, generating an internal collision normal. Consider Figure 6.7 in which a box is sliding to the right on two joined edges. A ghost collision occurs when the box hits the vertex that joins them, If Edge 1 did not exist, this collision would seem fine. With Edge 1 present, the internal

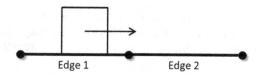

Figure 6.7 • A ghost collision is created between the box and the vertex joining Edge 1 to Edge 2.

collision is unnecessary and may cause spurious behavior if processed like a normal collision. If Edge 1 weren't present, the box would bounce off the vertex at the end of Edge 2. With Edge 1 present, the box should behave as if the vertex weren't there. The edge shape provides a mechanism for eliminating ghost collisions by storing a ghost vertex at each end, as shown in Figure 6.8. Box2D uses these ghost vertices to prevent internal collisions. For example, suppose we start with the following four vectors:

```
b2Vec2 v0(1.7f, 0.0f);  //ghost
b2Vec2 v1(1.0f, 0.25f); //real
b2Vec2 v2(0.0f, 0.0f);  //real
b2Vec2 v3(-1.7f, 0.4f); //ghost
```

The following creates an edge between v1 and v2 with ghost vertices v0 and v3.

```
b2EdgeShape edge;
edge.Set(v1, v2); //real
edge.m_hasVertex0 = true; //ghost
edge.m_hasVertex3 = true; //ghost
edge.m_vertex0 = v0; //ghost
edge.m_vertex3 = v3; //ghost
```

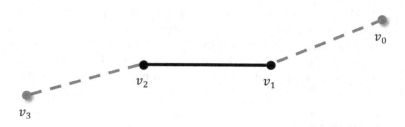

Figure 6.8 • v_0 and v_3 are ghost vertices.

A *chain* is an open series of connected edges. Box2D provides a b2Chain Shape derived from b2Shape, defined in files b2ChainShape.h and b2Chain Shape.cpp. To create a chain, start with an array of b2Vec2s.

```
b2Vec2 vs[4];
vs[0].Set(1.7f, 0.0f);
vs[1].Set(1.0f, 0.25f);
vs[2].Set(0.0f, 0.0f);
vs[3].Set(-1.7f, 0.4f);
```

The following creates a chain of edges from v[0] to v[1] to v[2] to v[3].

```
b2ChainShape chain;
chain.CreateChain(vs, 4);
```

Connect chains with ghost vertices. There are more functions to create loops. Self-collision of chain shapes may or may not work. Each edge in the chain is treated as a child shape and can be accessed by index.

```
for(int32 i=0; i<chain.GetChildCount(); i++){
  b2EdgeShape edge;
  chain.GetChildEdge(&edge, i);
  . . .
} //for
```

6.5 The Dynamics Module

The Dynamics Module provides the Physics World (Section 6.5.1) and the things that appear in it, for example, fixtures (Section 6.5.2), bodies (Section 6.5.3), contacts and joints (Section 6.6).

6.5.1 The Physics World

b2World is Box2D's implementation of the Physics World that we saw in Figure 5.3. As shown in Figure 6.9, the Box2D Physics World consists of objects such as bodies and joints, plus the code for managing them. We begin by defining a direction and a magnitude for the force of gravity as a 2D vector; then, we provide that vector as a parameter to the b2World constructor.

```
b2Vec2 gravity(-9.8f);
b2World g_b2dPhysicsWorld(gravity);
```

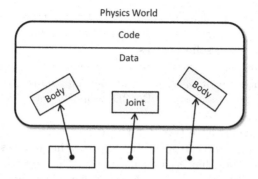

Figure 6.9 • The Physics World in Box2D.

6.5.2 Fixtures

As I mentioned above, a *fixture* consists of a shape plus some additional physical coefficients such as density, friction, and restitution. Multiple fixtures can be attached to a body. Fixtures on the same body never collide with each other. Fixtures are defined using a `b2FixtureDef` structure, which is defined as follows:

```
struct b2FixtureDef {
  b2FixtureDef ();
  const b2Shape* shape;
  void* userData;
  float32 friction;
  float32 restitution;
  float32 density;
  bool isSensor;
  b2Filter filter;
};
```

The first six members of `b2FixtureDef` are fairly straightforward. Let me pick out a few of them for comment. The constructor zeroes out the member variables with the exception of `friction`, which is set to a default value of `0.2f`, and `filter`, which has its own constructor. `userData` can be used for custom user data, remembering that we can typecast it from `void*` later. The coefficient of `friction` and the `restitution` are real numbers that are usually, but not necessarily, in the range $[0, 1]$. The last two members deal with sensors and collision filtering, respectively, which require a little more explanation.

Sometimes, game logic needs to know when two fixtures overlap, yet there should be no collision response. This is done by using *sensors*. You can flag any fixture as being a sensor. Sensors may be static or dynamic. Remember that you may have multiple fixtures per body. These may be any mix of sensors and solid fixtures.

Collision filtering allows you to prevent unwanted collision between fixtures. Not only does it prevent them from happening, it prevents them from taking up processor time. Box2D supports such collision filtering using *categories* and *groups*.

Fixture definitions have two 16-bit words of category flags: `category Bits`, which indicate the categories the fixture is in, and `maskBits`, which indicate the categories that it can collide with. The next block of code declares two fixture definitions, `pcFrDef` for the player character and `npcFrDef` for a nonplayer character, and sets their collision-filter categories.

```
b2FixtureDef pcFrDef , npcFrDef ;

pcFrDef . filter . categoryBits  =  0x0002;
npcFxtrDef . filter . categoryBits  =  0x0004;

pcFrDef . filter . maskBits  =  0x0004;
npcFrDef . filter . maskBits  =  0x0002;
```

After the declaration, the next two lines of code set the categories that the fixtures are in. The player character fixture is in Category 2, while the nonplayer character fixture is in Category 3 (remember that to set bit 3, we need to set the category bits to $0000000000000100 = 4_{10}$). The next two lines of code set the categories that the fixtures can collide with. The player character can collide with fixture Category 4 (the nonplayer character fixture), while the nonplayer character fixture can collide with Category 2 (the player character fixture).

Collision groups are indicated by an integer `groupIndex`. You can have all fixtures with the same group index always collide (positive `groupIndex`) or never collide (negative `groupIndex`). Group indices are usually used for things that are somehow related, like the parts of a game object. In the following example, fixtures `f1` and `f2` always collide, but `f3` and `f4` never collide.

```
b2FixtureDef  f1,  f2,  f3,  f4;
f1 . filter . groupIndex  =  42;
f2 . filter . groupIndex  =  42;
f3 . filter . groupIndex  =  -7;
f4 . filter . groupIndex  =  -7;
```

Group filtering has higher precedence than category filtering.

6.5.3 Bodies

A *body* is really only a carrier for a collection of fixtures. Box2D has three distinct types of body: *static, kinematic,* and *dynamic.* Static bodies do not move automatically in the Physics World, although the programmer can move them manually. Fixtures on a static body can only collide with fixtures on a dynamic body. Kinematic bodies move but do not respond to forces, so they have velocity but no acceleration. Fixtures on a kinematic body can only collide with fixtures on a dynamic body. Dynamic bodies are fully simulated: they have velocity, they respond to forces, and their fixtures collide with fixtures on bodies of all three types. By default, all created bodies are static unless you explicitly ask the Physics World to create them as dynamic bodies by setting the appropriate parameter.[7]

It takes four steps to create a body. The first step is to create a b2BodyDef structure that you will use to define the properties of your body, such as position.

```
b2BodyDef myboxBodyDef ;
myboxBodyDef . position . Set (0.0f, -100.0f);
```

If you want your box to be dynamic or kinematic rather than static, simply add the property b2_dynamicBody or b2_kinematicBody to your b2BodyDef structure's type field.

```
myboxBodyDef . type = b2_dynamicBody ;
```

Step 2 is to ask the Physics World object (Section 6.5.1) to create a body described by your b2BodyDef structure. The body will have no fixtures at this point. You will have to attach them later.

```
b2Body* myboxBody =
    g_b2dPhysicsWorld . CreateBody (&myboxBodyDef );
```

Step 3 is to define fixtures (Section 6.5.2) with properties such as shape (Section 6.4).

```
b2PolygonShape myboxShape ;
myboxShape . SetAsBox (50.0f, 10.0f);
```

Finally, Step 4 is to attach fixtures on the body.
....

[7]This means that if your bodies fail to move as expected, the first thing you should check is whether you remembered to make them dynamic.

```
myboxBody ->CreateFixture (&myboxShape ,  0.0f );
```

The second parameter is the shape density in kg/m². Although density
is not used in static bodies, it's probably a good idea to set it to zero
to remind yourself of this fact. Dynamic bodies usually have more fixtures
besides their shape. We can define a fixture with density 1.0 and coefficient
of friction 0.42 as follows:

```
b2FixtureDef myfixtureDef ;
myfixtureDef .shape = &myboxShape ;
myfixtureDef .density = 1.0f ;
myfixtureDef .friction = 0.42f ;
```

The CreateFixture function is given a pointer to the fixture (containing
the shape and other properties) instead of a pointer to the shape:

```
myboxBody ->CreateFixture (&myfixtureDef );
```

This automatically updates the mass of the body from its size and density.
If you add multiple fixtures to a body, each one contributes to the total
mass.

6.5.4   The Integrator

The Integrator simulates the physics equation in discrete time. Generally,
physics engines for games like a time step at least as fast as 60 hertz or 1/60
seconds. You can get away with larger time steps, but you will have to be
more careful about setting up your world. A fixed time step means better
convergence, and reproducible results (which is, of course, very important
when debugging). Don't tie the time step to the render frame rate.

```
const float32 timeStep = 1.0f/60.0f ;
```

6.5.5   The Constraint Solver

The constraint solver solves all the constraints in the simulation one at a
time. It has two phases: In the *velocity phase*, the solver computes the
impulses necessary for the bodies to move correctly. In the *position phase*,
the solver adjusts the positions of the bodies to reduce overlap and joint
detachment. A single constraint can be solved perfectly. However, when
we solve one constraint, we slightly disrupt other constraints. As we saw

earlier in Section 2.4, we will need to iterate over all constraints a number of times to get a good solution.

The position phase may exit early if errors are small. The suggested iteration count for Box2D is 8 for velocity and 3 for position.

```
const int32 velocityIterations = 8;
const int32 positionIterations = 3;
```

Note that the time step and the iteration count are completely unrelated. An iteration is not a sub-step. One constraint-solver iteration is a single pass over all the constraints within a time step. You can have multiple passes over the constraints within a single time step. Here is the simulation loop that simulates 60 time steps for a total of 1 second of simulated time.

```
for(int32 i=0; i<60; i++){
  g_b2dPhysicsWorld.Step(timeStep, velocityIterations,
    positionIterations);
  b2Vec2 p = myboxBody->GetPosition();
  float32 a = myboxBody->GetAngle();
  //render myboxBody at (p.x, p.y) at angle a radians
}
```

● 6.6 Joints

The Stoners amongst the readers of this book may think otherwise, but for us the term *joint* means a constraint used to hold two or more bodies together. For example, your elbow joint attaches your upper arm to your lower arm and constrains the angle between them to be concave.

Box2D provides eight joint types[8] derived from the generic b2Joint. Each joint type has a corresponding *joint definition* derived from b2Joint Def that specifies various parameters of the joint. To make a joint, you first describe it with a joint definition structure, then pass the joint definition to the Physics World's CreateJoint function, which gives you a pointer to the new joint in return. The eight joint types and their corresponding joint definition types are described in Table 6.14. Box2D joint files are contained

....

[8]The sci-fi author Robert Heinlein wrote that there are two artistic ways of lying, the first of which is "Tell the truth, but not all of it." I lied to you. Box2D actually has nine joint types, the ninth of which is the *mouse joint*. I'm going to ignore it because it crosses world boundaries.

Joint	Joint Type	Joint Definition Type
Distance	b2DistanceJoint	b2DistanceJointDef
Revolute	b2RevoluteJoint	b2RevoluteJointDef
Prismatic	b2PrismaticJoint	b2PrismaticJointDef
Pulley	b2PrismaticJoint	b2PrismaticJointDef
Gear	b2GearJoint	b2GearJointDef
Weld	b2WeldJoint	b2WeldJointDef
Rope	b2RopeJoint	b2RopeJointDef
Friction	b2FrictionJoint	b2FrictionJointDef

Table 6.14 • Joints and joint definitions.

File	Joint Class
b2DistanceJoint.h,cpp	b2DistanceJointDef, b2DistanceJoint
b2FrictionJoint.h,cpp	b2FrictionJointDef, b2FrictionJoint
b2GearJoint.h,cpp	b2GearJointDef, b2GearJoint
b2Joint.h,cpp	b2JointDef, b2Joint
b2MouseJoint.h,cpp	b2MouseJointDef, b2MouseJoint
b2PrismaticJoint.h,cpp	b2PrismaticJointDef, b2PrismaticJoint
b2PulleyJoint.h,cpp	b2PulleyJointDef, b2PulleyJoint
b2RevoluteJoint.h,cpp	b2RevoluteJointDef, b2RevoluteJoint
b2RopeJoint.h,cpp	b2RopeJointDef, b2RopeJoint
b2WeldJoint.h,cpp	b2WeldJointDef, b2WeldJoint
b2WheelJoint.h,cpp	b2WheelJointDef, b2WheelJoint

Table 6.15 • The joint files in folder Joints with the classes they contain.

in a folder called Joints in the Dynamics Module folder Dynamics. There you will find the files in Table 6.15 with their corresponding class names.

Suppose we have created two bodies pointed to by pb2bBody1 and pb2b Body2 and computed anchor points b2v2Anchor1 and b2v2Anchor2 declared as follows.

```
b2Body* pb2bBody1 , pb2bBody2;
b2Vec2 b2v2Anchor1 , b2v2Anchor2;
```

The next few sections will show how to create the joint definitions for various types of joints connecting the bodies pointed to by pb2bBody1 and pb2bBody2 at anchor points b2v2Anchor1 and b2v2Anchor2.

● 6.6.1 Distance Joint

A *distance joint* fixes the distance between two points on two bodies (see Figure 6.10). Once you specify the two anchor points in world coordinates,

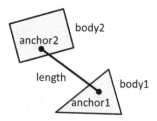

Figure 6.10 • Distance joint.

world-space distance between them is kept fixed during the simulation. The
initialization function assumes that the bodies are already in the correct
position.

```
b2DistanceJointDef b2djdExample1;
djdExample1.Initialize(pb2bBody1, pb2bBody2,
   b2v2Anchor1, b2v2Anchor2);
```

The `Initialize` function used above is a shortcut for specifying the
corresponding member variables directly:

```
b2DistanceJointDef b2djdExample1;
b2djdExample1.bodyA = pb2bBody1;
b2djdExample1.bodyB = pb2bBody2;
b2djdExample1.anchorPoint = b2v2Anchor1;
```

Distance joints can be made soft, like a spring-damper connection. Soft-
ness is achieved by tuning two constants in the definition, the frequency,
and the damping ratio. The *frequency* is specified in hertz, or cycles per
second. Typically, the frequency should be less than half the frequency of
the time step (this is related to the *Nyquist frequency*). The *damping ratio*
is non-dimensional and is typically between 0 and 1, but can be larger. At 1,
the damping is *critical*, which means that all oscillations should vanish.

```
b2djdExample1.frequencyHz = 10.0f;
b2djdExample1.dampingRatio = 0.6f;
```

6.6.2   Revolute Joint

The *revolute joint* forces two bodies to share a common anchor point, also
known as the *hinge point* (see Figure 6.11). The revolute joint has a single

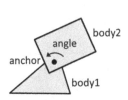
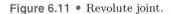
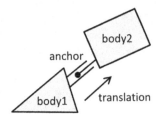

Figure 6.11 • Revolute joint.   **Figure 6.12** • Prismatic joint.

degree of freedom: the relative rotation of the two bodies. This is called the *joint angle*. To specify a revolute joint you need to provide two bodies and a single anchor point in world space. The initialization function assumes that the bodies are already in the correct position. The following declaration creates a revolute joint between two bodies at the first body's center of mass.

```
b2RevoluteJointDef b2djdExample2;
b2djdExample2.Initialize(pb2bBody1, pb2bBody2,
    b2v2Anchor1);
```

6.6.3 Prismatic Joint

The *prismatic joint*, often called a *slider*, allows only linear motion along an axis (see Figure 6.12). The following declaration creates a prismatic joint between two bodies attached to the first body with axis at 45° as shown in Figure 6.12.

```
b2PrismaticJointDef b2djdExample3;
b2djdExample3.Initialize(pb2bBody1, pb2bBody2,
    b2v2Anchor1, b2Vec2(1.0f, 1.0f));
```

6.6.4 Pulley Joint

The *pulley joint* is used to create an idealized pulley. As one body goes up the other goes down, conserving the total length of the pulley rope. You can use a *ratio* to simulate a block-and-tackle, in which one side of the pulley extends faster than the other. The block-and-tackle is used to create mechanical leverage since the constraint force is smaller on one side too. (See Figure 6.13.)

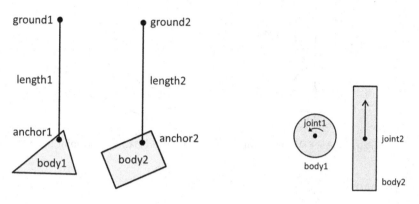

Figure 6.13 • Pulley joint.   Figure 6.14 • Gear joint.

```
b2Vec2 b2v2Ground1;
b2Vec2 b2v2Ground2;
float32 f32Ratio = 1.5f;
b2PulleyJointDef b2djdExample4;
b2djdExample4.Initialize(
    pb2bBody1, pb2bBody2, b2v2Anchor1, b2v2Anchor2,
    b2v2Ground1, b2v2Ground2, f32Ratio);
```

6.6.5   Gear Joint

The *gear joint* can only connect revolute or prismatic joints (see Figure 6.14). Like the pulley ratio, you can specify a gear ratio; however, in this case, the gear ratio can be negative. When one joint is a revolute joint (angular) and the other joint is prismatic (translation), the gear ratio will have units of either length or $1 - $ length.

Gear joints have no `Initialize()` function, so you'll have to initialize their member functions directly. Suppose we've already created a revolute joint pointed to by `b2djRevolute` and a prismatic joint pointed to by `b2djdPrismatic`. (Yes, I know we're getting a little ahead of ourselves. We'll see how to actually create joints from joint descriptors later in Section 6.6.10.)

```
b2GearJointDef b2djdExample5;
b2djdExample5.joint1 = &b2djRevolute;
b2djdExample5.joint2 = &b2djdPrismatic;
b2djdExample5.ratio = 1.0f;
```

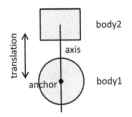

Figure 6.15 • Wheel joint.   **Figure 6.16** • Weld joint.

6.6.6   Wheel Joint

The *wheel joint* restricts a point on one body to a line on another (see Figure 6.15).

```
b2WheelJointDef  b2djdExample6 ;
b2djdExample6 . Initialize (pb2bBody1 ,  pb2bBody2 ,
   b2v2Anchor1,  b2Vec2(0.0f,  1.0f));
```

6.6.7   Weld Joint

The *weld joint* attempts to constrain all relative motion between two bodies (see Figure 6.16). However, chains of bodies connected by weld joints will flex.

```
b2WeldJointDef  b2djdExample6 ;
b2djdExample6 . Initialize (
   pb2bBody1 ,  pb2bBody2 ,  b2v2Anchor1 );
```

6.6.8   Rope Joint

The *rope joint* restricts the maximum distance between two points. Don't try to change the length of the rope at runtime. Use a distance joint instead.

```
b2RopeJointDef  b2djdExample7 ;
b2djdExample7 . localAnchorA  =  b2v2Anchor1 ;
b2djdExample7 . localAnchorB  =  b2v2Anchor2 ;
```

6.6.9   Friction Joint

The *friction joint* is used for z-axis friction, including both translational and angular friction. To create a friction joint between two bodies, you need to initialize the joint definition with anchor points on the bodies in body space and an anchor point in world space. The joint has a `SetMaxForce` function and a `SetMaxTorque` function that you can use to set its maximum friction force and torque, respectively.

6.6.10   Creating, Using, and Destroying Joints

Joints must connect different bodies. They are usually used to connect dynamic bodies, but one body may be static. Joints have no effect on kinematic bodies.

Joints must be created and destroyed using the Physics World factory methods. Do not use `new` or `malloc`. For example, a distance joint `pb2djExample1` is created from the distance joint definition `b2djdExample1` above as follows:

```
b2DistanceJoint* pb2djExample1 = (b2DistanceJoint*)
   g_b2PhysicsWorld->CreateJoint(&b2djdExample1);
```

Joints are deleted with the Physics World's `DestroyJoint` function. Be aware that when bodies are destroyed, the attached joints are also automatically destroyed. Make sure that you either destroy joints before bodies, or do a *safe delete* as in the code snippet below. It's probably best to do both.

```
if(pb2djExample1){ //safe delete
   g_b2PhysicsWorld->DestroyJoint(pb2djExample1);
   pb2djExample1 = NULL;
}
```

There's no need to keep joint definitions around after their joints have been created, because you can get that information back from the joint itself. For example, to get back the bodies and anchor points from the joint pointed to by `pb2djExample1`,

```
b2Body* pb2bBodyA   = pb2djExample1->GetBodyA();
b2Body* pb2bBodyB   = pb2djExample1->GetBodyB();
b2Vec2 b2v2AnchorA  = pb2djExample1->GetAnchorA();
b2Vec2 b2v2AnchorB  = pb2djExample1->GetAnchorB();
```

All joints have a reaction force and a torque, which can be retrieved as follows. The following functions compute torque and force on demand, which may require quite a bit of computation, so it's best use them sparingly.

```
b2Vec2 b2v2Force =
  pb2djExample1->GetReactionForce ();
float32 f32Torque =
  pb2djExample1->GetReactionTorque ();
```

● 6.7 Exercises

If you haven't already done so, go back to Section 5.1 and follow the instructions for downloading and installing Box2D before you attempt these problems.

1. Make a list of the functions and classes in the Common Module files b2Math.h and b2Math.cpp. There are some I didn't include in Section 6.1. What are they?

2. Evaluate the speed of the approximate inverse square-root function b2InvSqrt from b2Math.h in the Common Module compared to the obvious alternative of inverting the output of the standard sqrt function. Write a program that compares the running time for the two approaches. You may need to repeat each function call a thousand or more times and divide by the same to get a meaningful time measurement.

3. Evaluate the accuracy of the approximate inverse square-root function b2InvSqrt from b2Math.h in the Common Module compared to the obvious alternative of inverting the output of the standard sqrt function. Write a program that compares the accuracy of the two approaches. Collect data for a sample of randomly chosen n-bit integers, for all $1 \leq n \leq 16$. Draw a graph with n on the x-axis and the average absolute value of the ratio of the approximated value b2InvSqrt(m) to the real value $1/\sqrt{m}$ over the n-bit integers m on the y-axis. Can you discern any pattern? Explain.

4. Examine the code for function GetSymInverse33 from b2Math.cpp in the Common Module. Where exactly does it assume that the matrix is symmetrical? Can you explain in one sentence what it returns if the matrix isn't symmetrical?

7

The Cannon Game

The Cannon Game gives the player control of a cannon in a world with a tempting tower of books. The player's job is to knock down the tower in 60 seconds or less by firing cannonballs at it. The temperature of the cannon goes up every time it is fired, and it cools down slowly afterwards. The current temperature of the cannon barrel and the maximum temperature reached so far are indicated on a temperature gauge (as shown in Figure 7.1). If the cannon barrel is overstressed by heating it above the maximum allowable temperature, then it will explode the next time it is fired. (See Figures 7.2–7.6.) The player controls the cannon using the keyboard. Table 7.1 shows the keyboard bindings.

Although this 60-second minigame is very basic, it exhibits in rudimentary form all of the required characteristics of a game, which are the following:

1. It has a virtual world.

2. The world has stuff in it.

3. The player can interact with the stuff.

4. The player can win.

5. The player can lose.

The "virtual world" is the screen space, the "stuff" is the cannon and the books, the "interaction" is firing the cannon and knocking down the books, the player "wins" when the books are knocked down and "loses" when the cannon overheats. What's not to like?

Figure 7.1 • The temperature gauge.

Key	Action
ESC	Quit
Enter	Restart
↑	Barrel up
↓	Barrel down
←	Move left
→	Move right
Backspace	Stop moving
Space	Fire

Table 7.1 • The keys used in the Cannon Game.

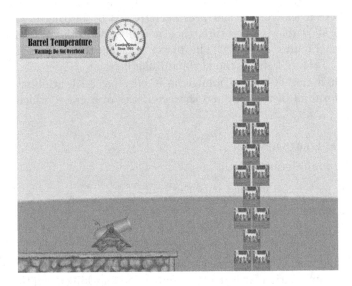

Figure 7.2 • The start of the cannon game.

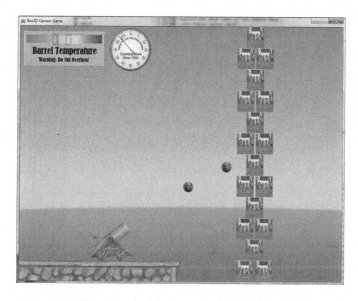

Figure 7.3 • The cannon game is underway, the barrel is starting to heat up.

Figure 7.4 • The tower of books is toppled.

Figure 7.5 • The tower has been vanquished.

Figure 7.6 • This is what happens when you let the cannon overheat.

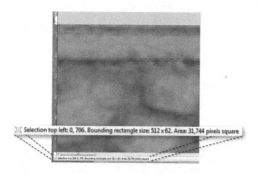

Figure 7.7 • The ledge is 512 × 62 pixels.

• 7.1 The Platform and the Tower

I began by taking the Getting Started app from Section 5.4 and stripping out the code in `NonPlayerObjects.cpp`. We'll replace it with code to create the cannon and the tower of books.

I want a platform for the cannon to sit on. In my favorite image editing program,[1] I create a ledge that is half the width of the image in Physics World units, and I see in Figure 7.7 that it is 62 pixels high, which is `RW2PW(62)` in Physics World units. There's no need to make it a sprite, so I just paint it into the background image `background.png`, as shown in Figure 7.8. This code gets added to function `CreateWorldEdges` to add the corresponding edge to Physics World, as shown in Figure 7.9 (remembering that it has already computed w, the world width in Physics World units):

```
const float lh = RW2PW(62);
shape.Set(b2Vec2(0, lh), b2Vec2(w/2, lh));
edge->CreateFixture(&shape, 0);
```

While we were a little cavalier about how we created the edge bodies for the boundaries of our Physics World, it's time we got a little more careful about how we structure our code. We're going to create the rest of the physics bodies for our game in the following order:

1. Shape: `b2Shape` or any of the shapes derived from it, see Section 6.4.
2. Fixture: `b2FixtureDef`, see Section 6.5.2.
3. Body definition: `b2BodyDef`, see Section 6.5.3.
4. Body: `b2Body`, see Section 6.5.3.

....

[1]I like to use either Gimp or paint.net, depending on the task. They are both Open Source, and between them, I have all the functionality that a lowly programmer could need, for free.

Figure 7.8 • The game background from `background.png` with the platform for the cannon.

Figure 7.9 • The ledge in Render World with the edge in Physics World.

The dependencies between shape, fixture, body definition, and body are illustrated in Figure 7.10. You can create them in any order that respects these dependencies, but it makes sense to do so in the same order every time to ensure that you don't forget anything and to make your code more readable. Consistency is good.[2]

Function `PlaceBook` in `NonPlayerObjects.cpp` looks a little like function `CreateBook` from Section 5.4. It's been streamlined so it can be used for multiple books, reusing the Fixture Definition which is passed as a new parameter. It starts with a `b2BodyDef` that describes a `b2_dynamicBody` at `(x, y)`.

....

[2]Notwithstanding the Ralph Waldo Emerson quote "A foolish consistency is the hobgoblin of little minds." This is by no means a foolish consistency. It is a sensible one.

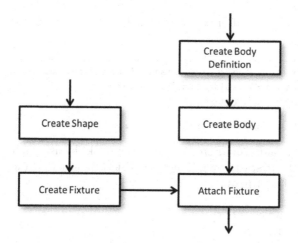

Figure 7.10 • Steps needed to create a Box2D body.

```
void PlaceBook(float x, float y,
  const b2FixtureDef& fd)
{
b2BodyDef bd;
bd.type = b2_dynamicBody;
bd.position.Set(x, y);
```

It creates the book in Object World first.

```
CGameObject* pGameObject =
  g_cObjectWorld.create(BOOK_OBJECT);
```

Then, it creates the book in Physics World and gives the Object World object a link to the Physics World object. Remember that the Object World is the central place where we go to learn about objects as abstractions that are instantiated in Physics World and Render World. We are on potentially dangerous ground here. The Object World now has a pointer deep into Physics World that it can use to get into a whole lot of pain if that pointer gets written to. We'll only use it to read, but there's no guarantee that future generations of coders maintaining your code will continue to do so.

• IMPORTANT POINT •

Don't forget that getting pointers to things deep inside Box2D gives you great power that comes with great responsibility. If you abuse that power, you may be heading for a world of pain.

We're ready to leave after we attach the fixture defined by `fd` to the new book body.

```
   b2Body* pBook = g_b2dPhysicsWorld.CreateBody(&bd);
   pGameObject->SetPhysicsBody(pBook);
   pBook->CreateFixture(&fd);
} //PlaceBook
```

Function `CreateTower` creates a tower of books by using a bunch of calls to `PlaceBook`. It starts by getting the Object World width and height in Render World coordinates.

```
void CreateTower(){
  float w, h;
  g_cObjectWorld.GetWorldSize(w, h);
```

Next, we create a `b2FixtureDef` called `bookfd` and set it to a box that is 27×32 in Render World units, just as we did in function `CreateBook` from Section 5.4.

```
   b2PolygonShape bookshape;
   bookshape.SetAsBox(RW2PW(27), RW2PW(32));
   b2FixtureDef bookfd;
   bookfd.shape = &bookshape;
   bookfd.density = 1.0f;
   bookfd.restitution = 0.3f;
```

We'll build the tower of books 12 layers high one layer at a time using a loop structure like this. The "then" part of the if statement places a single book and gets executed in odd-numbered layers, that is, in layers 1, 3, 5, 7, 9, 11. The "else" part of the if statement places a pair of books and gets executed in even-numbered layers, that is, in layers 0, 2, 4, 6, 8, 10. It remains for us to figure out the coordinates to be given to `PlaceBook`.

```
   for(int i=0; i<12; i++){
     if(i&1)
       PlaceBook(?, ?, bookfd);
     else{
       PlaceBook(?, ?, bookfd);
       PlaceBook(?, ?, bookfd);
     } //else
   } //for
```

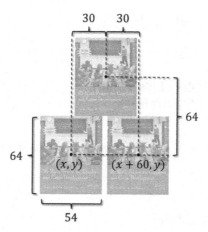

Figure 7.11 • The relative positions of alternate layers of books. Their centers are at (x, y), $(x + 60, y)$ on the bottom layer and $(x + 30, y + 64)$ on the top layer (in Render World coordinates).

Figure 7.11 shows that in an even-numbered layer, if the first book is placed at (x, y), then the second one is draw at $(x + 60, y)$. Similarly on an odd-numbered layer, the book is to be drawn with x-coordinate $x + 30$. Remembering to convert to Physics World units and remembering to add 32 pixels to y because things in Render World are drawn by specifying their center points, we can fill out the details of the final for loop in `CreateTower` as follows.

```
for(int i=0; i<12; i++){
  float x = RW2PW(0.7f*w), y = RW2PW(32 + 64*i);
  if(i&1)
    PlaceBook(x + RW2PW(30), y, bookfd);
  else{
    PlaceBook(x, y, bookfd);
    PlaceBook(x + RW2PW(60), y, bookfd);
  } //else
} //for
} //CreateTower
```

7.2 The Heads-Up Display

The cannon has a heads-up display or HUD (Figure 7.12) that registers the barrel's current and highest temperature at left and a stop watch

Current   Highest

Figure 7.12 • The Heads-up Display (HUD).

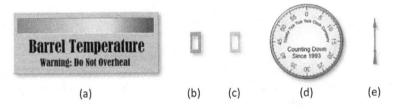

(a)   (b)   (c)   (d)   (e)

Figure 7.13 • Sprites for the objects that make up the HUD. (a) Thermometer background, (b) current temperature indicator, (c) highest temperature indicator, (d) stopwatch face, (e) stopwatch needle.

at right. For convenience, let's make it a class CHeadsUpDisplay in files hud.cpp, h. CHeadsUpDisplay is derived from CObjectManager since its job will be to the care and feeding of the objects that make up the HUD, a thermometer background, the current temperature indicator, the highest temperature indicator, the stopwatch background, and the stopwatch needle. The sprites corresponding to the HUD objects are shown in Figure 7.13. The key thing about the HUD is that it consists of objects that are outside of Object World and Physics World and need only be represented in Render World. CHeadsUpDisplay has its own constructor and it overrides the inherited CObjectManager draw function.

```
class CHeadsUpDisplay : public CObjectManager{
  public:
    CHeadsUpDisplay(int size);
    void draw(int secs, float temp, float maxtemp);
}; //CHeadsUpDisplay
```

The constructor simply passes its size parameter to the CObjectMan ager constructor, which uses it for the size of its object array. Since the number of HUD parts is small, the actual parameter for the CHeadsUpDis play should be small but clearly at least 5.

```
CHeadsUpDisplay::CHeadsUpDisplay(int size):
CObjectManager(size){} //constructor
```

CHeadsUpDisplay's draw function overrides the inherited CObjectMan
ager draw function. It has three parameters, the number of seconds to
display on the stopwatch, the current temperature, and the highest temperature seen so far in the level. It declares a handy CGameObject pointer
p and makes sure that the number of seconds is less than 60.

```
void CHeadsUpDisplay::draw(
    int secs, float temp, float maxtemp)
{
  CGameObject* p=NULL;
  secs = secs % 60;
```

It loops through its inherited Object List, sets p to point to the current
object, and assuming that the object actually exists (we can assume that
it does since we don't delete HUD objects, but you never know what might
happen in the future), it begins the task of determining where and at what
angle to draw the current HUD part.

```
for(int i=0; i<m_nSize; i++){
  p = m_pObjectList[i];
  if(p){
    float x=0.0f, y=0.0f, a=0.0f;
```

Naturally, these values depend on the type of the HUD object. I'll leave
you to puzzle out the details for yourself.

```
    switch(p->m_nObjectType){
    case TEMPGAUGE_OBJECT:
     x = 140.0f; y = 40.0f;
     break;
    case TEMPMAXNEEDLE_OBJECT:
     x = 25 + min(300.0f, 256.0f * maxtemp/178.0f);
     y = 40.0f;
     break;
    case TEMPNEEDLE_OBJECT:
     x = 25 + min(300.0f, 256.0f * temp/178.0f);
     y = 40.0f;
     break;
    case CLOCKFACE_OBJECT:
     x = 350.0f; y = 70.0f;
     break;
```

The clock needle orientation a might cause you to pause for thought. Take the number of seconds secs and divide by the number of seconds around a clock face, which is 60. We multiply this by 2π since that's the number of radians in a full circle.

```
    case CLOCKNEEDLE_OBJECT:
    x = 350.0f; y = 70.0f;
    a = ((float)secs/60.0f)*2.0f*b2_pi;
    break;
  } //switch
```

Now that we know what, where, and at what angle, we can go ahead and ask the Render World to do the actual drawing. Render World has a handy drawtop function that measures the vertical axis down from the top of the screen, so we'll use that.

```
    g_cRenderWorld.drawtop(
      p->m_nObjectType, x, y, a);
  } //if
 } //for
} //draw
```

• 7.3 The Object World

The class CObjectWorld declaration in ObjectWorld.h has had some things added to it from the original version that we saw in our Getting Started app in Section 5.4. It gets a new private member variable for the HUD and a new public member variable for the cannon. It also has three new public member functions, CreateHudObject, PlayerHasWon, and MakeSound.

```
 private:
   CHeadsUpDisplay* m_pHeadsUpDisplay;

 public:
   CCannon m_cCannon;
   void MakeSound();
   CGameObject* CreateHudObject(GameObjectType t);
   BOOL PlayerHasWon(float level);
```

The CObjectWorld constructor in ObjectWorld.cpp remains almost exactly the same as before but gets a new line of code to create the HUD.

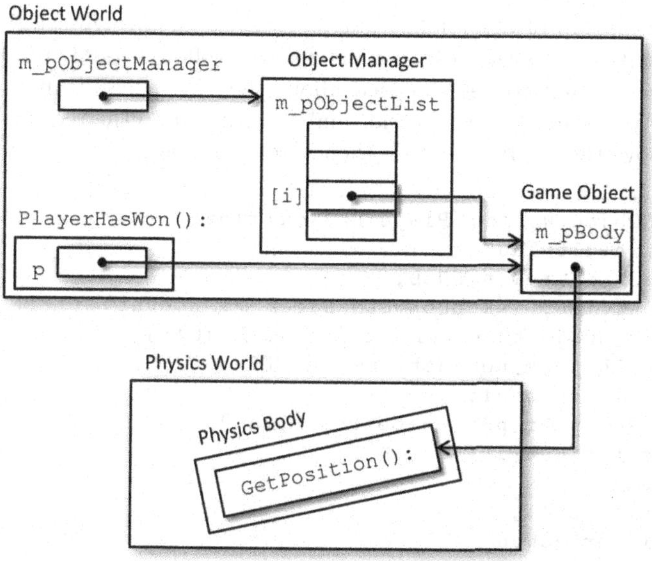

Object World

Figure 7.14 • Getting a Game Object's position.

There's a corresponding **delete** line in the destructor, too.

```
m_pHeadsUpDisplay = new CHeadsUpDisplay (32);
```

CreateHudObject asks **m_pHeadsUpDisplay** to create the requested HUD object.

```
CGameObject* CObjectWorld::
  CreateHudObject (GameObjectType t)
{
  return m_pHeadsUpDisplay ->create(t);
} //CreateHudObject
```

The player wins the game if all of the books are in, say, the bottom quarter of the screen. The term "quarter" is a guess, so we'd better make that value a parameter to this function. It might well vary from level to level when we flesh out the game, so call it **level**. It's intended to be a fraction between 0 and 1, but doesn't necessarily have to be that way. In order to get the book altitudes, we need to follow the chain of pointers from Object World to Physics World illustrated in Figure 7.14. We use a handy object pointer p that is set to **m_pObjectManager->m_pObjectList[i]** on the ith iteration of a for loop that loops through the Object Manager's Object List. It gets that object's height p->m_pBody->GetPosition().y, (remembering not to get confused about the difference in units between Physics World and Render World) and compares it to the required height. If it's above the required level, then it returns a fail.

```
BOOL CObjectWorld::PlayerHasWon(float level){
  BOOL result=TRUE;
  CGameObject* p = NULL;
  for(int i=0; i<m_pObjectManager->m_nCount; i++){
   p = m_pObjectManager->m_pObjectList[i];
   if(p && p->m_nObjectType == BOOK_OBJECT)
    result = result &&
     PW2RW(p->m_pBody->GetPosition().y) <
      m_fHeight/level;
  } //for
  return result;
} //PlayerHasWon
```

Function MakeSound asks m_pObjectManager to do the actual work.

```
void CObjectWorld::MakeSound(){
  m_pObjectManager->MakeSound();
} //MakeSound
```

● 7.4 The Cannon Object

Instead of placing variables and functions that represent the user directly into the Object World code as I did in the Pool End Game app in Chapter 3, I've chosen to wrap them up into their own class called CCannon in files Cannon.h, cpp. As you will see, there are quite a lot of them. We'll put an instance of CCannon into CObjectWorld later. CCannon starts by making CObjectWorld a friend, which is a lot easier than making a set of accessor functions just so that CObjectWorld can interact with the cannon.

```
class CCannon{
 friend class CObjectWorld;
```

The first set of private member variables are pointers to the b2Bodys for the parts of the cannon in Physics World. These represent the cannon's barrel, base, and wheels. Their Render World equivalents can be seen flying apart in Figure 7.6, but most of the time, they will be joined together using

Box2D joints and will look like a single cohesive object as shown in, for example, Figure 7.2.

```
private:
   b2Body* m_pCannonBarrel;
   b2Body* m_pCannonBase;
   b2Body* m_pWheel1;
   b2Body* m_pWheel2;
```

The second set of private member variables are pointers to Box2D joints. We'll need three of them, two wheel joints (Section 6.6.6) joining a wheel each to the base, and a revolute joint (Section 6.6.2) that joins the barrel to the base.

```
b2WheelJoint* m_pCannonWheelJoint1;
b2WheelJoint* m_pCannonWheelJoint2;
b2RevoluteJoint* m_pCannonBarrelJoint;
```

We'll be monitoring the cannon's state, including its current temperature, its maximum allowable temperature (after which it explodes when fired), the number of times it has been fired, and whether it has exploded yet.

```
float m_fCannonTemp;
float m_fCannonMaxTemp;
int m_nCannonBallsFired;
BOOL m_bCannonExploded;
```

CCannon's private member functions include helper functions to create the parts of the cannon in Physics World. Remember what a pain it is to create Physics World objects. It's not technically difficult, but you have to pay attention to detail. There are three functions, one for each type of cannon part, and each takes the coordinates of the part in Render World units and a collision group index. The collision group index parameter nIndex will be used to put the cannon parts in the same collision group (see Section 6.5.2), which will be negative to ensure that the cannon parts do not collide with each other. If we neglect to do this, then the cannon will look fine when it is still, but it will behave badly when forces are applied to parts of it as the collision constraints fight with the joint constraints.

```
b2Body* CreateCannonMount (
  int x, int y, int nIndex);
b2Body* CreateCannonBarrel (
  int x, int y, int nIndex);
b2Body* CreateWheel (int x, int y, int nIndex);
```

The final private member functions are `Impulse`, which provides an impulse to a particular `b2Body` along a vector `v` applied at point `ds`.

```
void Impulse(b2Body* b, b2Vec2& v, b2Vec2& ds);
void ResetCollisionGroupIndex(b2Body* b);
void StopMoving();
```

The public member functions start with three birth-and-death functions, a constructor, a `create` function that creates the cannon out of Physics body parts, and an `Explode` function that takes care of dismembering the cannon when it explodes.

```
public:
  CCannon();
  void create();
  void Explode();
```

The next three public member functions deals with the player's control of the cannon. `Fire` fires a cannonball. `BarrelUp` rotates the barrel up by a given `angle` (down if it is negative), subject to constraints that prevent it from reaching a ridiculous angle. `StartMovingLeft` starts the cannon moving left under its own power at a given `speed` (right if it is negative).

```
BOOL Fire();
void BarrelUp(float angle);
void StartMovingLeft(float speed);
```

The final group of four public member functions deals with the care and maintenance of the cannon. `BallsFired` returns the number of cannonballs fired, `IsDead` returns `TRUE` if called after the cannon has exploded, `CoolDown` cools the cannon down, and `Reset` resets the cannon back to its initial conditions.

```
  int BallsFired();
  BOOL IsDead();
  void CoolDown();
  void Reset();
}; //CCannon
```

Now lets look at `CCannon`'s member functions. The constructor does your basic constructor-y type things, `NULL`ing out pointers and calling `Reset` to set the rest of the private member variables to initial conditions.

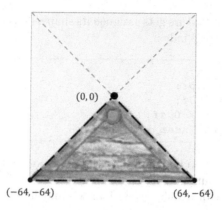

Figure 7.15 • The coordinates of the three triangle vertices of the cannon base in Render World.

```
CCannon::CCannon(){
  m_pCannonBarrel = m_pCannonBase = NULL;
  m_pWheel1 = m_pWheel2 = NULL;
  m_pCannonWheelJoint1 = m_pCannonWheelJoint2 = NULL;
  Reset();
} //constructor
```

CreateCannonMount has three parameters, the x and y coordinates of the cannon in Render World and the collision group index for the cannon parts, nIndex. It begins with a b2PolygonShape that is set to a triangle with a horizontal base. The cannon mount is 128 × 128 pixels in Render World, and if the top vertex of the triangle is at $(0,0)$, then the base vertices have a y-coordinate of -64 and x-coordinates of ± 64 in Render World (see Figure 7.15).

```
b2Body* CCannon::CreateCannonMount(
    int x, int y, int nIndex)
{
  b2PolygonShape shape;
  b2Vec2 vertices[3];
  const float s = RW2PW(64);
  vertices[0].Set(-s, -s);
  vertices[1].Set(s, -s);
  vertices[2].Set(0.0f, 0.0f);
  shape.Set(vertices, 3);
```

The cannon mount's fixture gets assigned its shape, density, and restitution, and the collision group index.

```
b2FixtureDef fd;
fd.shape = &shape;
fd.density = 1.0f;
fd.restitution = 0.4f;
fd.filter.groupIndex = nIndex;
```

The cannon mount's body definition receives its position from the first two parameters of the function (remembering to convert from Render World units to Physics World units using RW2PW), and it is, of course, set to a dynamic body type.

```
b2BodyDef bd;
bd.type = b2_dynamicBody;
bd.position.Set(RW2PW(x), RW2PW(y));
```

Finally, we create the cannon mount body, attach the fixture, and return a body pointer.

```
b2Body* body = g_b2dPhysicsWorld.CreateBody(&bd);
body->CreateFixture(&fd);
return body;
} //CreateCannonMount
```

Function `CreateCannonBarrel` also takes as parameters the location of the cannon barrel in the Render World and a collision group index. It does the same steps as function `CreateCannonMount` in the same order, but its shape is a box instead of a triangle.

```
b2Body* CCannon::CreateCannonBarrel(
      int x, int y, int nIndex){

//shape
b2PolygonShape shape;
shape.SetAsBox(RW2PW(67), RW2PW(22));

//fixture
b2FixtureDef fd;
fd.shape = &shape;
fd.density = 1.0f;
fd.restitution = 0.2f;
fd.filter.groupIndex = nIndex;
```

```
//body definition
b2BodyDef bd;
bd.type = b2_dynamicBody;
bd.position.Set(RW2PW(x), RW2PW(y));

//body
b2Body* body = g_b2dPhysicsWorld.CreateBody(&bd);
body->CreateFixture(&fd);
return body;
} //CreateCannonBarrel
```

Function CCannon::CreateWheel is similar, but its shape is a circle of radius 16 units in Render World.

```
b2Body* CCannon::CreateWheel(
int x, int y, int nIndex)
{
//shape
b2CircleShape shape;
shape.m_radius = RW2PW(16);

//fixture
b2FixtureDef fd;
fd.shape = &shape;
fd.density = 0.8f;
fd.restitution = 0.6f;
fd.filter.groupIndex = nIndex;

//body definition
b2BodyDef bd;
bd.type = b2_dynamicBody;
bd.position.Set(RW2PW(x), RW2PW(y));

//body
b2Body* body;
body = g_b2dPhysicsWorld.CreateBody(&bd);
body->CreateFixture(&fd);
return body;
} //CreateWheel
```

The create function uses the above private member functions to put together the cannon from the mount, barrel, and wheels, connecting them with joints. nCannonCollisionGroup is the cannon's collision group index, which we set arbitrarily[3] to 42. It will be created on the ground in the Physics World at x-coordinate fCannonX, which we set arbitrarily[4] to 300 Render World units, which is about a third of the way across the screen.

```
void CCannon::create(){
  const int nIndex = -42;
  const int nX = 300;
  const int nY = 62;
```

The first thing we do is create the four cannon parts in Object World.

```
CGameObject* pBarrel =
  g_cObjectWorld.create(CANNONBARREL_OBJECT);
CGameObject* pMount =
  g_cObjectWorld.create(CANNONMOUNT_OBJECT);
CGameObject* pWheel1 =
  g_cObjectWorld.create(WHEEL_OBJECT);
CGameObject* pWheel2 =
  g_cObjectWorld.create(WHEEL_OBJECT);
```

Then, we create their counterparts in Physics World. You'll notice that the cannon mount was created at 84 pixels above the ground in Render World. The cannon mount image is 128 pixels high (which is an artifact of DirectX preferring textures that are square and a power of 2 in size), but the top of the mount is at 64 pixels. The 84 pixels represents "64 plus a little bit" that was found by trial and error. After attaching the cannon barrel, I found that the weight of mount-plus-barrel caused the mount to sink on its springs (which we will see in a moment) to about 13 pixels off the ground, which looked about right. Creating the cannon barrel at the Physics World equivalent of 72 pixels above the ground in Render World was adjusted until it too looked about right. Putting the wheels 30 pixels in from the edge of the base looked about right too. So, being completely honest about it, the numbers 84, 72, and 30 in the following code were determined by trial and error.[5] The 16 is the radius of the wheels in Render World, which are 32×32 pixels.

```
m_pCannonBase = CreateCannonMount(
  nX, nY + 84, nIndex);
m_pCannonBarrel = CreateCannonBarrel(
```
....

[3]Well, not completely arbitrarily. It must, as I've said before, be negative to prevent the cannon's parts from colliding, and 42 is the "Answer to Life, the Universe, and Everything" in Douglas Adams' *Hitchhiker's Guide to the Galaxy* trilogy.

[4]This one *is* arbitrary.

[5]Kluged.

```
    nX, nY + 72, nIndex);
  m_pWheel1 = CreateWheel(
    nX - 30, nY + 16, nIndex);
  m_pWheel2 = CreateWheel(
    nX + 30, nY + 16, nIndex);
```

Naturally, we are going to use wheel joints to connect the wheels to the cannon mount. We declare a b2WheelJointDef, declare a vertical axis for the suspension,[6] and call the b2WheelJointDef's Initialize function to connect the first wheel to the cannon mount at the wheel's position with vertical axis.

```
  b2WheelJointDef wd;
  b2Vec2 axis(0.0f, 0.9f);
  wd.Initialize(m_pCannonBase, m_pWheel1,
    m_pWheel1->GetPosition(), axis);
```

The next few settings illustrate a simple way to put a little resistance on the axle joints. We enable a joint motor with a high damping ratio and set its speed to zero. We will use the wheel joints' motors later to move the cannon at the player's command.

```
  wd.dampingRatio = 0.9f;
  wd.motorSpeed = 0.0f;
  wd.maxMotorTorque = 1000.0f;
  wd.enableMotor = TRUE;
```

Now, we can create the wheel joints for wheels 1 and 2, pausing in between to change the b2WheelJointDef's position to the second wheel's position. It's important to remember that Box2D's CreateJoint function connects up the joint between the objects *in their current positions* in the Physics World. This means, for example, that the length of the invisible springs in the wheel joints connecting up the wheel to the chassis will be exactly the right length to go from the current position of the wheel to the current position of the body. Recall that in function CreateCannon above, we created the cannon mount with the function call CreateCannonMount(fCannonX, 8.4f, nCannonCollisionGroup). The 8.4 is the height of the cannon mount above the ground in Physics World. If we changed the 8.4 to 16.4 or even 24.4, we'd see the cannon as depicted in Figure 7.16. More importantly, the cannon would *stay that way*; that

....

[6]Remember that the wheel's axis of rotation is parallel to the z-axis, which is perpendicular to the wheel.

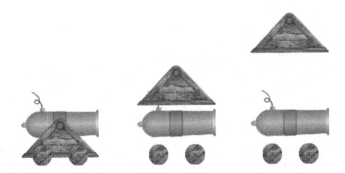

Figure 7.16 • The cannon mount created at heights 8.4, 16.4, and 24.4.

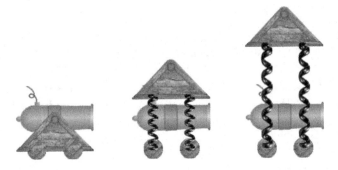

Figure 7.17 • The cannon will behave as if there are invisible springs between the wheels and the mount when they are created in the positions in Figure 7.16.

is, it would behave as if the invisible springs connecting the wheels to the body were like Figure 7.17.

• IMPORTANT POINT •

You must ensure that the bodies connected by your joint are in the correct relative position in Physics World when the joint is created.

```
//create wheel joint for wheel 1
m_pCannonWheelJoint1 =
  (b2WheelJoint *) g_b2dPhysicsWorld.CreateJoint(&wd);

//create wheel joint for wheel 2
wd.Initialize(m_pCannonBase, m_pWheel2,
   m_pWheel2->GetPosition(), axis);
m_pCannonWheelJoint2 =
   (b2WheelJoint *) g_b2dPhysicsWorld.CreateJoint(&wd);
```

A revolute joint is used to connect the cannon barrel to the cannon mount. The process is similar to the wheel joints above.

```
b2RevoluteJointDef jointDef;
jointDef.Initialize(m_pCannonBarrel, m_pCannonBase,
 m_pCannonBarrel->GetWorldCenter());
jointDef.maxMotorTorque = 1000.0f;
jointDef.motorSpeed = 0.0f;
jointDef.enableMotor = true;
```

It wouldn't look good for the cannon to be able to point in all directions, so we set the revolute joint's upper and lower angles and enable joint limits. These lower and upper angles are measured from the barrel and mount's initial orientations in Physics World. Since the barrel is initially horizontal and pointing to the right, we set the upper limit to zero (meaning that the barrel is horizontal) and the lower limit to 45° counterclockwise, which is $-\pi/4$ radians.[7]

```
jointDef.lowerAngle = -b2_pi/4.0f;
jointDef.upperAngle = 0.0f;
jointDef.enableLimit = TRUE;
```

Having now completed the joint definition, we can now create the revolute joint between the cannon barrel and mount.

```
m_pCannonBarrelJoint = (b2RevoluteJoint*)
  m_b2dPhysicsWorld.CreateJoint(&jointDef);
```

Finally, we leave `create` after passing a link to the Physics Bodies for the cannon parts across to their matching Object World objects.

```
pBarrel->SetPhysicsBody(m_pCannonBarrel);
pMount->SetPhysicsBody(m_pCannonBase);
pWheel1->SetPhysicsBody(m_pWheel1);
pWheel2->SetPhysicsBody(m_pWheel2);
} //create
```

CCannon's `BarrelUp` function has a single parameter `angle`, and its job is to increment the cannon barrel's angle of rotation by `angle`. It does this by calling the cannon barrel body's `SetTransform` function. `SetTransform`

....

[7]It may seem a little strange that the lower limit puts the cannon mouth higher in the air than the upper limit, but it all makes sense when you remember that $-\pi/4 < 0$.

requires a position and an angle, which is a bit inconvenient if you only want
to change one and not the other. We have to query the cannon body to
get something we can provide to SetTransform as its position parameter,
and we need its current angle of rotation to add angle to. Fortunately
for us, b2Body has a GetPosition function that returns position in the
correct units and coordinate space and a GetAngle function that returns
orientation.

```
void CCannon::BarrelUp(float angle){
  m_pCannonBarrel->SetTransform(
    m_pCannonBarrel->GetPosition(),
    m_pCannonBarrel->GetAngle() + angle);
} //BarrelUp
```

CCannon's StartMovingLeft function has a single parameter speed,
and its job is to start the cannon moving at speed speed. We're going to
use Box2D's built-in joint motors to do this. The cannon will be two-wheel
drive, so we need to activate the joint motors on both of the wheel joints.
Each activation takes two steps: first, call the wheel joint's SetMotorSpeed
function to pass along the speed parameter, then start the motor by calling
the wheel joint's EnableMotor function with parameter TRUE. First, however, we check that the joints actually exist. They might not if the player
is experimentally mashing the arrow keys after the cannon has exploded.
It might get picked up somewhere else in the code, but it's best to be safe.

```
void CCannon::StartMovingLeft(float speed){
  if(m_pCannonWheelJoint1){
    m_pCannonWheelJoint1->SetMotorSpeed(speed);
    m_pCannonWheelJoint1->EnableMotor(TRUE);
  } //if
  if(m_pCannonWheelJoint2){
    m_pCannonWheelJoint2->SetMotorSpeed(speed);
    m_pCannonWheelJoint2->EnableMotor(TRUE);
  } //if
} //StartMovingLeft
```

StopMoving does the opposite. It's not enough to call StartMoving(0),
though, since we need to deactivate the motors with EnableMotor(FALSE).

```
void CCannon::StopMoving(){
  if(m_pCannonWheelJoint1){
    m_pCannonWheelJoint1->SetMotorSpeed(0.0f);
    m_pCannonWheelJoint1->EnableMotor(FALSE);
  } //if
```

```
if (m_pCannonWheelJoint2 ){
  m_pCannonWheelJoint2 ->SetMotorSpeed (0.0f);
  m_pCannonWheelJoint2 ->EnableMotor (FALSE);
} //if
} //StopMoving
```

Impulse(b, v, ds) applies an impulse to body b with direction and magnitude specified by a vector v to be applied at point p, where p is in local Object Space. b2Body's ApplyLinearImpulse function will get the job done. It is awfully tempting to just call b->ApplyLinearImpulse(v + ds), but this won't work because ApplyLinearImpulse requires the position parameter to be in World Space. We transform from Object Space to World Space by adding the body's World Space position to the Object Space ds.

```
void CCannon :: Impulse (
b2Body* b, b2Vec2& v, b2Vec2& ds)
 {
 b->ApplyLinearImpulse (v, b->GetPosition () + ds);
}; //Impulse
```

Remember that the parts of the cannon were set to the same collision group index so that they don't collide with each other. Now would be a perfect time to write a short piece of code to reverse that. Box2D lets us read a collision filter, change its settings, and then write it back to the fixture it is connected to. Since we will need to do this for all of the bodies that make up the cannon, we'll make a handy function ResetCollisionGroupIndex.

```
void CCannon::ResetCollisionGroupIndex(b2Body* b){
  b2Filter f = b->GetFixtureList ()->GetFilterData ();
  f.groupIndex = 0;
  b->GetFixtureList ()->SetFilterData (f);
} //ResetCollisionGroupIndex
```

Function ExplodeCannon is what gets called when the cannon explodes due to overheating. It asks Physics World to destroy the three joints holding the cannon together, carefully making this a safe destroy by setting the global joint pointers to NULL. There's more work to do after that, though.

```
void CCannon::Explode (){
  //break joints
  if (m_pCannonWheelJoint1 ){
```

```
  g_b2dPhysicsWorld.
    DestroyJoint(m_pCannonWheelJoint1);
  m_pCannonWheelJoint1 = NULL;
}
if(m_pCannonWheelJoint2){
  g_b2dPhysicsWorld.
    DestroyJoint(m_pCannonWheelJoint2);
  m_pCannonWheelJoint2 = NULL;
}
if(m_pCannonBarrelJoint){
  g_b2dPhysicsWorld.
    DestroyJoint(m_pCannonBarrelJoint);
  m_pCannonBarrelJoint = NULL;
}
```

We then apply impulses to the parts of the cannon using CCannon's Impulse function, described above, so that they fly apart most satisfactorily. The magnitudes and directions of the impulses are kluged up values that seem to look appropriately amusing.

```
Impulse(m_pCannonBase,
  b2Vec2(0, 50), b2Vec2(80, 80));
Impulse(m_pCannonBarrel,
  b2Vec2(0, 100), b2Vec2(40, 40));
Impulse(m_pWheel1,
  b2Vec2(-50, 200), b2Vec2(1, 1));
Impulse(m_pWheel2,
  b2Vec2(50, 220), b2Vec2(-1, -1));
```

Now, we set the collision group indices of the cannon bodies to zero so that they can collide with each other, making use of CCannon's ResetCollision GroupIndex function that we described earlier.

```
ResetCollisionGroupIndex(m_pCannonBase);
ResetCollisionGroupIndex(m_pCannonBarrel);
ResetCollisionGroupIndex(m_pWheel1);
ResetCollisionGroupIndex(m_pWheel2);
```

Lastly, we set m_bCannonExploded to TRUE to indicate that the cannon has exploded, and we're ready to go.

```
  m_bCannonExploded = TRUE;
} //Explode
```

Now we get to write code to fire the cannon. We'll use the timer to slow down the maximum rate of fire.[8] We'll use a `static` local integer variable[9] `nLastFireTime` to remember the last time that the cannon fired.

```
BOOL CCannon::Fire(){
  static int nLastFireTime=0;
```

The cannon can't fire if it has exploded, and it can't fire until a quarter of a second has passed since the last time it fired. Otherwise, it's going to fire, so its temperature will increase by an arbitrary 50°.

```
if(!m_bCannonExploded &&
g_cTimer.elapsed(nLastFireTime, 250)){
  m_fCannonTemp += 50.0f;
```

We need a shape, a fixture definition, and a body definition for the new cannonball. Since the cannonball sprite in `ball.png` is 32 × 32 pixels, the ball's radius is 16 units in Render World, and therefore, `RW2PW(16)` units in Physics World. I've chosen reasonable values for the cannonball's density and coefficient of restitution. Naturally, the cannonball needs to be a dynamic body.

```
    b2CircleShape ballshape;
    ballshape.m_radius = RW2PW(16);

    b2FixtureDef ballfd;
    ballfd.shape = &ballshape;
    ballfd.density = 0.5f;
    ballfd.restitution = 0.3f;

    b2BodyDef bd;
    bd.type = b2_dynamicBody;
```

The initial placement of the cannonball needs some linear algebra.[10] Clearly, it depends on both the position and the orientation of the cannon barrel. The more the barrel is pointed up, the higher the cannonball's initial position will be, as you can see in Figure 7.18. Let's put the initial position of

·······················

[8]Not only can the player emulate a machine-gun style cannon by holding down the space bar so that it autorepeats, in extreme cases he or she might be tempted to change their computer's autorepeat timing to get a faster rate of fire—serious geek stuff.
[9]I could have made it a `CCannon` private member variable, but this makes it clear that it is to be used by this function only.
[10]If you are still rusty about linear algebra, consult [Dunn and Parberry 11].

Figure 7.18 • The initial position of the cannonball depends on both the cannon barrel position and orientation.

$$64 + 5 + 16 = 85$$

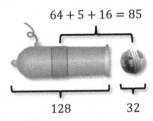

128   32

Figure 7.19 • The initial position of the cannonball should be 85 pixels from the center of the cannon barrel.

the cannonball 5 pixels beyond the muzzle in Render World. The cannon barrel image is 128×128 pixels, and the ball is 32×32 pixels, making the total distance $64 + 5 + 16 = 85$ pixels from the center of the barrel to the center of the ball, as shown in Figure 7.19.

The initial distance from barrel to ball in Physics World is RW2PW(85). b2Vec2(RW2PW(85),0) is a horizontal vector of that length. The barrel's orientation is m_pCannonBarrel->GetAngle(), as we saw above when discussing CCannon's BarrelUp function. A transformation for a rotation by that amount is b2Rot(m_pCannonBarrel->GetAngle()) (b2Rot has a constructor that takes an angle parameter, as you may[11] recall from Table 6.8). Applying that rotation transformation to b2Vec2(RW2PW(85),0) gives us a vector displacement from the center of the barrel to the center of the ball. This is done with b2Mul, as follows:

```
b2Mul(b2Rot(m_pCannonBarrel->GetAngle()), b2Vec2(RW2PW(85),0)).
```

The center of the barrel is at m_pCannonBarrel->GetPosition(). Therefore, we compute the initial position of the ball v and use it to set the ball's initial position in bd, as follows.

```
b2Vec2 v =
    m_pCannonBarrel ->GetPosition () +
```

....

[11]But probably won't.

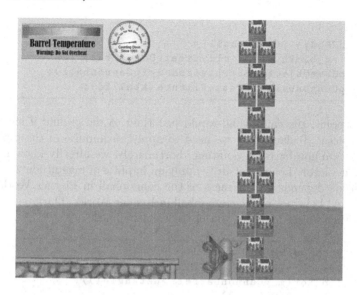

Figure 7.20 • Firing the cannon in this position should lead to an explosion.

```
    b2Mul(
      b2Rot(m_pCannonBarrel->GetAngle()),
      b2Vec2(RW2PW(85),0)
    );

bd.position.Set(v.x, v.y);
```

If the cannon's mouth is pointing towards the ground, then the cannon explodes. This can happen if the player drives the cannon off the edge of the platform as shown in Figure 7.20. The easiest way to detect this is to check whether the cannonball's y-coordinate v.y is less than zero since we create the cannonball object a little beyond the mouth of the cannon.

```
if(v.y < 0.0f)
    Explode();
```

Otherwise, the barrel is free and clear, so we can go ahead and fire. At last! We start by creating the cannonball in Object World and in Physics World, telling the Object World object about the Physics World one.

```
  else{
    CGameObject* pGameObject =
      g_cObjectWorld.create(BALL_OBJECT);
```

```
b2Body* pCannonball =
  g_b2dPhysicsWorld.CreateBody(&bd);
pGameObject->SetPhysicsBody(pCannonball);
pCannonball->CreateFixture(&ballfd);
```

At this point, the cannonball would just thud to the ground if left to its
own devices. To launch it, we need to apply an impulse in the direction
that the cannon barrel is pointing. Fortunately, we already know how to
find that vector. Let's arbitrarily apply an impulse of magnitude 200. The
magnitude depends on the mass of the cannonball in Physics World and
the desired behavior of the cannonball in Render World. Thirty seconds of
playtesting will at least get you in the right ballpark.

```
StopMoving();
b2Vec2 vImpulse = b2Mul(
  b2Rot(m_pCannonBarrel->GetAngle()),
  b2Vec2(200, 0));
```

It would be cool to apply a recoil impulse to the cannon barrel in the other
direction so that the cannon is rocked on its springs and pushed backwards.
We use the CCannon member function Impulse to apply the right impulses.
Let's make the recoil impulse have half the magnitude of the launch impulse
in the other direction by multiplying the b2Vec2 vImpulse vector by the
scalar −0.5f using the b2Vec2 overloaded multiplication operator to make
it look clean. After applying the pair of impulses, we increment the counter
m_nCannonBallsFired and return TRUE to indicate that we succeeded.

```
Impulse(pCannonball, vImpulse);
Impulse(m_pCannonBarrel, -0.5f * vImpulse);

m_nCannonBallsFired++;
return TRUE;
} //else
```

If we failed for any reason, we return FALSE instead.

```
  } //if
  return FALSE;
} //Fire
```

CCannon has a BallsFired function that returns the number of balls
that have been fired. We're going to use this later for the "You've won"

message displayed on the screen. It's just a simple reader function for the private member variable m_nCannonBallsFired.

```
int CCannon::BallsFired(){
 return m_nCannonBallsFired;
} //BallsFired
```

Function CoolDown reduces the cannon's temperature by a small amount. We're going to call this regularly to emulate the gradual cooling of a hot object. If the barrel is hotter than it has ever been before, then we change the maximum registered temperature to the current one. Then we linearly reduce the cannon's temperature by an arbitrary factor[12] of 64.0f. Finally, if the cannon is too hot (and it hasn't exploded already), then make it explode.

```
void CCannon::CoolDown(){
 if(m_fCannonTemp > m_fCannonMaxTemp)
   m_fCannonMaxTemp = m_fCannonTemp;

 if(m_fCannonTemp > 0)
   m_fCannonTemp -= m_fCannonTemp/64.0f;

 if(m_fCannonTemp >= CANNONEXPLODETEMP &&
 !m_bCannonExploded)
   Explode();
} //CoolDown
```

IsDead is another reader function, this time for the private member variable m_bCannonExploded.

```
BOOL CCannon::IsDead(){
 return m_bCannonExploded;
} //IsDead
```

Reset puts the cannon back to the initial conditions at the start of a level. This is used in the CCannon constructor and in the code to restart a level.

....

[12]Dividing the temperature by a constant emulates the linear cool-down of hot objects in the Real World, in which temperature loss is proportional to temperature difference, meaning that the hotter an object is, the faster it cools down. I'm not sure this is worth the trouble. It's a playability issue that can probably be resolved through playtesting.

```
void CCannon::Reset(){
  m_fCannonTemp = m_fCannonMaxTemp = 0.0f;
  m_nCannonBallsFired = 0;
  m_bCannonExploded = FALSE;
} //Reset
```

7.5   The Frame Loop and the Keyboard Handler

MyGame.cpp has a function RenderFrame to render a frame of animation. It starts by asking Render World to start the rendering pipeline. If that fails, it bails. Otherwise, it asks Render World to draw the background. Then it asks Object World to draw the game objects. Object World will ask Render World to draw them based on the position information that it gets from Physics World. Finally, Render World is given the opportunity to write a winning or losing message to the screen. It is told about the game state, the number of shots fired, and the elapsed time, the former so that it can make a decision about whether to write or not, and the latter two values so it can write them to the screen for boasting purposes. RenderFrame ends by asking the Render World to shut down the graphics pipeline in preparation for the next animation frame.

```
void RenderFrame(){
  if(g_cRenderWorld.BeginScene()){
    g_cRenderWorld.DrawBackground();
    g_cObjectWorld.draw();
    g_cRenderWorld.DrawWinLoseMessage(
      g_cObjectWorld.m_cCannon.BallsFired(),
      g_nGameState,
      g_cTimer.GetLevelElapsedTime()/1000);
    g_cRenderWorld.EndScene();
  } //if
} //RenderFrame
```

ProcessFrame begins with some start-of-frame housekeeping. The timer and the Sound Manager are notified that the frame is starting, the former so that it returns the same time measurement over the course of the entire frame, and the latter so that there are no double plays.

```
void ProcessFrame(){
  g_cTimer.beginframe();
  g_pSoundManager->beginframe();
```

Object World is then asked to move the game objects (which task it will, of course, subcontract out to Physics World), to make the appropriate sounds, and to cool the cannon down a little. Then the largest per-frame task begins, a call to function RenderFrame to draw a frame of animation.

```
g_cObjectWorld.move();
g_cObjectWorld.MakeSound();
g_cObjectWorld.m_cCannon.CoolDown();

RenderFrame();
```

Next, some stuff that is only done during PLAYING_GAMESTATE, managing the clock, and checking whether the player has won or lost. We start with the clock. We grab the elapsed time in seconds into a local variable t and compare it to a static local variable lasttick which, as you should know already, persists from frame to frame. If they are different, we play a "tick" sound and set lasttick to t to delay the next "tick" for another second.

```
if(g_nGameState == PLAYING_GAMESTATE){
  int t = g_cTimer.GetLevelElapsedTime()/1000;
  static int lasttick=0;

  if(lasttick != t){
    g_pSoundManager->play(TICK_SOUND);
    lasttick = t;
  } // if
```

While we're still in the PLAYING_GAMESTATE if statement, we should check for game over. The player has lost if either the cannon has exploded or time has run out. If so, change g_nGameState to LOST_GAMESTATE, play a disapproving sound, and stop the clock.

```
  if(g_cObjectWorld.m_cCannon.IsDead() ||
  t >= g_nMaxPlayingTime){
    g_nGameState = LOST_GAMESTATE;
    g_pSoundManager->play(LOSE_SOUND);
    g_cTimer.StopLevelTimer();
  } //if lost
```

Otherwise, ask the Object World whether the player has won. We'll define winning to be knocking all of the books into the bottom quarter of the screen. The Object World's PlayerHasWon function takes a single parameter, let's call it f, and returns TRUE if the y-coordinates of all of the books

are less than 1/f of the screen height. I've made it a parameter because it's
an obvious thing to use later to increase the difficulty level.[13] If so, change
g_nGameState to WON_GAMESTATE, play an approving sound, and stop the
clock. That ends function ProcessFrame.

```
    else
      if(g_cObjectWorld.PlayerHasWon(4.0f)){
        g_nGameState = WON_GAMESTATE;
        g_pSoundManager->play(WIN_SOUND);
        g_cTimer.StopLevelTimer();
      } //else if won
  } //if playing
} //ProcessFrame
```

Finally, the keyboard handler lets the player interact with the cannon,
which, you will recall, is represented by a CCannon class public member variable m_cCannon inside the Object World. We arbitrarily pick an angle of
0.01f radians as the amount that the cannon barrel rotates in response to
the appropriate key click and 2.0f the speed that the cannon moves. These
values are named CANNONBARREL_DELTA_ANGLE and CANNONMOVE_DELTA, respectively. While we're at it, we grab a pointer to the CCannon from Object
World and store it in a local pointer variable cannon. This is not so much
for efficiency, since any decent optimizing compiler should be able to do
the same thing at compile time, but it certainly increases the readability
of the source code.

```
BOOL KeyboardHandler(WPARAM k){
  const float CANNONBARREL_DELTA_ANGLE = 0.01f;
  const float CANNONMOVE_DELTA = 2.0f;
  CCannon* cannon = &(g_cObjectWorld.m_cCannon);
```

VK_ESCAPE has to work in any game state so that the player can quit the
game at any time.

```
  if(k ==   VK_ESCAPE)return TRUE;
```

Then, there's a switch statement for keystrokes during PLAYING_GAMESTATE.
Each keystroke gets tied to the corresponding CCannon member function.

```
  if(g_nGameState == PLAYING_GAMESTATE)
    switch(k){
```
....

[13]When I get around to it.

```
case VK_UP:
  cannon->BarrelUp(CANNONBARREL_DELTA_ANGLE);
  break;

case VK_DOWN:
 cannon->BarrelUp(-CANNONBARREL_DELTA_ANGLE);
  break;

case VK_LEFT:
  cannon->StartMovingLeft(CANNONMOVE_DELTA);
  break;

case VK_RIGHT:
  cannon->StartMovingLeft(-CANNONMOVE_DELTA);
  break;
```

If the cannon fires successfully, then the Sound Manager plays the appropriate sound.

```
case VK_SPACE:
  if(cannon->Fire())
    g_pSoundManager->play(CANNONFIRE_SOUND);
  break;
} //switch
```

Now, we'll look at the keystrokes that only work when you're not playing. The only one is the key to restart the game. That's the last thing to be done in KeyboardHandler.

```
else
  if(k == VK_RETURN)
    BeginGame();

return FALSE;
} //KeyboardHandler
```

• 7.6 Son et Lumière

Son et Lumière is French for a "sound and light show," a traditional form of outdoor entertainment that uses, as one might guess, sound and light. That's all we have left to do in this code example: sounds and light. Sounds involve knowing when objects hit each other, and light involves knowing where to draw them. Both of these involve interacting with Physics World. We'll start with sound. The Object Manager's MakeSound asks each object in the Object List to make its own sounds.

```
void CObjectManager::MakeSound(){
  for(int i=0; i<m_nSize; i++)
    if(m_pObjectList[i])
      m_pObjectList[i]->MakeSound();
} //MakeSound
```

For this game, those will be the sounds of collisions. A quick and dirty way to figure out when a collision happens is to check each object's change in velocity from the previous animation frame. We can logically assume that if the change in velocity is large enough in magnitude, then a collision must have happened. (There is a more efficient way of doing this using a Box2D *contact listener*, but we'll postpone that to Section 8.2.)

After a quick safety check of the m_pBody body pointer, we use the Box2D body's GetLinearVelocityFromWorldPoint to put the object's velocity vector in the Physics World's frame of reference into a local variable vNewV. I forgot to mention that we need to add a new private member variable m_b2vOldV to hold the old velocity vector. The velocity change vector vDelta is the difference between the new and old velocities. We then check that its change in speed, the length vDelta, is large enough to warrant making a noise about it. Notice that we compute length-squared using the LengthSquared function instead of Length to save the unnecessary square root calculation, taking care to square the right-hand side of the comparison that it's used in (which was kluged anyway).

```
void CGameObject::MakeSound(){
  if(!m_pBody)return;

  b2Vec2 vNewV = m_pBody->
    GetLinearVelocityFromWorldPoint(b2Vec2(0, 0));
  b2Vec2 vDelta = m_b2vOldV - vNewV;

  if(vDelta.LengthSquared() > 25000.0f)
```

Now we enter a switch statement to play the correct thump or clang sound based on object type.

```
    switch(m_nObjectType){
      case BALL_OBJECT:
      case WHEEL_OBJECT:
```

```
      g_pSoundManager ->play (THUMP_SOUND );
      break;

   case BOOK_OBJECT :
   case CANNONMOUNT_OBJECT :
      g_pSoundManager ->play (THUMP2_SOUND );
      break;

   case CANNONBARREL_OBJECT :
      g_pSoundManager ->play (CLANG_SOUND );
      break;
 } //switch
```

On the way out, we remember to update m_b2vOldV so it's ready for the next animation frame.

```
  m_b2vOldV = vNewV;
} //MakeSound
```

The Object Manager's draw function must query Physics World to get each object's position in Physics World units and angle in radians. It then asks Render World to draw the correct sprite in the correct screen position in Render World units. Throw in a bit of safety code to make sure that the body pointer is not NULL, and we're done:

```
void CObjectManager :: draw (){
  CGameObject * p;
  for(int i=0; i<m_nSize; i++){
    p = m_pObjectList [i];
    if (p){
      float a = p->m_pBody ->GetAngle ();
      b2Vec2 v = p->m_pBody ->GetPosition ();
      g_cRenderWorld .draw (p->m_nObjectType ,
        PW2RW(v.x), PW2RW(v.y), a);
    } //if
  } //for
} //draw
```

• 7.7 Exercises

1. The collision shape for the cannon barrel is currently a box, but the barrel is not really box-shaped. Change function CreateCannon Barrel in MyGame.cpp to replace the collision box with a polygon.

Figure 7.21 • The cannon gets crushed under books and cannonballs. Notice that it is hunkered down on its suspension like a lowrider.

2. Modify the code so that the cannonballs disappear after a lifetime of 15 s.
3. You may notice that as objects fall on it, the cannon can get pushed down on its suspension so that the mount meets the ground as shown in Figure 7.21. Write code to detect when this happens, and make the cannon explode.
4. *Rocket jumping* is the technique of using the recoil from a rocket launcher as a method of propulsion in first-person shooters.[14] Modify the Cannon Game so that the player can point the cannon at the ground and use the recoil from cannonfire to loft the cannon into the air as shown in Figure 7.22. You will need to make the following changes to `MyGame.cpp`.

    (a) Disable the limits on the revolute joint between the cannon barrel and the mount so that the cannon can point vertically downwards.
    (b) Disable the countdown timer so that you have time to experiment (optional).
    (c) Disable the cannon temperature change so that the barrel won't explode.
    (d) Disable the cannon explosion when the barrel is pointing at the ground.
    (e) Make the cannonball appear closer to the barrel.
    (f) Increase the amount of recoil. I recommend modifying the recoil to have double the magnitude of the impulse given to the cannonball.

....

[14]It first appeared in *Doom* in 1993. There was a place where you had (almost, it turns out) no option but to rocket jump. It was horizontal rocket jumping, but the principle is still the same.

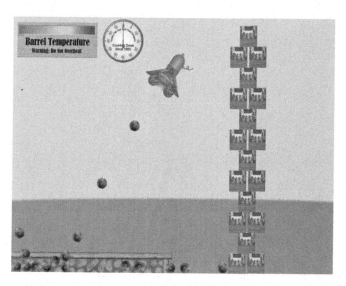

Figure 7.22 • Cannon jumping.

★ 5. Use the Cannon Game code to make a two-player cannon game in which a pair of cannons face each other behind a wall of blocks. The first player to hit their opponent's cannon ten times wins. Remap the keys so that Player 1 uses keys on the left-hand side of the keyboard and Player 2 uses keys on the right-hand side of the keyboard.

★ 6. Add code to the Cannon Game to give it multiple levels with varying amounts of difficulty. For example, you could start by limiting the number of shots allowed as well as the time. You should also consider putting extra objects into the game to make it harder and powerups to make it easier. The one who comes up with the best game idea wins.

8

The Collision Module

The aim of this chapter is to drill down into some of the Box2D Collision Module code that you probably don't need to mess with in the normal course of making a game with Box2D. It's here for the curious and for the advanced programmer who needs to get more features of more performance out of Box2D by messing with its internals.

● 8.1 Contacts and Manifolds

Section 6.3.1 gave us a quick peek into Box2D contact manifolds, which, you will recall, are a discrete approximation to a continuous region of contact. Now it's time to look into contacts and contact manifolds more carefully. Let's do this bottom-up, starting with the most basic structures in b2Collision.h and moving up to more complicated ones.

A *contact feature* is a very small structure that indicates which features, either vertices or edges, on the colliding bodies are actually doing the colliding. It begins with a local definition of a Type, which can be either a vertex e_vertex or an edge e_face. The structure consists of exactly four bytes, two for the indices of the contacting features in the edge or vertex array of the colliding fixtures, and two for the Types of those features. The naming convention used throughout this code is that the two colliding bodies are thought of as Body A and Body B and, for example, indexA and typeA belong to Body A.

```
struct b2ContactFeature{
  enum Type{
    e_vertex , e_face
  };
```

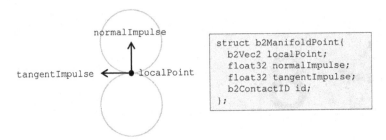

Figure 8.1 • A b2ManifoldPoint structure for two colliding circles.

```
    uint8 indexA;
    uint8 indexB;
    uint8 typeA;
    uint8 typeB;
};
```

The b2ContactFeature structure is kept to four bytes so that it can be unioned with a 32-bit integer in b2ContactID to allow fast comparison.

```
union b2ContactID{
    b2ContactFeature  cf;
    uint32 key;
};
```

A *manifold point* structure b2ManifoldPoint stores the information associated with a contact point inside a contact manifold. It has four fields (see Figure 8.1): localPoint holds the position of the point of contact in local space; normalImpulse holds the normal impulse, which prevents the bodies from interpenetrating; tangentImpulse holds the tangent impulse, which is used for friction; and id holds the contact id as described above.

```
struct b2ManifoldPoint{
    b2Vec2 localPoint;
    float32 normalImpulse;
    float32 tangentImpulse;
    b2ContactID id;
};
```

Now for the forbidden and mysterious[1] b2Manifold structure. It starts with a local definition of an enumerated type Type. More about that in

[1]If the words "hidden and mysterious" don't ring a bell, you should probably refresh yourself on the material in Section 6.3.1.

Type	Vector	Used For
e_circles	localPoint	local center of circleA
	localNormal	not used
e_faceA	localPoint	center of faceA
	localNormal	normal on polygonA
e_faceB	localPoint	center of faceB
	localNormal	normal on polygonB

Table 8.1 • What the vectors localPoint and localNormal are used for in a b2Manifold structure, depending on the type field.

a moment. The fields begin with an array points of b2ManifoldPoint, which, as you recall from above, store information about the contact points, including locations and impulse vectors. Before you get too excited, recall from Section 6.3.1 that b2_maxManifoldPoints is #defined to be 2. We can deduce from this that the last field pointCount, which counts the number of points in the manifold, can be either 1 or 2. Returning to the three fields that I skipped over, type is of type Type, which is an enumerated type[2] that consists of three values, e_circles, e_faceA, and e_faceB. Type e_circles is used when two circles collide; otherwise, one of e_faceA and e_faceB is used, depending on whether the contact manifold is for Body A or Body B.[3] The usage of the remaining two vectors localPoint and localNormal depends on the value of the type field, as shown in Table 8.1.

```
struct b2Manifold{
  enum Type{
    e_circles , e_faceA , e_faceB
  };

  b2ManifoldPoint points [b2_maxManifoldPoints ];
  b2Vec2 localNormal ;
  b2Vec2 localPoint ;
  Type type ;
  int32 pointCount ;
};
```

As noted in Section 6.3.1, the preferred way for a programmer to interact with a contact manifold is through the b2WorldManifold structure,

. . . .

[2]Yes, I really just did find a legitimate way to use the word "type" four times in a ten-word phrase. I'm rather proud of it, although any grammarian with any kind of sensibility at all will probably be on the floor writhing in pain.

[3]Look back at the intro to this section if you've forgotten what Body A and Body B mean.

Figure 8.2 • Collision points marked by stars.

which has a handy `Initialize` function that builds it from a `b2Manifold`.
Remember to keep the original `b2Manifold` around though, since it contains information not available through `b2WorldManifold`, such as the number of contact points.

The `Initialize` function will set `normal` to be the contact normal and the vector array `points` to be the contact points, all in world space coordinates (recall that they are in local space coordinates in `b2Manifold`). Function `Initialize` has five parameters, the first of which is a pointer to the `b2Manifold` structure for the contact, `manifold`. The second and fourth parameters `xfA` and `xfB` are the body-to-world space transforms for the two colliding bodies, Body A and Body B. The third and fifth parameters `radiusA` and `radiusB` are the radii of Body A and Body B, respectively. These should be computed from the shapes attached to them.

```
struct b2WorldManifold{
  void Initialize(const b2Manifold* manifold,
    const b2Transform& xfA, float32 radiusA,
    const b2Transform& xfB, float32 radiusB);

  b2Vec2 normal;
  b2Vec2 points[b2_maxManifoldPoints];
};
```

For example, if I wanted to do some sexy collision response such as using a particle engine to put a star at contact points like in Figure 8.2, I would write a function `MyStarMaker` as follows.

```
void MyStarMaker(const b2Manifold* m,
  const b2Transform& tA, const b2Shape& sA,
  const b2Transform& tB, const b2Shape& sB)
{
  b2WorldManifold w;
  w.Initialize(m, tA, sA.m_radius, tB, sB.m_radius);
  for(int32 i=0; i<m.pointCount; i++){
```

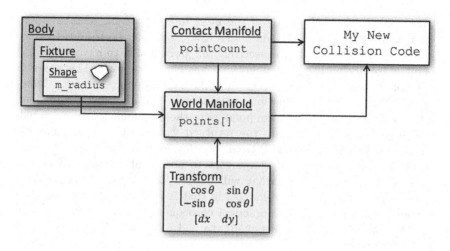

Figure 8.3 • How to use a contact manifold in your own collision-response code.

```
    b2Vec2 p = w.points[i];
    //Animate a star at point p in Physics World
    ...
  } //for
} //MyStarMaker
```

The flow of information between code and structures is summarized in Figure 8.3. Each of the bodies involved in the contact will have an attached shape, which will have a radius m_radius. We have a transform from each body's local space to its current position and orientation in world space and a contact manifold. These are used to construct a world manifold using the latter's Initialize function. The contact manifold and the world manifold are both needed in MyStarMarker.

There is a better way of doing this using a *contact listener*, which we will examine in the next section. It is useful to be able to test whether anything has changed in a contact manifold from the last time step to the current one, in particular, whether a contact point has been added or removed from the manifold. Box2D has a b2GetPointStates function that compares two manifolds and reports back on the *point state* of each of the manifold points using the following enumerated type.

```
enum b2PointState{
  b2_nullState, b2_addState,
  b2_persistState, b2_removeState
};
```

The point states likely to be of the most interest are `b2_addState` and `b2_removeState`, which indicate that the point has been added or removed from the manifold, respectively. `b2_persistState` means that the point is totally boring in that nothing has changed. `b2_nullState` is a kind of sentinel state indicating that the point does not exist. Function `b2GetPointStates` has four parameters. The last two parameters, `manifold1` and `manifold2`, are pointers to the manifolds to be compared. The first two parameters are the returned values, `state1` and `state2`. These are arrays of `b2PointState`, one for each of the (two) possible points in the manifold. It's important to note that `state1` is forward-looking in that it records what will happen to a point in `manifold1`, whereas `state2` is backward-looking in that it records what happened to a point in `manifold2`. The practical consequences of this are that only `state1` can have state `b2_removeState` and only `state2` can have state `b2_addState`.

8.2 Contact Listeners

We're wasting processor time by investigating every contact manifold for every body to see whether there are contact points that need stars on them because most of the time, most game objects probably won't be doing any colliding with anything. It would be better to look at only the nonempty contact manifolds, meaning the ones that actually have points in them. Box2D gives us a class called a *contact listener* that lets us select only the nonempty contact manifolds. All we have to do is write a function that Box2D is to call once for each nonempty contact manifold.

This is done by deriving a class from `b2ContactListener`, which has four member functions. `BeginContact` gets called from within a physics time step when a contact begins. `EndContact` gets called from within a physics time step when a contact ends and will also get called from outside a time step if a contacting body is destroyed. Both functions have a single parameter of type `b2Contact*` that the solver will use to give you a pointer to the contact structure. `PreSolve` gets called after collision detection but before collision resolution, and `PostSolve` gets called after collision resolution. These have two parameters, the same `b2Contact*` pointer, plus a `b2Manifold*` pointer that points to the old contact manifold as described at the end of Section 8.1.

```
class b2ContactListener {
  public:
    void BeginContact(b2Contact* contact);
    void EndContact(b2Contact* contact);
```

```
      void PreSolve(b2Contact* contact,
        const b2Manifold* oldManifold);
      void PostSolve(b2Contact* contact,
        const b2ContactImpulse* impulse);
};
```

We're going to derive a contact listener called `CMyContactListener` for the Cannon Game as follows:

```
class CMyContactListener: public b2ContactListener{
   public:
     void PreSolve(b2Contact* contact,
       const b2Manifold* oldManifold);
}; //CMyContactListener
```

We declare an instance of `CMyContactListener` as a global variable.

```
CMyContactListener g_cMyContactListener;
```

That just creates a contact listener but does not activate it. To activate it, we need to call the Physics World's `SetContactListener` function. Function `InitGame` in `MyGame.cpp` is a good place to do this. We can just add the following line of code to the end of that function.

```
g_b2dPhysicsWorld.SetContactListener(
   &g_cMyContactListener);
```

`g_cMyContactListener` has been declared and activated, but we have yet to implement function `PreSolve`. Algorithm 3 gives an overview of the major steps involved.

Algorithm 3 • `CMyContactListener::PreSolve`

Get the two bodies Body A and Body B that are contacting
if there is a new contact point **then**
    wp ← the contact point in Physics World Space
    speed ← the relative speed between Body A and Body B
    if speed is large enough **then**
        Play a "bonk" sound
        Create a star particle at point wp
    end if
end if

Our function PreSolve begins by getting the contact manifold into world space in a b2WorldManifold structure by calling the contact's GetWorld Manifold manifold as described at the end of Section 8.1.

```
void CMyContactListener :: PreSolve(
    b2Contact* contact ,
    const b2Manifold* oldManifold )
{
    b2WorldManifold worldManifold ;
    contact ->GetWorldManifold(& worldManifold );
```

We then declare two b2PointState arrays, state1 and state2. Recall that each of these has two b2PointStates for the (at most) two possible contact points. Calling b2GetPointStates tells us what has changed from the old contact manifold oldManifold that came in as a parameter to the new contact manifold, which we get by calling contact->GetManifold(). We're only really interested in state2, we can ignore the rest.

```
    b2PointState state1[2] , state2[2];
    b2GetPointStates(state1 , state2 ,
        oldManifold , contact ->GetManifold ());
```

If state2[i] is b2_addState, then it means that a new contact point has been created, in which case we want to play a "bonk" sound and display a star at the contact point. So, we get b2Body* pointers to the two bodies involved in the contact, bodyA and bodyB, by calling the contact's GetFixtureA and GetFixtureB functions to get the fixtures and then calling their GetBody functions.

```
    for(int i=0; i<2; i++)
     if(state2[i] == b2_addState ){
        const b2Body* bodyA =
            contact ->GetFixtureA ()->GetBody ();
        const b2Body* bodyB =
            contact ->GetFixtureB ()->GetBody ();
```

Next, we compute speed, the relative speed of Body A and Body B. We start by getting a point wp on the worldManifold to measure from, then calling each body's GetLinearVelocityFromWorldPoint function to get their relative velocities vA and vB measured from that point. The velocity of Body A relative to Body B deltavee is then the vector difference vA – vB. Finally, speed is the dot product of that vector with the worldManifold normal:

```
b2Vec2 wp = worldManifold.points[0];
b2Vec2 vA =
  bodyA->GetLinearVelocityFromWorldPoint(wp);
b2Vec2 vB =
  bodyB->GetLinearVelocityFromWorldPoint(wp);
b2Vec2 deltavee = vA - vB;
float32 speed =
  b2Dot(deltavee, worldManifold.normal);
```

Next, we need to find out what kinds of objects are colliding so we can play the appropriate sound. For example, anything hitting the cannon barrel should go "bong," not "thud." Remember that when we created each body, we used the handy userData in its b2BodyDef structure to hold a pointer to the object's CGameObject in Object World. We use the physics body's GetUserData function to retrieve that pointer now. Notice that since GetUserData returns the pointer as a void*, we must typecast it to CGameObject*.

```
CGameObject* objectA =
  (CGameObject*)bodyA->GetUserData();
CGameObject* objectB =
  (CGameObject*)bodyB->GetUserData();
```

Now that we have object pointers, we can use them to retrieve the sprite types in local variables typeA and typeB.

```
SpriteType typeA = UNKNOWN_SPRITE;
SpriteType typeB = UNKNOWN_SPRITE;
if(objectA) typeA = (SpriteType)objectA->m_nSprite;
if(objectB) typeB = (SpriteType)objectB->m_nSprite;
```

I'm going to use the number of balls, books, and barrels that are colliding in order to decide what kind of response to make.

```
int nBallCount=0, nBookCount=0;
if(typeA == BALL_SPRITE)nBallCount++;
if(typeB == BALL_SPRITE)nBallCount++;
if(typeA == BOOK_SPRITE)nBookCount++;
if(typeB == BOOK_SPRITE)nBookCount++;
BOOL bCannonBarrel =
  typeA == CANNONBARREL_SPRITE ||
  typeB == CANNONBARREL_SPRITE;
```

Based on those numbers, I set `starSprite` to indicate the color of the star I'd like to draw. Book-to-ball contacts have a white star, book-to-book a yellow star, ball-to-ball a magenta star, and everything else a red star.

```
SpriteType starSprite = REDSTAR_SPRITE;
if(nBookCount>0 && nBallCount>0)
  starSprite = WHITESTAR_SPRITE;
else if(nBookCount == 2)
  starSprite = YELLOWSTAR_SPRITE;
else if(nBallCount == 2)
  starSprite = MAGENTASTAR_SPRITE;
```

Now I'm ready to code the contact response. If `speed` is large enough, I want to play the appropriate collision sounds and create a star particle at the collision point `wp`. First the sounds:

```
if(speed > 0.5f){
  if(nBallCount>0)
    g_pSoundManager->play(THUMP_SOUND);
  if(nBookCount>0)
    g_pSoundManager->play(THUMP2_SOUND);
  if(bCannonBarrel)
    g_pSoundManager->play(CLANG_SOUND);
```

Finally, I create the star that I decided on in `starSprite`.

```
    CParticle* pParticle = (CParticle*)
      g_cParticleManager.create(starSprite);
    if(pParticle)pParticle->Set(
      D3DXVECTOR2(PW2RW(wp.x), PW2RW(wp.y)),
      500, 1.0f);
  } //if
  } //if
} //PreSolve
```

Let's run an experiment to see when the Contact Listener's `PreSolve` actually gets called. Suppose we drop a single book onto one corner, from which position it thunks down onto one side, rocks to the right, then the left, then comes to rest. To be precise,

1. I drop a book tilted slightly counterclockwise so that it will hit the ground on its bottom left corner (facing the book).
2. The left corner of the book makes contact with the ground. It begins to pivot clockwise on that corner.

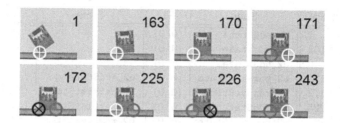

Figure 8.4 • What the dropped book looks like in Render World when the Contact Listener's PreSolve function is called.

3. The right corner of the book makes contact. Both corners are down, but the book still has some clockwise angular momentum.

4. The left corner lifts and the book begins to pivot clockwise on its right corner.

5. The book pivots clockwise until it accedes to the pull of gravity, at which point it begins to pivot back counterclockwise.

6. The left corner of the book makes contact. Both corners are down, but the book still has some counterclockwise angular momentum.

7. The right corner lifts and the book begins to pivot counterclockwise on its left corner.

8. The book pivots counterclockwise until it accedes to the pull of gravity, at which point it begins to pivot clockwise.

9. The right corner of the book makes contact. Both corners are down and the book has exhausted its angular momentum with all this thunking around, so it stays that way.

The events that get recorded by PreSolve are listed in Table 8.2. The first column of that table lists the frame number in which PreSolve gets called in Physics World. Figure 8.4 shows what the book looks like in Render World in those animation frames. The white circle with the plus sign indicates a point that has been added to the contact manifold, the grey circle indicates a point that has persisted, and the black circle with the cross indicates a point that has been removed. The numbers are frame counts that correspond with the frame counts in Table 8.2. The following is an analysis of the calls to the Contact Listener's PreSolve function during the experiment. Coordinates are given in Render World units (pixels), and they are normalized so that the corner of the book hits at $(0,0)$. The book is, you will undoubtedly recall, 54 pixels wide.

Frame 1: b2_addState for point 0 at $(0,0)$. The corner of the book has made first contact with the platform. (Table 8.2, line 1 and Figure 8.4, top row).

S	FN	State	Pt	State	Pt
N	1	b2_addState	(0, 0)	–	–
N	163	b2_addState	(0, 0)	–	–
N	170	b2_addState	(0, 0)	–	–
N	171	b2_persistState	(0, 0)	b2_addState	(53, 0)
O	172	b2_removeState	(0, 0)	b2_persistState	(53, 0)
N	225	b2_addState	(0, 0)	b2_persistState	(53, 0)
O	226	b2_persistState	(0, 0)	b2_removeState	(53, 0)
N	243	b2_persistState	(0, 0)	b2_addState	(53, 0)

Table 8.2 • The Contact Listener's PreSolve function gets called with this information. Column 1 shows whether information came from the old or the new manifold. Column 2 shows the frame number. Columns 3 and 4 show the state and the location in Render World of contact point 0. Columns 5 and 6 show the state and the location in Render World of contact point 1.

Frame 163: b2_addState for point 0 at (0,0) The contact has probably shifted enough in Physics World to trigger the Contact Listener but not enough to actually see in Render World. (Table 8.2, line 2 and Figure 8.4, top row).

Frame 170: b2_addState for point 0 at (0,0). Again, the contact has probably shifted enough in Physics World to trigger the Contact Listener but not enough to actually see in Render World. (Table 8.2, line 3 and Figure 8.4, top row).

Frame 171: b2_persistState for point 0 at (0,0) and b2_addState for point 1 at (53,0). For the third time, the contact has probably shifted enough in Physics World to trigger the Contact Listener but not enough to actually see in Render World. This tells me that I'd better allow for consecutive adds in my code. (Table 8.2, line 4 and Figure 8.4, top row).

Frame 172: b2_removeState for point 0 at (0,0) and b2_persistState for point 1 at (53,0). The book is rocking on its right corner. (Table 8.2, line 5 and Figure 8.4, bottom row).

Frame 225: b2_addState for point 0 at (0,0) and b2_persistState for point 1 at (53,0). The book has both corners on the ground. (Table 8.2, line 6 and Figure 8.4, bottom row).

Frame 226: b2_persistState for point 0 at (0,0) and b2_deleteState for point 1 at (53,0). The book is rocking on its left corner this time. (Table 8.2, line 7 and Figure 8.4, bottom row).

Frame 243: `b2_persistState` for point 0 at $(0,0)$ and `b2_addState` for point 1 at $(53,0)$. The book has both corners on the ground, finally. (Table 8.2, line 8 and Figure 8.4, bottom row).

I've simplified things by not giving you the `PreSolve` calls that are (`b2_persistState`, `b2_persistState`) or (`b2_persistState`, `b2_null State`). Not only are these less interesting, but there are hundreds of them. In fact, after the book comes to rest in Frame 243, `PreSolve` gets a (`b2_persistState`, `b2_persistState`) call once per frame, indicating that the book is (still) still. What can we learn from this analysis? One is that we should ignore all calls except the ones with a `b2_addState` (and possibly a `b2_removeState`). That given, our code should assume that it will probably get consecutive `b2_addState` calls for the same point in Render World coordinates without a `b2_removeState` in between.

● 8.3 AABBs

The aim of broad-phase collision detection is to construct a list of object pairs that may collide with a small number of false positives and no false negatives. That is, all colliding pairs are in the list, but not much else is. Naturally, we would like to be able to do it blindingly fast.

In order to achieve these goals, broad-phase collision detection works with bounding boxes instead of the original object. Each bounding box is larger than the actual object,[4] so it gives false positives, but it has fewer edges to test on so it is faster. Even better, we can make the collision tests blindingly fast by aligning the edges of the bounding box with the world-space axes. This kind of bounding box is called an *axially aligned bounding box*, or AABB for short. Figure 8.5 shows two polygonal objects

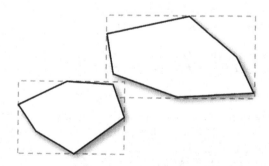

Figure 8.5 • Two polygon shapes and their AABBs.

....
[4]Obvious exception excepted.

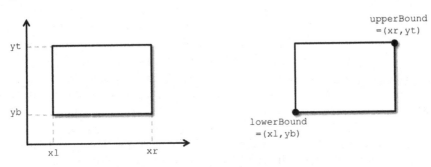

Figure 8.6 • Specifying an AABB using two points.

and their AABBs. Notice that these objects would give a false positive in broad-phase collision detection since their AABBs collide but the objects themselves do not.

An AABB can be specified by listing its left and right x-coordinates xl and rl and its top and bottom y-coordinates yt and yb. Box2D stores these as two points, the top-right point upperBound and the bottom-right point lowerBound, as shown in Figure 8.6. We will call these the *upper* and *lower* vertices, respectively. b2AABB is defined in b2Collision.h:

```
struct b2AABB{
  bool IsValid() const; //verify bounds are sorted
  b2Vec2 GetCenter() const;
  b2Vec2 GetExtents() const; //extents are half-widths
  float32 GetPerimeter() const;
  void Combine(const b2AABB&); //combine with AABB
  void Combine(const b2AABB&,
    const b2AABB&); //combine with two AABBs
  bool Contains(const b2AABB&) const;
  bool RayCast(b2RayCastOutput*,
    const b2RayCastInput&) const;

  b2Vec2 lowerBound; //lower vertex
  b2Vec2 upperBound; //upper vertex
};
```

The first Combine function works in the obvious way. The new left bound, for example, is the smaller of the left bounds of the two AABBs.

```
void Combine(const b2AABB& aabb){
  lowerBound = b2Min(lowerBound, aabb.lowerBound);
  upperBound = b2Max(upperBound, aabb.upperBound);
}
```

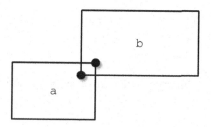

Figure 8.7 • Testing for AABB collision.

The functions b2Min and b2Max used in the above function are defined in b2Math.h as component-wise min and max as follows:

```
template <typename T> inline T b2Min(T a, T b){
  return a<b? a: b;
}

inline b2Vec2 b2Min(
 const b2Vec2& a, const b2Vec2& b)
{
  return b2Vec2(b2Min(a.x, b.x), b2Min(a.y, b.y));
}

template <typename T> inline T b2Max(T a, T b){
  return a>b? a: b;
}

inline b2Vec2 b2Max(
 const b2Vec2& a, const b2Vec2& b)
{
  return b2Vec2(b2Max(a.x, b.x), b2Max(a.y, b.y));
}
```

Two AABBs collide if both coordinates of the upper vertex of one of them are greater than the corresponding coordinates of the lower vertex of the other and vice versa (see Figure 8.7). Box2D uses the function b2TestOverlap in b2Collision.h:

```
inline bool b2TestOverlap(const b2AABB& a,
                          const b2AABB& b){
  b2Vec2 d1 = b.lowerBound - a.upperBound;
  b2Vec2 d2 = a.lowerBound - b.upperBound;

  if(d1.x>0.0f || d1.y>0.0f)return false;
```

```
    if(d2.x>0.0f || d2.y>0.0f)return false;
    return true;
}
```

We will make use of functions `b2AABB::Combine` and `b2TestOverlap` in the next section on dynamic trees.

8.4 Dynamic Trees

Box2D's broad-phase collision detection uses a 2D version of the dynamic bounding volume trees from Nathanael Presson's Bullet physics engine [Presson 12]. In the Box2D code, they are simply referred to as *dynamic trees*, so to avoid possible confusion when you read the code, I will do the same here.[5] A good place to start reading about them is [Ericson 05], but by far the best description is in the original paper [Goldsmith and Salmon 87].

Dynamic trees are full binary trees, that is, every nonleaf node has exactly two children. Each node of a dynamic tree contains an AABB. The AABBs in the leaves are the AABBs of the objects in your game. The AABB in each node is the smallest AABB that contains the AABBs of its leaves using function `b2AABB::Combine` from the previous subsection. Dynamic trees are intended to be used for fast broad-phase collision detection for AABBs and rays with the AABBs in your game. We will concentrate on AABB collision detection here. The ray-casting version is similar enough that you should be able to read it directly from the code after you've mastered this section.

Figure 8.8 shows a dynamic tree for the AABBs at top left of that diagram. To help you understand, I've redrawn it in Figure 8.9 with the AABBs of the objects in every node, but please remember that it is not stored that way. Since there are $n = 8$ AABBs, the dynamic tree has 8 leaves. I've made it a complete binary tree, but dynamic trees are not necessarily complete, even when n is a power of 2. They can be completely unbalanced to the point where they degenerate to a linked list.

8.4.1 Search

Suppose we are given an AABB B, and we want to find which of the AABBs in the game intersect with it. For example, Figure 8.10 shows B on the left and the desired result on the right, the three AABBs shown in white. Remember that we want to compute that result as fast as we can.

....

[5]Although I am tempted to call them DBV-trees for obvious reasons.

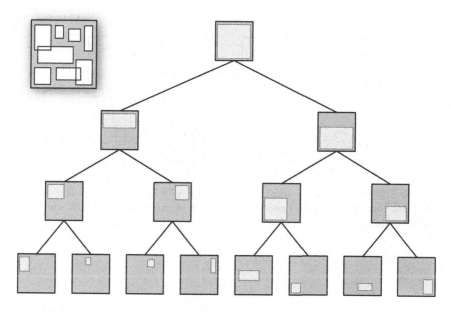

Figure 8.8 • A dynamic tree for the set of AABBs shown at top left.

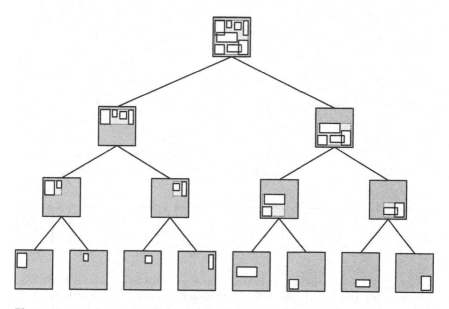

Figure 8.9 • The dynamic tree from Figure 8.8 drawn with the underlying AABBs filled in as an aid to comprehension only; they are not actually stored in the data structure.

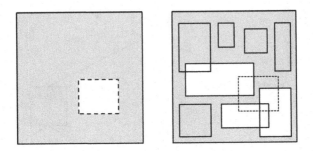

Figure 8.10 • Suppose we want to find which AABBs collide with the one on the left. The answer we're expecting is the set of three white AABBs shown in white at right.

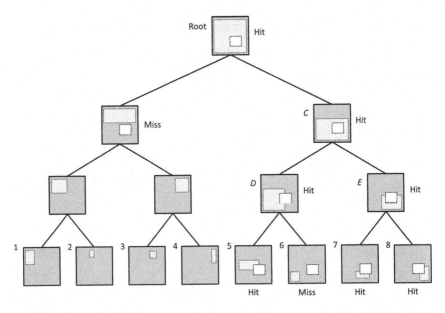

Figure 8.11 • Using the dynamic tree from Figure 8.9 to find the AABBs that intersect the AABB in Figure 8.8. The three leaves with hits (numbered 5, 7, and 8) correspond to the AABBs that are intersected in Figure 8.10 (right).

Figure 8.11 shows the process. We start in the root node. Since B overlaps the AABB in the root node, we look in both of its children. B does not overlap with its left child's AABB, so we go to the right child, C. Since B overlaps with C's AABB, we test both of its children D and E and find overlaps in both cases. The left child of D overlaps with B (leaf number 5), but its right child doesn't (leaf number 6). Both of the children of E (leaves number 7 and 8) overlap with B. The AABBs that overlap with B are therefore the ones in nodes 5, 7, and 8, which, as expected, are exactly the three white AABBs shown at right in Figure 8.10.

The best dynamic tree for our purpose is one in which the AABB sizes are small (which means that the AABBs of siblings should be close together), and the tree itself is very shallow, ideally as close to a complete binary tree as we can get. Unfortunately, this is very computationally intensive to achieve. Fortunately, we can fake it and still get good results.

8.4.2   Insertion and Deletion

The dynamic tree is called that because[6] it needs to be dynamic; that is, it needs to change when objects move. Box2D cheats by making the AABBs slightly larger than their enclosed objects. These are called *fat AABBs* in the code. Fat AABBs are larger than the objects they surround by a factor of `b2_fatAABBFactor`. Objects are allowed to wander within their fat AABBs without penalty. However, once an object moves outside its fat AABB, the leaf containing that object is deleted from the tree and then reinserted with its new fat AABB.

So how do we delete leaves from and insert leaves into a dynamic tree? Deleting one isn't too difficult. Suppose we want to delete a leaf node L with parent P and sibling S. We simply need to remove L, replace P with S (Figure 8.12), then follow a path from P to the root, recomputing the combined AABBs along the way. That isn't too time consuming provided the tree isn't too deep.

The mechanics of inserting a node B doesn't appear too difficult either. If you think about it, it's almost the reverse of the deletion algorithm above. Suppose we've found a potential sibling S for N hidden somewhere in the guts of the dynamic tree. Here's how we can insert N as the sibling of S, as shown in Figure 8.13.

1. Create a new parent node P.
2. Replace S in the tree with P.
3. Make S and N the children of P.
4. Follow a path from P to the root adjusting the AABBs.

....

[6]Surprise, surprise.

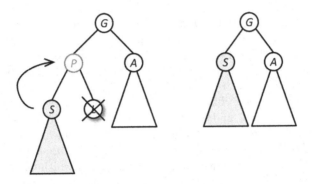

Figure 8.12 • Deleting a leaf node L from a dynamic tree, before deletion (left) and after deletion (right). Remove L, replace its parent P with L's sibling S.

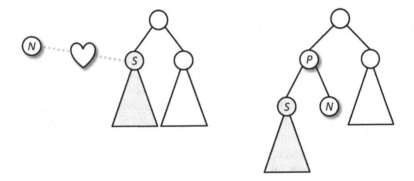

Figure 8.13 • Inserting a new node N into a dynamic tree so that it has sibling S, before insertion (left) and after insertion (right). Create a new node P, make it the parent of N and S, and put it in place of S.

The hard part is finding a good sibling S for the new node N (see Figure 8.14), where "good" means that we should try to keep the time required for AABB search as small as we can. In order to talk more succinctly about dynamic tree nodes and their AABBs, let's adopt the following conventions:

1. If N is a dynamic tree node, $\boxed{N}$ is its AABB.

2. If $\boxed{A}$ and $\boxed{B}$ are AABBs, then $\boxed{A} \cup \boxed{B}$ is the smallest AABB containing both $\boxed{A}$ and $\boxed{B}$.

As we noted at the end of Section 8.4.1, we can reduce search time by keeping AABB sizes small. We want to avoid a situation in which $\boxed{N}$ is very far from $\boxed{S}$ because then the smallest AABB that surrounds them both, $\boxed{P} = \boxed{A} \cup \boxed{B}$, will be very large.

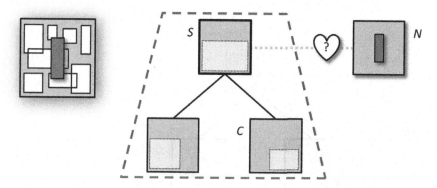

Figure 8.14 • Left: The AABBs in the dynamic tree in white, and the new AABB in dark gray. Right: Consider inserting N, the node containing the new AABB, as a sibling of S,

We do this using a *greedy algorithm*,[7] that is, an algorithm that makes the best local choices without bothering to compute whether these choices lead to a global optimum. We proceed from the root of the dynamic tree down to a leaf, making locally optimal choices at each nonleaf node as to whether we go left, right, or stay at the current node.

Define the *cost* of a node S, denoted $\Gamma(S)$, to be the sum over all of its children C of the probability of having to do an AABB intersection test between $\boxed{N}$ and $\boxed{C}$. We test both the children of S when the intersection test of $\boxed{N}$ with $\boxed{S}$ succeeds, which happens with probability $\text{Area}(\boxed{S})/W$, where W is the area of the game world. Therefore

$$\Gamma(S) = 2 \cdot \text{Area}(\boxed{S})/W.$$

(The factor of 2 is because we have to test both children.) The cost of the whole dynamic tree is defined to be the sum of the costs of its nodes. Note that the cost of a leaf is zero since it has no children.

Suppose we make a new parent node P for S and N, as shown in Figure 8.15, with AABB $\boxed{P} = \boxed{N} \cup \boxed{S}$. Since P is new, the extra cost added to the tree by making N the sibling of S is

$$\Gamma(P) = \Gamma(\boxed{P}) = 2 \cdot \Gamma(\boxed{N} \cup \boxed{S})/W.$$

However, it might be cheaper to push N down to one of S's children C. What would that cost?

If C is a leaf, we would replace it with a new node P and make C and N the children of P, as shown in Figure 8.16. That would increase the

....

[7]If you are unfamiliar with the concept of a greedy algorithm, consult any reputable algorithms textbook such as [Cormen et al. 01].

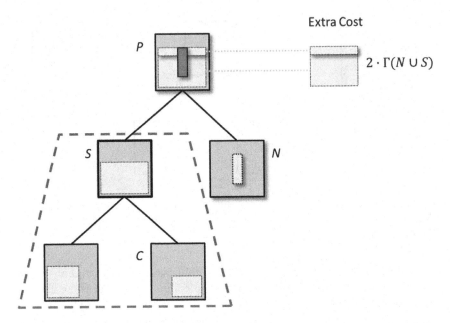

Figure 8.15 • Make a new parent node P for S and N with area equal to their combined areas.

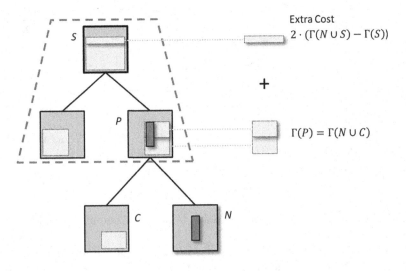

Figure 8.16 • If S's child C is a leaf, replace it with a new node P, and make C and N the children of P.

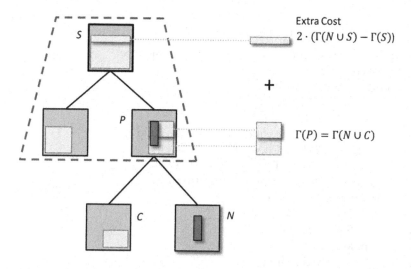

Figure 8.17 • If S's child C is not a leaf, estimate the cost of making N a descendant of C.

area of S from Area($\boxed{S}$) to Area($\boxed{N} \cup \boxed{S}$), increasing it by Area($\boxed{N} \cup \boxed{S}$) − Area($\boxed{S}$). This will increase the cost of S by an amount that we will call the *inheritance cost*:

$$\text{Cost}_I = 2 \cdot (\text{Area}(\boxed{N} \cup \boxed{S}) - \text{Area}(\boxed{S}))/W.$$

The cost of the new node P, which has children N and C, will be $\Gamma(\boxed{N} \cup \boxed{C})/W$. The total increase in cost is therefore

$$(\text{Cost}_I + \Gamma(\boxed{N} \cup \boxed{C}))/W.$$

If C is not a leaf, we have no way of determining the cost of pushing N down to the subtree rooted at C exactly, but it is at least

$$(\text{Cost}_I + \Gamma(\boxed{N} \cup \boxed{C}) - \Gamma(\boxed{C}))/W,$$

as shown in Figure 8.17. Finally, since all of the costs have a factor of W, the area of the game world, we can simply ignore it. The whole procedure is summarized in Algorithm 4.

Unfortunately, every time an AABB moves outside its fat AABB, it triggers a deletion followed by an insertion, which almost certainly will make the dynamic tree move out of balance. `b2DynamicTree` has a `Balance` function that rebalances the tree using a *tree rotation* operation borrowed from the classical red-black tree[8] data structure. If any left child C is 2 deeper

....

[8]Once again, if you are unfamiliar with this concept, consult any reputable algorithms textbook such as [Cormen et al. 01].

Algorithm 4 • Make S the best sibling of N

Require: S is the root of a nonempty dynamic tree
1: finished $\leftarrow$ "S is a leaf"
2: **while** not finished **do**
3:     $\text{Cost}_S \leftarrow 2 \cdot \Gamma(\boxed{N} \cup \boxed{S})$
4:     $\text{Cost}_I \leftarrow 2 \cdot (\Gamma(\boxed{N} \cup \boxed{S}) - \Gamma(\boxed{S}))$
5:     Suppose S has left child C_L and right child C_R
6:     $\text{Cost}_L \leftarrow \text{Cost}_I + \Gamma(\boxed{N} \cup \boxed{C_L}) - \Gamma(\boxed{C_L})$
7:     $\text{Cost}_R \leftarrow \text{Cost}_I + \Gamma(\boxed{N} \cup \boxed{C_R}) - \Gamma(\boxed{C_R})$
8:     finished $\leftarrow \text{Cost}_S < \min(\text{Cost}_L, \text{Cost}_R)$
9:     **if** not finished **then**
10:       **if** $\text{Cost}_L < \text{Cost}_R$ **then**
11:         $S \leftarrow$ Left child of S
12:       **else**
13:         $S \leftarrow$ Right child of S
14:       **end if**
15:       finished $\leftarrow$ "S is a leaf"
16:     **end if**
17: **end while**

---

than its sibling B, perform a *left rotation* as described in Figure 8.18 or Figure 8.19, depending on which of its children is the cause of the discrepancy. If any right child B is 2 deeper than its sibling C, perform a *right rotation* as described in Figure 8.20 or Figure 8.21, depending on which of its children is the cause of the discrepancy. Naturally, the combined AABBs will need to be recomputed on a path back to the root, which won't be too expensive provided the dynamic tree is rebalanced periodically.

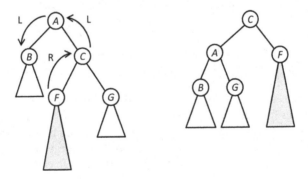

Figure 8.18 • If C is 2 deeper than B because of its left child F, perform an RLL rotation.

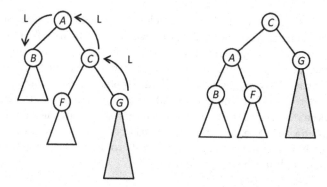

Figure 8.19 • If C is 2 deeper than B because of its right child G, perform an LLL rotation.

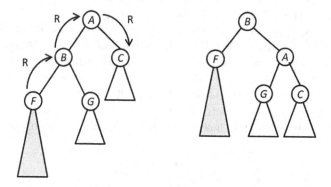

Figure 8.20 • If B is 2 deeper than C because of its left child F, perform an RRR rotation.

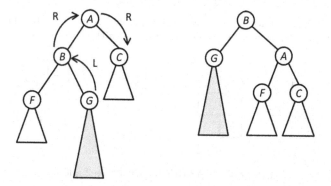

Figure 8.21 • If B is 2 deeper than C because of its right child G, perform an LRR rotation.

There is one more thing before we close this section on dynamic trees. While I've been talking about AABB *area* as a measure of the cost of a dynamic tree node, b2DynamicTree uses AABB *perimeter* instead, presumably because perimeter is cheaper to compute than area, the latter requiring a pesky floating-point multiplication. Unfortunately, the variable and function names are based on the concept of area, for example, b2DynamicTree has a GetAreaRatio function, and you will find local variables named area, combinedArea, oldArea, newArea, totalArea, and rootArea scattered throughout b2DynamicTree.cpp. This leads to a certain amount of cognitive dissonance, but what's in a name?[9]

● 8.5 Exercises

1. We saw in Section 8.2 that the Contact Listener is prone to detecting consecutive b2_addStates for the same point. If you look closely enough, you can detect evidence of this happening in the Cannon Game with stars. You'll see a curious and fleeting "star within a star" pattern as shown in Figure 8.22. Design a fast and effective method for preventing "star in star" from happening. Implement your algorithm in the Cannon Game with stars.

2. For each of the four sets of AABBs in Figure 8.23, starting with an empty dynamic tree, insert each of the AABBs in the order shown.

Figure 8.22 • Evidence of consecutive b2_addStates detected by the Contact Listener for the same point in the Cannon Game with stars. See Exercise 1.

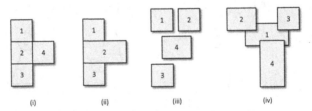

Figure 8.23 • AABBs for Exercises 2 and 3.

....

[9] "What's in a name? That which we call a rose by any other name would smell as sweet." William Shakespeare, *Romeo and Juliet* (II, ii, pp. 1–2).

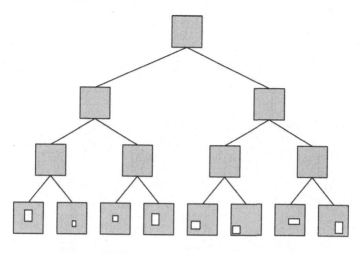

Figure 8.24 • Dynamic tree for Exercise 4.

3. For each of the four sets of AABBs in Figure 8.23, starting with an empty dynamic tree, insert each of the AABBs in the reverse of the order shown.

4. Fill in the AABBs in the nonleaf nodes of the dynamic tree shown in Figure 8.24.

5. Delete the node indicated with an "X" in the dynamic tree given in Figure 8.25.

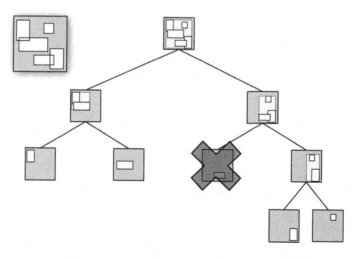

Figure 8.25 • Dynamic tree for Exercise 5.

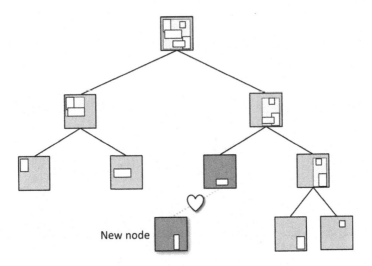

Figure 8.26 • Dynamic tree for Exercise 6.

6. Insert the node flagged "New node" into the dynamic tree in Figure 8.26 as a sibling of the indicated leaf node.

Part III

Appendices

 **A**

For Math Geeks Only

For the math geeks among you, let's try to prove the identities

$$\cos(\alpha + \beta) = \cos\alpha \cos\beta - \sin\alpha \sin\beta$$
$$\sin(\alpha + \beta) = \sin\alpha \cos\beta + \cos\alpha \sin\beta.$$

that we used in Section 2.1.4. Actually, I'm going to do the first one carefully and leave the second one for you, and I'm only going to do it in the first quadrant, that is, the case where $\alpha + \beta \leq 90°$. The following elegant geometric proof is from [Smiley 99].[1]

Step 1. (Figure A.1, top left.) Start by drawing a right triangle $\triangle ABC$ with $\angle ABC = 90°$, $\angle CAB = \beta$, and hypotenuse AC of length $\|AC\| = 1$. Then, $\|BC\| = \sin\beta$ and $\|AB\| = \cos\beta$.

Step 2. (Figure A.1, top right.) Assuming that $\beta \leq 90° - \alpha$, extend $\triangle ABC$ into a larger right triangle $\triangle ABD$ where $\angle ADB = \alpha$.

Step 3. (Figure A.1, middle left.) Extend a line from C perpendicular to AD. Let E be the point where this line intersects AD.

Step 4. (Figure A.1, middle right.) Since the internal angles of a triangle sum to 180°, $\angle BAD = 90° - \alpha$, which implies that $\angle CAD = \angle BAD - \beta =$

....

[1] These identities are one of those horrible things that are easy to prove when you have heavy machinery (in this case complex numbers will do), but annoyingly intricate otherwise. Smiley's proof is the simplest that I know of to date.

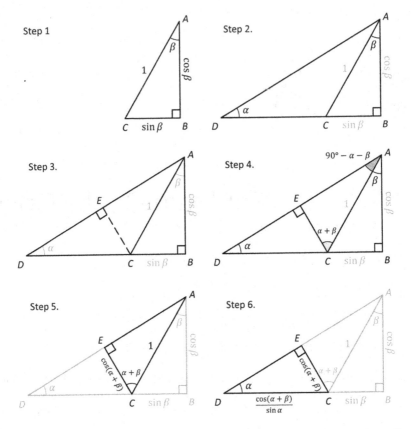

Figure A.1 • The first six steps of Smiley's geometric proof that $\cos(\alpha + \beta) = \cos\alpha\cos\beta - \sin\alpha\sin\beta$.

$90° - \alpha - \beta$. Therefore,

$$\begin{aligned} \angle ACE &= 90° - \angle CAD \\ &= 90° - (90° - \alpha - \beta) \\ &= \alpha + \beta. \end{aligned}$$

Step 5. (Figure A.1, bottom left.) Therefore, since $\|AC\| = 1$, $\|CE\| = \cos(\alpha + \beta)$.

Step 6. (Figure A.1, bottom right.) Since $\sin\alpha = \|CE\|/\|CD\|$ and $\|CE\| = \cos(\alpha + \beta)$,

$$\|CD\| = \frac{\cos(\alpha + \beta)}{\sin\alpha}.$$

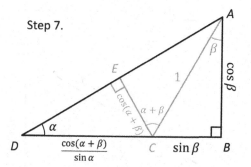

Figure A.2 • The seventh and last step of Smiley's geometric proof that $\cos(\alpha + \beta) = \cos\alpha\cos\beta - \sin\alpha\sin\beta$.

Step 7. Here's where we put it all together. Since $\|AB\| = \cos\beta$ and

$$\|BD\| = \|BC\| + \|CD\| = \sin\beta + \frac{\cos(\alpha + \beta)}{\sin\alpha},$$

we can conclude from Figure A.2 that

$$\tan\alpha = \frac{\|AB\|}{\|BD\|} = \frac{\cos\beta}{\sin\beta + \frac{\cos(\alpha+\beta)}{\sin\alpha}}.$$

Now we're making progress. This means that

$$\frac{\sin\alpha}{\cos\alpha} = \frac{\cos\beta}{\sin\beta + \frac{\cos(\alpha+\beta)}{\sin\alpha}}.$$

It's getting a little hairy on the right-hand side of the equation, but hang in there for a moment. Solving for $\cos(\alpha + \beta)$, we see that

$$\frac{\sin\beta + \frac{\cos(\alpha+\beta)}{\sin\alpha}}{\cos\beta} = \frac{\cos\alpha}{\sin\alpha}$$

$$\sin\beta + \frac{\cos(\alpha + \beta)}{\sin\alpha} = \frac{\cos\alpha\cos\beta}{\sin\alpha}$$

$$\frac{\cos(\alpha + \beta)}{\sin\alpha} = \frac{\cos\alpha\cos\beta}{\sin\alpha} - \sin\beta$$

$$\cos(\alpha + \beta) = \cos\alpha\cos\beta - \sin\alpha\sin\beta,$$

which is the first identity we were looking for.

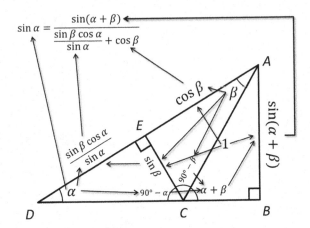

Figure A.3 • Smiley's proof that $\sin(\alpha + \beta) = \sin \alpha \cos \beta + \cos \alpha \sin \beta$ in one diagram.

I'm going to leave it at that by saying that similarly, we can show from Figure A.3 that $\sin(\alpha + \beta) = \sin \alpha \cos \beta + \cos \alpha \sin \beta$. I'm sure you don't want to read the details of that one. Work it out with a pencil if you do.

 **B**

The Blacke Arte of
Program Debugging

The use of the term "bug" to describe a problem with a computer is usually attributed to the computing pioneer Admiral Grace Murray Hopper in 1947. When colleagues traced a fault in Harvard University's Mark II Computer to a moth stuck in Relay 70 of Panel F, she remarked that they were "debugging" the system. The remains of the moth can still be seen in the log book entry for that day.

Theodore Rubin once said, "The problem is not that there are problems. The problem is expecting otherwise and thinking that having problems is a problem." That's true of bugs too. The problem is not that there are bugs. The problem is expecting otherwise and thinking that having bugs is a problem. Unfortunately, we spend much more time teaching programming than we do teaching debugging skills even though the professional programmer typically spends a large fraction of their time debugging. That tends to make students think that bugs are things to be ashamed of. Steve McConnell writes, "An average programmer generates 15–50 bugs per 1000 lines of code."

There are useful debugging tools for programmers, for example, the debugger that is a part of Visual Studio. This lets you interrupt the computation and examine the contents of memory. Debuggers are good for catching low-level bugs, but often the big picture is hidden by too much information (aka "can't see the forest for the trees").

● B.1 The Debug `printf`

What do you do when your program crashes? Experiment with your program and *think*. Try to get some idea about where in the code the crash occurs if you can. The first task is to reproduce the bug—find a series of actions that is guaranteed to make the bug occur every time. That should give you some clue as to where the bug might be. Reproducing bugs is quite often very difficult. Some bugs are not easily reproducible. In your professional life, you may have a Quality Assurance (abbreviated QA) team tasked with finding bugs, but they may not tell you how to reproduce it. Knowing how to reproduce it alone may tell you enough about the bug to figure out what's causing it. Start by adding `printf`s that output messages on function entry and exit. Do this for the suspicious functions, all of them if you have to. Look at the output file after your program crashes. If you see an `Entering function foo()` message and no `Exiting function foo()` message, then you know in which function the crash occurred. Then, add code to localize on which line it happened. When you've found the line of code that's bad, add code that prints out the values used on that line before you get to it. Look at the values output immediately before the crash. Think Hard. Are they right? If not, what should they be? And how did they get to be bad? The actual cause of the bug may be elsewhere, in which case you will have to work backwards until you find it.

There are some bugs that can't be caught with debug `printf`s, in particular, bugs in timing and scheduling of multithreaded processes. Adding debug output will slow down your program and change its execution profile, which may make the bug go away. Try using as few debug outputs as possible.

Albert Einstein once said, "It's not that I'm so smart, it's just that I stay with problems longer." That may be true, but it was also that he was Albert Einstein. The same thing is true with debugging: you have to stick with it through to the end. After all, as Voltaire said, "No problem can stand the assault of sustained thinking." According to Norman Vincent Peale, "When a problem comes along, study it until you are completely knowledgeable. Then find that weak spot, break the problem apart, and the rest will be easy." That's often true of debugging. The most challenging bugs are the ones that take three weeks to find and 30 seconds to fix.

● B.2 Zen and the Art of Debugging

Coding defensively makes a lot of sense. If you're careful, you can make sure that the damage caused by a bug is kept localized to one area of the code. Test for preconditions even when you know they're going to be true because you made it so. Write your code in small chunks and debug each chunk before moving on to the next one. Keep old versions. Use a Revision Control System (RCS) to keep track of them.

Diff is a Unix utility (also available on Windows) that compares two text files and tells you where they differ. Run diff on the latest two versions of your code to see what has changed. Selectively comment out new code until the bug goes away. This can take quite a lot of time.

There is also what I like to call the *Facepalm Method* or *Social Debugging*. Walk through your code line by line with another person, explaining it as you go along. Nine times out of ten, you will spot the bug yourself and be horribly embarrassed by it. Never underestimate the power of embarrassment as a debugging tool. This works best with somebody you would prefer to impress.

During the long and arduous debugging process, you will be tempted to stop for coffee, go on Facebook, and generally procrastinate. The impartial observer might think that you aren't making any actual progress. However, the unconscious part of your brain is *always* on the job. Keeping the conscious part of your brain distracted can actually help the unconscious part work on the problem.

When debugging, you should emulate Sherlock Holmes: Gather evidence and use logic. Remember what he said: "When you have eliminated the impossible, whatever remains, however improbable, must be the truth."

Douglas Adams in *Mostly Harmless* said, "We all like to congregate at boundary conditions. Where land meets water. Where earth meets air. Where bodies meet mind. Where space meets time. We like to be on one side and look at the other." Bugs like to collect around boundary conditions, so start looking there first. These include

- the first time around a loop,
- the last time around a loop,
- the code following a loop,
- the code at the start of a function,
- the code after a function returns.

For each unit of code (block, function, loop): Are the preconditions met? That is, do the conditions required for its correct execution hold at the time of execution? Does it meet the postconditions? That is, does it meet the conditions required for the correct execution of subsequent code?

Of course there is always the method of last resort: the *trace*. Grab a pencil and paper and pretend to be a computer executing your program. Draw boxes for variables and step through your code putting the computed values into their boxes. It is a method of desperation because it is so time consuming and tedious.

As the great philosopher Scooby Doo once said, "Rotsa Ruck!"

 **C**

There Are, in Fact, Dumb Questions

I stop answering dumb questions about programming once my students reach a certain level of programming skill. Don't let anybody tell you that there's no such thing as a dumb question. My definition of a dumb question about programming is a question that can be answered by experimenting with code. I tell the student "Why don't you code it up and see for yourself?" They probably assume that I'm being lazy or that I don't know the answer, but years later they recognize that moment for what it is, the transitional point from being a novice to a journeyman programmer. Naturally, I'm not asking them to do anything that I don't do myself. Here are two examples from this book.

C.1 Lies of π

I was excited when my wife brought home a book called *Life of Pi* by Yann Martel, thinking that it was about the irrational number π, the ratio of the circumference of a circle to its diameter. I was a little chagrined when I found that it was about a man on a lifeboat instead, but I kept reading it because it has animals in it and I like animals.[1]

There's enough known about π to write several books, and in fact, several books have been written. It's well established that π is an irrational number and has an infinite number of digits after the decimal point. You

....

[1] I felt cheated when I realized that they were only metaphorical animals, not real ones, but fortunately I didn't realize it until the end.

can compute it to as much precision as you've got patience for using any
number of algorithms, for example, the Gregory-Leibniz series,

$$\pi = 4 \cdot \sum_{i=1}^{\infty} \frac{(-1)^{i+1}}{i},$$

and the faster converging Nilakantha series,

$$\pi = 3 + \sum_{i=1}^{\infty} \frac{(-1)^{i+1}}{i(i+1)(2i+1)}.$$

We mostly get by in the Real World with a finite number of digits.
Elementary School kids find that $\pi = 22/7$ is perfectly satisfactory for
things that they can make with paper, scissors, and glue. The Box2D
header file b2Settings.h contains a definition of π that has 12 digits,
which is 11 decimal places of accuracy.

```
#define b2_pi 3.14159265359f
```

Being persnickety, I fell to wondering why 12 digits. Why not 11 or 13? Is
12 digits accurate enough? Single precision floating-point numbers effec-
tively have a 24-bit mantissa, which as we saw in Section 5.3 is enough for
about sevenish decimal digits. When rounded to 24 bits,

$$\pi = 11.0010010000111111011011,$$

which in decimal is 3.141592741012573242187. So while the #define was
made in good faith, the float value that results is actually different in the
seventh decimal place. That means we get an accuracy of seven significant
digits including the digit in front of the decimal point.

#define b2_pi		3.14159265359
(float) b2_pi	is	3.141592741012573242187

Wait a second, is that last value actually right? It doesn't hurt to check. It
takes only seconds to whomp up a quick C program using union to output
the decimal equivalent of the floating-point representation of b2_pi.

```
#include <stdio.h>

#define b2_pi 3.14159265359f

union mung{
  int nValue;
```

```
    float fValue;
};

int main(){
    mung pi;
    pi.fValue = b2_pi;
    printf("Pi = %d\n", pi.nValue);
    return 0;
}
```

When we run it, our program outputs 1078530011, and

$$1078530011_{10} = 0\,\underbrace{10000000}_{\text{exponent}}\,\underbrace{10010010000111111011011}_{\text{mantissa}}.$$

Therefore, the exponent x is[2] 1, and the mantissa m is

$$m = 10010010000111111011011_2 = 4788187_{10}.$$

According to Section 5.3, this represents the number $(1+m/2^{23})2^x$. Doing the math,

$$(1+m/2^{23})2^x = 2 + m/2^{22}$$
$$= 2 + 4788187/4194394$$
$$\approx 2 + 1.1415927410125732421875$$
$$= 3.1415927410125732421875,$$

which is exactly what we expected. A little experimentation will show you that #define b2_pi 3.1415927f gets the same output of 1078530011_{10}, but #define b2_pi 3.141593f is just not good enough, resulting in an output of 1078530012_{10}. Therefore, I can say quite unequivocally, the last four digits of the declaration of b2_pi are redundant; 7 digits after the decimal place are quite enough.

```
#define b2_pi 3.1415927f
```

It turns out that 11 decimal places are sufficient to measure the circumference of any circle with diameter smaller than that of the Earth with accuracy down to the millimeter level. The Earth has diameter about 1.3×10^4 km, let's round that up to 10^8 m. A millimeter is 10^{-3} m. Therefore, since circumference equals π times diameter, we need π to $8 + 3 = 11$ decimal places.

....

[2]Wait a second, I didn't tell you that the exponent x is stored backwards. That was a detail you didn't need to know yet in Section 5.3.

How far can we take this? A galactic civilization might need to measure the circumference of a circle whose diameter is that of our galaxy (10^6 light years $= 10^{22}$ m) down to the size of a hydrogen atom (10^{-10} m), which requires $22 + 10 = 32$ decimal places,

$$\pi = 3.14159265358979323846264338327950.$$

Since the diameter of the Universe is reputed to be 10^{11} light years $= 10^{27}$ m, and there appears to be[3] no particle smaller than 10^{-35} m, the maximum number of digits of π that one could ever need is $35 + 27 = 62$. Here it is:

3.14159265358979323846264338327950288419716939937510582097494459.

If you define π to be the ratio of the circumference to the diameter of a circle, and you insist on a real, actual circle, then all of those programs that compute π to a million decimal places are simply lies. Coming at it from another angle, 62 decimal digits is the equivalent of about 206 bits. I would hazard a guess that Deep Thought[4] uses 256-bit floating-point numbers, maybe 512 bits, just to be on the safe side. Those who argue that it is an analog computer are unclear on the concept that the Universe is discrete and so is everything in it. There is also the possibility that Deep Thought is a quantum computer, but I'm thinking probably not.

C.2   Quis Custodiet Ipsos Auditores?

> "Quis custodiet ipsos custodes?" —Juvenal

Who shall watch the listeners? Me, that's who. While writing the section on Contact Listeners (Section 8.2), I decided that to fully understand them, I needed to actually watch one in action to see what it does. I started with the code from Chapter 8. First, I went into functions CreateTower and PlaceBook and made the obvious changes to create a single book at the right orientation and position. After that, I replaced my Contact Listener's PreSolve code in ContactListener.cpp with the following code that calls function DescribeManifold (described below) twice.

....

[3] Any smaller particle with any meaningful mass would have radius less than its Schwartzchild radius, and would therefore be a black hole.

[4] The computer that determined that the answer to the question of life, the universe, and everything is 42.

```
void CMyContactListener :: PreSolve (
  b2Contact* contact, const b2Manifold* oldManifold)
{
 b2Manifold* newManifold = contact ->GetManifold ();
 b2PointState state1[2], state2[2];
 b2GetPointStates (state1, state2,
   oldManifold, newManifold);

 DescribeManifold ("Old", oldManifold, state1);
 DescribeManifold ("New", newManifold, state2);
} //PreSolve
```

Function `DescribeManifold` prints out a manifold's contact points by calling functions `DescribeState` and `DescribePoint` (both described below) twice each.

```
void DescribeManifold (const char* type,
 const b2Manifold* m, b2PointState state[]){

 if(!(state[0] == b2_persistState &&
   state[1] == b2_persistState) &&
   !(state[0] == b2_persistState &&
   state[1] == b2_nullState) &&
   !(state[0] == b2_nullState &&
   state[1] == b2_persistState) &&
   !(state[0] == b2_nullState &&
   state[1] == b2_nullState)
 ){
   b2Vec2 wp0 = m->points[0].localPoint;
   b2Vec2 wp1 = m->points[1].localPoint;
   int pointcount = m->pointCount;

   printf ("%s&%d&", type, g_nFrameNumber);

   if(pointcount<1)
     printf ("&");
   else{
     DescribeState (state[0]);
     printf ("&");
     DescribePoint (wp0);
   } //else

   printf ("&");
```

```
  if (pointcount <2)
    printf ("&");
  else{
    DescribeState (state [1]);
    printf ("&");
    DescribePoint (wp1);
  } //else
  printf ("\\\\\n");
 } //if
} //DescribeManifold
```

Function `DescribePoint` converts a Physics World point into Render World units, normalizes it so that $(26, 31)$ is the origin, and prints it out.

```
void DescribePoint (const b2Vec2 p){
  const int XOFFSET = 26;
  const int YOFFSET = 31;
  printf ("(%d,%d)",
    (int)(p.x*10.0f + 0.5f) + XOFFSET,
    (int)(p.y*10.0f + 0.5f) + YOFFSET);
} //DescribePoint
```

Function `DescribeState` prints out a `b2PointState`.

```
void DescribeState (b2PointState s){
  switch(s){
    case b2_nullState :
      printf ("b2_nullState ");
      break;
    case b2_addState :
      printf ("b2_addState ");
      break;
    case b2_persistState :
      printf ("b2_persistState ");
      break;
    case b2_removeState :
      printf ("b2_removeState ");
      break;
  } //switch
} //DescribeState
```

This is what it outputs, all ready to be put into a LaTeX table with a little extra formatting. That's how I got Table 8.2.

```
N&1&b2_addState&(0,0)&&\\
N&163&b2_addState&(0,0)&&\\
N&170&b2_addState&(0,0)&&\\
N&171&b2_persistState&(0,0)&b2_addState& (53,0)\\
O&172&b2_removeState&(0,0)&b2_persistState&(53,0)\\
N&225&b2_addState&(0,0)&b2_persistState&(53,0)\\
O&226&b2_persistState&(0,0)&b2_removeState&(53,0)\\
N&243&b2_persistState&(0,0)&b2_addState&(53,0)\\
```

I also wanted to get some screenshots that are synchronized with the Contact Listener's PreSolve rather than faking it all with Paint.NET, so I modified the Renderer code (which you don't have access to) to put a frame number down near the book so I could get the matching screenshots in Figure 8.4. I ran the experiment while using a screen capture program to make a movie of the program running, while simultaneously saving the text output into a file. Finally, I used a movie editing program to grab the frames I wanted out of the movie.

If there's something you don't understand about a feature in a programming language or a programming library like Box2D, you should experiment with it. Naturally, you can and probably will get into a whole lot of trouble along the way because you don't actually understand the thing you're trying to experiment with, but that's how you learn.

When you think about it, that's the reason why you do any kind of experiment, isn't it? The contrived experiments that you did in school where you know what the answer is beforehand are nothing but a pale shadow of the real thing.

 # D

Bullet Physics

The Bullet physics manual tells us that "Bullet Physics is a professional Open Source collision detection, rigid body and soft body dynamics library." It consists of Open Source C++ code released under the Zlib license and is free for any commercial use on all platforms including Playstation 3, XBox 360, Wii, PC, Linux, Mac OSX and iPhone. Bullet physics is a lot more sophisticated that Box2D, but once you start working with it, you will find that they have some concepts in common, for example, where Box2D has the Physics World b2World, Bullet physics has the Dynamics World btDiscreteDynamicsWorld. Tables D.1 and D.2 contain a few more equivalences.

Box2D	Bullet Physics
Physics World	Dynamics World
Joint	Constraint
Body	Rigid Body
Body Definition	Rigid Body Construction Info
Kinematic body	Kinematic rigid body
Dynamic body	Dynamic rigid body
Static body	Static rigid body
Shape	Collision shape

Table D.1 • Bullet equivalents for some Box2D concepts.

Box2D	Bullet Physics
b2World	btDiscreteDynamicsWorld
b2Body	btRigidBody
b2BodyDef	btRigidBodyConstructionInfo
b2Shape	btCollisionShape

Table D.2 • Bullet equivalents for some Box2D classes.

● D.1   Getting Started

You can download Bullet physics from [Presson 12]. Once you have done that, add the following projects to your Visual Studio Solution:

1. BulletDynamics.vcxproj,
2. BulletCollision.vcxproj,
3. LinearMath.vcxproj.

Next,

1. add the include path Bullet-2.79/src,
2. add the library path Bullet-2.79/lib,
3. add to your source file the line

```
#include "btBulletDynamicsCommon.h"
```

Check out CcdPhysicsDemo to see how to create a btDiscreteDynamics World, btCollisionShape, btMotionState, and btRigidBody. Call step Simulation on the Dynamics World once per frame of animation, and synchronize the world transform for your graphics object.

Basic order of operations:

1. Create Core Objects

   - btDefaultCollisionConfiguration.
   - btCollisionDispatcher.
   - btBroadphaseInterface.
   - btSequentialImpulseConstraintSolver.
   - btDiscreteDynamicsWorld.

2. Physics Loop (repeat until done)

   (a) Add any new rigid bodies, soft bodies, etc.
   (b) Modify physics parameters.
   (c) Step simulation.

3. Clean Up

   (a) Delete objects created in Physics Loop.
   (b) Clear various arrays.
   (c) Delete core objects.

● D.2   The Dynamics World

A *Dynamics World* provides a high-level interface that manages your physics objects and constraints and implements the update of all objects each frame. There are a number of things to declare first, however. Declare the default Collision Configuration.

```
btDefaultCollisionConfiguration*
 collisionConfiguration = new
  btDefaultCollisionConfiguration();
```

Use the Collision Configuration to declare the default Collision Dispatcher:

```
btCollisionDispatcher *
 dispatcher = new
  btCollisionDispatcher (
   collisionConfiguration);
```

Declare a broad-phase Interface:

```
btBroadphaseInterface *
 overlappingPairCache  = new
  btDbvtBroadphase ();
```

Declare the default Constraint Solver:

```
btSequentialImpulseConstraintSolver*
 solver = new
  btSequentialImpulseConstraintSolver;
```

Now, you can declare the Dynamics World.

```
btDiscreteDynamicsWorld*
dynamicsWorld = new
 btDiscreteDynamicsWorld(
  dispatcher, overlappingPairCache ,
  solver, collisionConfiguration);
```

● D.3 Adding Objects

To construct a btRigidBody or btCollisionObject, you need to provide mass (positive for dynamic moving objects and zero for static objects), CollisionShape (such as Box, Sphere, Cone, Convex Hull, or
Triangle Mesh), and material properties (such as friction and restitution).
You can then add it to the btDynamicsWorld. First, we define its mass
and local inertia.

```
btScalar mass(1.f);
btVector3 localInertia(0, 0, 0);
```

Then, we define its MotionState.

```
btTransform startTransform;
startTransform.setIdentity();
startTransform.setOrigin(
  btVector3(2, 10, 0));
btDefaultMotionState*
myMotionState = new
  btDefaultMotionState(
    startTransform);
```

Finally, we declare its collision shape.

```
btCollisionShape* colShape = new
  btSphereShape(btScalar(1.0));
colShape->calculateLocalInertia(
  mass, localInertia);
```

Now, we can make an rbInfo structure filled in with all of the information
about the required body and use it to declare the rigid body body.

```
btRigidBody::btRigidBodyConstructionInfo
  rbInfo(mass, myMotionState, colShape,
    localInertia);
btRigidBody* body = new
  btRigidBody(rbInfo);
dynamicsWorld->addRigidBody(body);
```

D.4   Rigid Body Dynamics

Rigid body dynamics is implemented on top of the collision-detection module. It adds forces, mass, inertia, velocity, and constraints. The main rigid body object is `btRigidBody`, which is derived from `btCollisionObject` so that it inherits its world transform, friction, and restitution and adds linear and angular velocity. `btTypedConstraint` is the base class for rigid body constraints, including

- `btHingeConstraint`,
- `btPoint2PointConstraint`,
- `btConeTwistConstraint`,
- `btSliderConstraint`,
- `btGeneric6DOFConstraint`.

Moving objects must have nonzero mass and inertia.

There are three different types of rigid bodies in Bullet. *Dynamic rigid bodies* have positive mass, and on every simulation frame, they update their world transform. *Static rigid bodies* have zero mass, cannot move, but can collide. *Kinematic rigid bodies* have zero mass, can be animated by the user, but there will be only one-way interaction. Dynamic objects will be pushed away by kinematic rigid bodies, but there is no influence from them.

The world transform of a rigid body is, in Bullet, always equal to its center of mass, and its basis also defines its local frame for inertia. The local inertia depends on the shape, and the `btCollisionShape` class provides a method to calculate the local inertia, given a mass. This world transform has to be a rigid body transform, which means it should contain no scaling, shear, etc. If the collision shape is not aligned with the center of mass transform, it can be shifted to match with a `btCompoundShape`, using the child transform to shift the child collision shape.

D.5   Motion States

Motion states are a way for Bullet to get the world transform of objects being simulated into the rendering part of your game. Your game loop will iterate through all the objects before each frame render. For each object, update the position of the render object from the physics body using motion states. Other benefits of motion states are as follows:

- Computation involved in moving bodies around is only done for bodies that have moved.

- You don't just have to do render stuff in them. They could be effective for notifying network code that a body has moved and needs to be updated across the network.
- Interpolation is usually only meaningful in the context of something visible on screen. Bullet manages body interpolation through motion states.

Motion states are used in two places in Bullet.

1. When a body is first created, Bullet gets the initial position of a body from its motion state when the body enters the simulation, calls `getWorldTransform` with a reference to the variable it wants you to fill with transform information.
2. After the first update, during simulation, Bullet calls the motion state for a body to move it around. It calls `setWorldTransform` with the transform of the body for you to update your object appropriately. To implement one, derive a class from `btMotionState`, and override `getWorldTransform` and `setWorldTransform`.

Although recommended, it is not necessary to derive your own motion state from `btMotionState`. Bullet provides a default `MotionState` for you. Simply construct it with the default transform of your body:

```
btDefaultMotionState * ms = new
  btDefaultMotionState ();
```

• D.6   Render Frames and Physics Frames

Once per render frame, call `stepSimulation` on the Dynamics World. The Dynamics World automatically takes into account variable time step by performing interpolation instead of simulation for small time steps. It uses an internal fixed time step of 60 hertz. Function `stepSimulation` will perform collision detection and physics simulation. It updates the world transform for active objects by calling the `btMotionState`'s `setWorldTransform` function.

By default, Bullet physics simulation runs at an internal fixed frame rate of 60 hertz. Your render loop will have a different or even variable frame rate. To decouple the render frame rate from the simulation frame rate, an automatic interpolation method is built into `stepSimulation`. If the application delta time is smaller then the internal fixed time step, Bullet will interpolate the world transform and send it to the `btMotionState` without performing physics simulation. If the application time step is larger than 60 hertz, one or more simulation steps can be performed during each `stepSimulation` call. You can limit the maximum number of simulation steps by passing a maximum value as second argument.

Bibliography

[Catto 11] Erin Catto. "Box2D v2.2.0 User Manual." http://box2d.org/manual. pdf, 2007–2011.

[Catto 12] Erin Catto. "Box2D: A 2D Physics Engine for Games." http://box2d. org/, last accessed 2012.

[Cormen et al. 01] Thomas H. Cormen, Charles E. Leiserson, Ronald L. Rivest, and Clifford Stein. *Introduction to Algorithms*, Second edition. Cambridge, MA: MIT Press and McGraw-Hill Book Company, 2001.

[Dunn and Parberry 11] Fletcher Dunn and Ian Parberry. *3D Math Primer for Graphics and Game Development*, Second edition. Natick, MA: A K Peters, 2011.

[Ericson 05] Christer Ericson. *Real-Time Collision Detection*. San Francisco: Morgan Kaufman, 2005.

[Goldsmith and Salmon 87] Jeffrey Goldsmith and John Salmon. "Automatic Creation of Object Hierarchies for Ray Tracing." *IEEE Computer Graphics and Applications* 7:5 (1987), 14–20.

[Parberry et al. 07] Ian Parberry, Jeremy R. Nunn, Joseph Scheinberg, Erik Carson, and Jason Cole. "SAGE: A Simple Academic Game Engine." In *Proceedings of the Second Annual Microsoft Academic Days on Game Development in Computer Science Education*, pp. 90–94. http://larc.unt.edu/ian/Cruise2007/madgdcse2007.pdf, 2007.

[Parberry 97] Ian Parberry. "Knowledge, Understanding, and Computational Complexity." In *Optimality in Biological and Artificial Networks?*, edited by D. S. Levine and W. R. Elsberry, Chapter 8, pp. 125–144. Hillsdale, NJ: Lawrence Erlbaum Associates, 1997.

[Parberry 12] Ian Parberry. "Intro to Game Physics with Box2D." http://larc. unt.edu/ian/books/gamephysics/, 2012.

[Presson 12] Nathanael Presson. "Bullet Physics Library." http://bulletphysics. org/, last accessed 2012.

[Smiley 99] Leonard M. Smiley. "Proof without Words: Geometry of Subtraction Formulas." *Mathematical Magazine* 72 (1999), 366.

[Stroustrup 97] Bjarne Stroustrup. *The C++ Programming Language*, Third edition. Reading, MA: Addison-Wesley, 1997.

Index

Printed in the United States
by Baker & Taylor Publisher Services